POLITICAL TRADITIONS IN FOREIGN POLICY SERIES
Kenneth W. Thompson, Editor

The values, traditions, and assumptions undergirding approaches to foreign policy are often crucial in determining the course of a nation's history. Yet, the interconnections between ideas and policy for landmark periods in our foreign relations remain largely unexamined. The intent of this series is to encourage a marriage between political theory and foreign policy. A secondary objective is to identify theorists with a continuing interest in political thought and international relations, both younger scholars and the small group of established thinkers. Only occasionally have scholarly centers and university presses sought to nurture studies in this area. In the 1950s and 1960s the University of Chicago Center for the Study of American Foreign Policy gave emphasis to such inquiries. Since then the subject has not been the focus of any major intellectual center. The Louisiana State University Press and the series editor, from a base at the Miller Center of Public Affairs at the University of Virginia, have organized this series to meet a need that has remained largely unfulfilled since the mid-1960s.

THE TWO FACES
OF NATIONAL INTEREST

THE TWO FACES
OF NATIONAL INTEREST

W. DAVID CLINTON

LOUISIANA STATE UNIVERSITY PRESS

Baton Rouge and London

Designer: Glynnis Phoebe
Typeface: Sabon
Typesetter: G & S Typesetters, Inc.
Printer and binder: Thomson-Shore, Inc.

Library of Congress Cataloging-in-Publication Data
Clinton, W. David.
    The two faces of national interest / W. David Clinton.
       p.   cm. — (Political traditions in foreign policy series)
    Includes bibliographical references and index.
    ISBN 0-8071-1841-9. — ISBN 0-8071-1895-8 (pbk.)
    1. United States—Foreign relations—1945–1989—Case studies.
    2. United States—Foreign relations—1989–   —Philosophy. I. Title.
    II. Series.
    E840.C63   1994
    327.73—dc20   93-24206
                                            CIP

Portions of this book appeared in slightly different form as "The National Interest: Normative Foundations," *Review of Politics*, XLVIII (Fall, 1986), 495–519. This material is used with permission. Quotations from "The National Interest and the Pentagon Papers," by Hans Morgenthau, Noam Chomsky, *et al.*, which first appeared in *Partisan Review*, XXXIX (1972), are used with permission.

The paper in this book meets the guidelines for permanence and durability of the Committee on Production Guidelines for Book Longevity of the Council on Library Resources.♾

CONTENTS

PREFACE

NATIONAL INTEREST (along with the related terms *national interests* and *public interest*) readily finds a place in the discourse of contemporary politics. Indeed, it is so pervasive that one can hardly avoid coming across it in news articles and commentary on a host of subjects, most of which have little in common other than the appearance of this phrase. Several examples will illustrate the point:

—Speaking at the Center for Strategic and International Studies on May 4, 1989, Secretary of State James Baker warned, "Judgments and words ultimately have to be turned into action if we are going to serve the public interest."[1] This usage implied that serving the public interest was a responsibility of political leaders, and perhaps all participants in politics, though it did not indicate why this should be so.

—"The Bar recognises that it is such fun knocking lawyers that the public good may be ignored," read a statement by Great Britain's Bar Council upon the publication of a government proposal to rewrite the laws regulating the legal profession. "What interests the public is not necessarily in the public interest." Here, the public interest is seen in contradistinction to the wishes of many or perhaps most individual members of the public; it is what is good for the public rather than what the public wants.[2]

—Former senator Gary Hart, announcing his candidacy for the 1988 Democratic presidential nomination, charged, "We've let personal greed replace a sense of social justice and equity and national good. . . . We've increasingly let narrow single interests finance our campaigns and control our political process. Most of all, I think we've lost a sense of the national interest, and we're in serious danger of letting our future pass us by." Simi-

1. U.S. Department of State, Current Policy No. 1170, "The Challenge of Change in U.S.-Soviet Relations."

2. *Economist,* March 4, 1989, p. 56.

larly, a former chairman of the United States International Trade Commission opposed efforts to require a president to accept recommendations from the ITC to protect industries hurt by import competition: "While the commission studies only the impact of imports on a given industry, the President weighs the industry's plight against the effect of relief on other sectors of the economy—exporters, consumers and retailers. He also takes into account the diplomatic fallout of imposing restrictions. In short, he considers the national interest." These statements employing the term echo the difference between the national interest and narrower interests, whether those of specific sectors of the economy or those of individual offices within the federal bureaucracy.[3]

—In a two-part article on education for world affairs, J. David Singer, the president of the International Studies Association, argued that "' the national interest' is a smokescreen by which we all too often oversimplify the world, denigrate our rivals, enthrall our citizens, and justify acts of dubious morality and efficacy." He lamented, "When that hoary concept of 'the national interest' is invoked, products of such a culture—and the educational structure that spawns them—snap to attention, do their duty, and turn off their ethical and intellectual equipment."[4] National interest may itself be seen as a narrow, special interest, as compared with the world's common good. This treatment views it as an invitation to xenophobia.

—As the chain of Soviet-supported Communist governments in Eastern Europe collapsed during the fall of 1989 with startling rapidity, analysts in Moscow tried to understand why the Soviet Union accepted this turn of events, and some found the explanation in the hope that new, popularly based regimes would be more stable neighbors for Moscow than their discredited predecessors. "I think the interests of East and West have come into balance in Eastern Europe," one was quoted as remarking. Another added, "These events have brought a coincidence of Soviet and Western interests. . . . I think the top leadership . . . agree that we must accept whatever happens in Eastern Europe as long as it does not directly threaten our geopolitical and geostrategic interest."[5] These comments imply a view of interests as concerns, requirements, or needs of states, which can sometimes co-

3. New York *Times*, April 14, 1987, Sec. A, p. 16, June 24, 1987, Sec. A, p. 27.

4. "Education for World Affairs: Beyond Conventional Vision and Revealed Truth" (two parts), *International Studies Newsletter* XIII (February–March, 1986), 1, (June–July, 1986), 6.

5. New York *Times,* November 14, 1989, Sec. A, p. 7.

incide, and also change, but on which at any one time there are irreducible limits, the violation of which raises the danger of conflict.

—In an article appearing in the summer of 1990, an American analyst of Soviet affairs spun out the thesis that the Soviet government was, in both word and action, turning to "the national interest" as a way of groping toward the changed policies demanded by the new circumstances of the 1990s. "The leadership apparently wanted a new political vocabulary for weighing—and justifying—changes in the Soviet Union's international role," he surmised. This new language, replacing traditional Marxist-Leninist slogans and insubstantial "spaceship-earth" rhetoric, would explain the necessity for Moscow's withdrawal from a host of foreign commitments and conflicts; and it would subject advocates of future foreign actions to the test of justifying their policy both in a newly vigorous domestic debate (to demonstrate that they would be materially beneficial and affordable) and before other members of the states-system (to preserve the Soviet Union's "reputation and self-respect"). The result of thinking in terms dictated by national interest, it seemed, was national restraint—self-restraint, in deference to one's capabilities, and mutual restraint by the need to appeal to a common interstate consensus on the acceptable bounds of state action, the existence of which was affirmed by recourse to the language of interest.[6]

—A newspaper story on the American response to the Iraqi invasion of Kuwait in August of 1990 quoted Secretary Baker as asserting, "Since 1949, every American President has said that the gulf is a vital U.S. and Western interest." The author of the piece went on to contend that "the real political and economic interests involved are not quite so lofty as some of the broad principles used by the President to explain the operation."[7] Used in this way, national interests (now in the plural) appear to refer to needs that may provide the motive force for actions, but are less altruistic, and therefore less likely to be employed in public rationales, than are general moral or legal duties.

Watching this inundation of the public discourse by references to national interest (and the examples could be multiplied many-fold), I have become convinced, or have convinced myself, of the need for a reexamina-

6. Stephen Sestanovich, "Inventing the Soviet National Interest," *The National Interest* XX (Summer, 1990), 3–16.

7. Thomas L. Friedman, "U.S. Gulf Policy: Vague 'Vital Interests,'" New York *Times*, August 12, 1990, Sec. A, p. 1.

tion of a term so frequently used as totem or whipping boy. In particular, I have been struck by the seemingly endless variety of meanings attached to it, and have wondered whether a phrase employed to prove the correctness of diametrically opposed policy stands, and to describe so many different things, might not have become too elastic for its (and our) own good. Likewise, the resort to national interest as a way of justifying foreign policies has also raised questions. They include the practical possibility of devoting oneself to the interest of the entire nation (as opposed to the "real" stuff of politics: narrower interests, such as particular industries or sectors of the economy, or other interest groups defined by ethnicity or belief, or purely personal desires) and the ethical desirability of devoting oneself to the interest of one nation (as opposed to the welfare of the entire human family).

Without attempting premature disquisitions on these concerns, I should note that I begin with a predisposition to master the concept of national interest, rather than to junk it, not least because looking at the international states-system through this lens has the simple but not inconsiderable advantage of being in accord with what national leaders say they are doing. This is not an argument for complete credulity in the face of disingenuous public posturing; it is a suggestion that, in a field already heavily marked by "a tongue not understood of the people," it is a mistake to diverge unnecessarily from the language employed in the world we observe. Indeed, it may be that it is only when we have in hand a clear definition of a term honed by our own use that we can recognize clumsy or misleading ways of wielding it by others.

Part One of this study is devoted to a search for definition. After a brief survey of the origins and development of the concept of national interest as it has been used to explain and justify the actions of states, this section goes on to lay out the critics' case against national interest, to suggest a definition that will meet the objections, and to consider the special case of the fit between national-interest thinking and the American diplomatic tradition. In Part Two, I put on the national-interest spectacles just ground and view through them the development of policy goals, punctuated by public statements by responsible decision-makers, for four departures in American foreign policy since World War II.

The four were chosen because each marked a significant turn in policy—that is, an occasion for the reexamination of the requirements of the national interest. Two came during the Truman presidency and together did much to define containment: the preparation of the Marshall Plan and the decision to enter the Korean War. Two others accompanied the end of the containment consensus and marked attempts to devise a new roster of asserted interests: the evolution of the Nixon Doctrine and of the Carter policy on human rights. These are brief case studies, not complete histories; they are concerned only with the initial setting of new policy goals. I make no effort to follow, say, the Korean War through to the armistice of 1953, though I recognize that policy is never static and the aims of the war changed over its course. The stopping point for each of the histories is an occasion on which, having defined for themselves a substantial shift in diplomatic goals, policy makers went to the American public and the world with a considered description of and rationale for this new definition of what the national interest demanded.

In each instance, then, the recounting of events is an effort to determine whether interpreting them as the formulation and clash of interests is useful to the analyst. If we look at these episodes in ways suggested by national interests as they are defined here, do we understand American actions better? Given all the other forces impinging on these decisions and actions, is this helpful in explaining why the United States asked some things and not others of foreign countries? That is the aim of this work—not to build an elaborate theoretical superstructure, or to assert that only one cause is at work, but to suggest that national interest is ubiquitous in discourse because it refers to something of substance and weight in the life of nations and states.

ACKNOWLEDGMENTS

A BOOK THAT goes through a long gestation period receives the aid of many midwives. In the present case, I am conscious of a debt owed to so many sources of advice, criticism, and support that to attempt a comprehensive list would be to double the length of the resulting volume, and so I shall necessarily rely on the memories and the tolerance of a long list of advisers, critics, and supporters whom I now thank *en masse*. Of those who deserve specific words of appreciation, let me begin with several sources of institutional funding and other aid: the Miller Center of Public Affairs, first and foremost, as well as the University of Virginia and Tulane University, including especially the staffs of their libraries, the Harry S. Truman Library, the Jimmy Carter Library, and the George C. Marshall Research Library.

Among the individuals who have helped to bring this project to term, my deepest debt of gratitude goes to Kenneth W. Thompson. His years of counsel, and his steadfast faith in the work, make him in a sense a coauthor, though neither he nor any of the other persons mentioned here bears any responsibility for what these pages contain. Others who knew the manuscript in its earlier manifestations and whose suggestions have helped immeasurably in improving it are James S. Young, Inis L. Claude, and Norman Graebner. Cecil Crabb provided cogent and welcome analysis of the arguments presented here. The physical preparation of the manuscript could not have been completed without the professional aid of Shirley Kohut and others on the Miller Center staff, and of the editors and staff of Louisiana State University Press. Finally, my most heartfelt appreciation goes to my parents, whose love and self-sacrifice will always be an inspiration to me.

ONE The Concept of National Interest

Interest, sir, has a most powerful influence over the
human mind, and is the basis on which all the trans-
actions of mankind are built.
> —William Richardson Davie, quoted in
> *The Records of the Federal Convention of 1787*

Virtues are swallowed up by self-interest as rivers are
lost in the sea.
> —François de La Rochefoucauld,
> *The Maxims of La Rochefoucauld*

I National Interest and the States-System

"INTEREST" AS AN organizing concept for the understanding of inter-national affairs is as old as the field of study itself. More than one volume has been written to trace the history of interest and its influence over the thinking of scholars and statesmen.[1] Thucydides expressed, through the speeches of the orators who appear throughout his history of the Peloponne-sian War, many of the ideas concerning the national interest that would later be rediscovered by observers of the emergence of the present states-system. The Greek historian defined interest in terms of the power position of the state, which in turn depended on its wealth and territorial possessions. He thus distinguished interest, as the exclusive advantage of a particular com-munity, from any overarching standard, such as justice, as a guide to state action. The distinction is made clear in the Athenians' debate over whether the men of Mytilene should be killed and their wives and children enslaved as punishment for the Mytilenians' revolt against Athens. Against the de-mand by Cleon for vengeance, Diodotus did not deny the guilt of the Myti-lenians but pled for clemency on the grounds of expediency: "I have not come forward either to oppose or to accuse in the matter of Mitylene; in-deed, the question before us as sensible men is not their guilt, but our interests. . . . I consider it far more useful for the preservation of our empire voluntarily to put up with injustice, than to put to death, however justly, those whom it is our interest to keep alive."[2]

1. Friedrich Meinecke, *Machiavellism: The Doctrine of Raison d'Etat and Its Place in Modern History,* trans. Douglas Scott (London, 1957); Charles A. Beard, *The Idea of National Interest: An Analytical Study in American Foreign Policy* (New York, 1934), 1–168; Albert O. Hirschmann, *The Passions and the Interests: Political Arguments for Capitalism Before Its Triumph* (Princeton, 1977), 7–66; Luigi Sturgo, *The International Community and the Right of War,* trans. Barbara Barclay Carter (New York, 1970), 183–86.
2. Thucydides, *The Peloponnesian War,* trans. Richard Crawley (New York, 1951), 3.9.44.

While interest could not be equated with justice, the character of the community in question—the justness of its public philosophy—did affect the way in which that community could define its interest. Thucydides favorably contrasts the Athenians' decision, after sober reflection, to heed Diodotus' argument, with the action of Sparta in carrying out against the citizens of Plataea what Athens had been dissuaded from doing to the Mytilenians. The actions of Sparta were untouched by the restraint and farsightedness of the Athenians' more enlightened conception of self-interest, and the contrast was the greater because, as great powers, the two had a special responsibility to define their interests in an enlightened, nonexclusive way. As Thucydides had a spokesman for the Corinthians say of the Spartans' responsibilities in leading the alliance against Athenian imperialism, "Supremacy has its duties. Besides equitably administering private interests, leaders are required to show a special care for the common welfare in return for the special honours accorded to them by all in other ways."[3]

This interest of states operated in both domestic and foreign politics. Internally, the interest of the state encompassed all private interests and, in the case of any seeming conflict between the two, overrode them. Pericles took this view when he called upon his fellow Athenians not to allow the sacrifices they were forced to make at home dissuade them from supporting the country's policy in its war abroad: "I am of the opinion that national greatness is more for the advantage of private citizens, than any individual well-being coupled with public humiliation. A man may be personally ever so well off, and yet if his country be ruined he must be ruined with it; whereas a flourishing commonwealth always affords chances of salvation to unfortunate individuals." Externally, the state's interest, if it was correctly perceived, showed statesmen those foreign states with which it was politic to ally and those that it was necessary to oppose. Enlightened self-interest could be carried only so far: it was not equivalent to surrender, and irreconcilably clashing interests demanded watchfulness and defensive preparations, if not immediate war. On the other hand, two states could find that what benefited one also benefited the other; it was the recognition of coinciding interests that caused the Corinthian delegate at the second Congress at Lacedaemon of states threatened by the growth of Athenian power to remind his fellow delegates, in the frequently quoted phrase, that "identity

3. Richard D. Sears, "The Classical Understanding of International Politics," in *Power, Principles and Interests: A Reader in World Politics*, ed. Jeffrey Salmon *et al.* (Lexington, Mass., 1985), 81–97; Thucydides, *Peloponnesian War*, 1.4.120.

of interests is the surest of bonds whether between states or individuals." The task of diplomacy was to recognize one's interest and to conduct policy toward other states and their interests accordingly.[4]

This system of thought was pushed into the background with the rise to intellectual and political supremacy of the Christian doctrine that the proper concern of man was not with the machinations of this world but with the promise of the next and that the actions of states ought not to be driven by their mundane interests but, like the lives of individuals, should be governed by a higher, universal natural law. Therefore, though Machiavelli did not employ the term *interest* in his writings, his challenge to the Christian heritage and his reliance on elements of the classical tradition mark the reopening of the history of interest as a guide to diplomatic conduct. Those in authority in the various political communities of the intervening period had frequently acted on the basis of their unstated interests; Machiavelli led the way for publicists and scholars, as well as rulers, to resume discussing and debating foreign policy in those terms.

In two important ways—unscrupulousness and prudence—the Florentine's work foreshadowed the reemergence of interest as an organizing principle for thought on international relations. While at first blush these two qualities might seem to rest uneasily together, in Machiavelli's mind they were consistent and complementary. They also revealed what was *not* a part of Machiavelli's conception of the goals of state action and thus remained to be developed, in thought and in practice, in later years.

First, Machiavelli identified as one of the characteristics of a great ruler the willingness to do wrong. His position is summed up in the well-known passage in *The Prince* in which he distinguished the advice he offered from that given by other writers still under the influence of the teachings of the Church: "There is such a difference between how men live and how they ought to live that he who abandons what is done for what ought to be done learns his destruction rather than his preservation, because any man who under all conditions insists on making it his business to be good will surely be destroyed among so many who are not good. Hence a prince, in order to hold his position, must acquire the power to be not good, and understand when to use it and when not to use it, in accord with necessity."[5]

This passage shows that Machiavelli was not as "machiavellian" as he

4. Thucydides, *Peloponnesian War*, 2.7.60, 1.5.124.

5. Allan H. Gilbert, ed., *Machiavelli: The Chief Works and Others* (3 vols.; Durham, N.C., 1965), I, 57–58, 66.

is sometimes portrayed: the prince was to know when not to use the power "to be not good," as well as when to use it; and he was counseled to hold to what was right when he could, doing wrong only when circumstances required it. Nevertheless, in saying that at times the ruler not only could but ought to abandon conventional ethics in the conduct of affairs of state, Machiavelli was undermining the authority of natural law over official actions, if not private ones, and opening the way for natural law as a guide to action to be replaced by the more morally neutral concept of interest.

Machiavelli's second contribution was his identification of prudence as a means of controlling and limiting those morally objectionable but at times necessary acts of injustice that the ruler was required occasionally to commit if he was to be successful. These transgressions of the moral law were not to be engaged in indiscriminately, by abandoning oneself to ungoverned cupidity, pride, or other passions, but were to be instrumental acts precisely geared to the attainment of specific limited political objectives and confined to the minimum wrong required for success. In Thucydides' terms, Machiavelli advised the prince to be a Diodotus rather than a Cleon. Reason, unclouded by emotion, would inform the statesman when it was necessary to commit wrongs; it would also channel those wrongs and prevent them from becoming undisciplined brutality or "a mere insensible greed for power."[6]

Even after making every allowance for this prudential restraint, however, one fails to see in Machiavelli the sense of responsibility to other states in the system, held by its most prominent and powerful members, that Thucydides portrayed in the wisest and best statesmen of his history. Machiavelli was primarily concerned with securing power against internal enemies. Moreover, the Italian states to which his writings were addressed were far too small even to think of holding a position of prominence comparable to that of Athens in the Hellenic age, and their narrow margin of security afforded them little opportunity for exercising the magnanimity to which Thucydides had alluded. It was left for others to recapture this element of national interest from desuetude.

The upheavals in European politics of the sixteenth and seventeenth centuries, beginning with the invasion of Italy by Charles VIII in 1494 that impelled Machiavelli to write *The Prince* as "an exhortation to grasp Italy

---

6. Meinecke, *Machiavellism*, 42; Gilbert, ed., *Machiavelli*, I, 401–404, 449–51.

and set her free from the barbarians," set off a series of diplomatic movements that extended well beyond the Italian peninsula. Throughout Europe—in England, in France, in Spain, and in their smaller emulators and competitors—the beginnings of the independent, modern state were replacing the older ideal of the universal *res publica christiana*. Feeling the need to observe with care the actions of their competitors, these states were engaged in vigorous efforts to construct a continental system of permanent diplomatic missions (accompanied by less public but equally active agents of espionage), and, in Meinecke's words, "it was the diplomat, sending in his reports, who was the acknowledged discoverer of the [modern] theory of the interests of States."[7] At the same time, centralized monarchial states were seeking a justification for the overall, common, "national," or "public," interest in their contest with feudalism's local or particularistic interests.

Both of these historical developments were mirrored in the life of the first great publicist of the interests of states, Duke Henri de Rohan. The commander of the Huguenot forces until the final defeat of this state within the French state, Rohan became a military lieutenant to his recent archenemy, the symbol of state interests, Cardinal Richelieu, in order to advance the power of the centralized French monarchy against its rivals at home and abroad. Thus, the duke wrote from practical experience as both friend and foe of the new, larger form of political organization taking shape in Europe.

It was Rohan's contribution to take the term *interest*—which had come into common use in the late sixteenth century to denote those aspirations of individuals that were prompted by rational calculation and pursued with prudence—and apply it to the goals and actions of states. His monograph, *De l'interet des Princes et Estats de la Chrestiente*, published posthumously in 1638 and dedicated to Richelieu, synthesized many of the ideas that were to become standard elements of works on international politics in the century ahead. There was the conviction, set out in the opening sentence of the preamble, that interest was the proper guidepost for state action: "Les princes commandent aux peuples, et l'interet commande aux princes." To try to construct a foreign policy from ethical principles alone would be impractical; but to rely on pure egoism would be self-defeating, for "*in matters of State* one ought not to suffer himself to be led by *inordinate desires,*

7. Meinecke, *Machiavellism,* 146–49.

which carrie us oftentimes to undertake things beyond our strength: nor by *violent passions* which doe diversely trouble us . . . : nor by *superstitious opinions,* whereby ill-conceived scruples are ministered unto us, but rather by our proper interest guided by reason [alone], which ought to be the rule of our actions." The role to be played by reason was central, both in directing the state's competition with other states and in restraining the state and preventing it from overreaching itself. Extraneous influences might cloud the vision of the statesman and lead the state astray; the state's interest was not always self-evident, and skill and coolness were required to ascertain it. Interest itself was infallible, however, and if the prince could surmount these obstacles he would be successful in maintaining or, possibly, adding to the power of his state. "The *Prince* may deceive himself, his *Counsell* may be corrupted but the interest alone can never fail. According as it is well or ill understood, it maketh *States* to live or die." In order to give these general arguments specific illustrations, Rohan described the interests of the major European powers of the day and to provide cautionary reminders of rulers who had failed because they had let themselves be carried away by passion instead of taking as their guide the reasonable dictates of interest.[8]

Rohan's short book was an immediate success, and its reception opened the way for a flood of imitations during the remainder of the seventeenth century and throughout the eighteenth century as other authors attempted to discern and explain the true interests of the states of Europe.[9]

In eighteenth-century thought, the advances in the natural sciences and the faith in rationalism that marked the age of the Enlightenment gave rise to a belief in an equally orderly political world in which statesmen acted after carefully calibrating nicely balanced diplomatic interests and states moved along predictable paths similar in their own way to those postulated by Newtonian physics for heavenly bodies. Moreover, as the passions of the religious wars and other disturbances that had necessarily colored the analyses and the prescriptions of Machiavelli and Rohan cooled, observers in the calmer atmosphere of the 1700s could entertain a broader, more tolerant

8. Henri, duc de Rohan, *A Treatise of the Interest of the Princes and States of Christendome* (London, 1643), I, 38–39.

9. See the references to the anonymous work *Interets et maximes des Princes et des Estats souverains* (1666) and the compendium by Jean Rousset, *Les interets presens et les pretentions des puissances de l'Europe* (1741), cited in Meinecke, *Machiavellism,* 165, 259. For further examples, see pp. 230–31.

view of state interest that acknowledged the legitimacy of the interests of other states in the system and of the system as a whole and could accept that one's own interest had to be reconciled with these other interests.

As frequently happens with ideas that impress themselves on scholarly opinion, the power of the insight of state interest carried hopes for the concept beyond what reality would support. On one side, the reasonable belief that rational calculation of interests was the hallmark of successful diplomacy sometimes slipped into unreasonably high expectations of the exactitude with which interests could be discerned. The interest of the state was less precise a concept than might be imagined from astronomical analogies. On the other side, the recognition that Europe formed a sort of society whose standards of true state interests ought to be consistent—an intellectual advance over the pure self-assertion of Machiavelli's Prince—could be taken to the unjustifiable extreme of faith in the automatic harmony of interests. Condorcet voiced a faith shared with many:

> If one considers the relationships of one people to another, one may say that the national interest does not exist, in the sense that one supposes these interests to be opposed. . . . The common interest of peoples is to be well governed at home, to be just toward foreigners as toward one's own citizens, to preserve peace with neighboring nations. Wars of vanity, wars of ambition, wars of commerce are equally without reason. A people can never have an interest in attacking another, nor in interfering with its liberty, nor in monopolizing to its exclusion, a branch of commerce; and one may say in general, and in the same sense, that the interest of one nation is in accord with the common interest of all, as we have said that the interest of each individual, properly understood, is in accord with the interest of society.[10]

Nevertheless, the eighteenth century did witness the flowering of a mature realization of state interest. Writers of the age preferred to rely on the calculation by each state of its own advantage in a world in which war was a juridically acceptable instrument of policy. Yet statesmen did not see them-

10. *Vie de M. Turgot* (London, 1786), 247–48, quoted in Robert E. Osgood and Robert W. Tucker, *Force, Order, and Justice* (Baltimore, 1967), 17.

selves in a war of all against all in which the only rule was to extend one's power by whatever means, fair or foul. Instead, Europe was viewed, according to Burke, as a "federative society—or, in other words, . . . [a] diplomatic republic." By the standards of this society, state interest was not simply the desire for aggrandizement, backed up by enough military power to make that desire a reality. As the result of rational deliberation, a state's definition of its interest had to be the conclusion of a reasoned argument that would convince other members of the society that the state, though looking after its own welfare as was its duty, was not aiming at hegemony and the destruction of the system. State interest was not altruism, though it was expected to be moderate. Nor was there any assurance that interests would never conflict; the standards of the society were relaxed enough to admit that reasonable cases could be made by opposing parties. Nor yet would state interest, even correctly understood, necessarily rule out war; when interests conflicted, war remained the *ultima ratio*, even among members of the society. Lastly, no guarantee existed that a state would not defy the society, define its objectives in excess of what the rules of interest allowed as reasonable, and still profit greatly. No less skilled a practitioner of eighteenth-century diplomacy than Frederick the Great admitted that his successful seizure of Silesia strained, if it did not break, the consensus that each state's conception of its interests was supposed to undergird and to reflect. Despite these limitations, however, state interest was the mainstay of *ottocento* international politics, which on the whole were restrained and mindful of the needs of the framework within which they were carried on.[11]

Both the limits and the possibilities of interest were revealed in the writings of the practitioners as well as the theorists of the diplomacy of the age. Two can be taken as representative of the rest: first, one who spent his life immersed in Europe's politics, Frederick the Great; second, a group of men who tried to escape from the European system, the founders of the American Republic.

Frederick labored under no illusions concerning the moral limitations of interest, as he made clear in a letter to friends in 1742: "You might cure all the ills of war, but I tell you candidly that you will not have achieved

11. Edward V. Gulick, *Europe's Classical Balance of Power: A Case History of the Theory and Practice of One of the Great Concepts of European Statecraft* (New York, 1967), 23; Friedrich Kratochwil, "On the Notion of 'Interest' in International Relations," *International Organization*, XXXVI (Winter, 1982), 1–30.

anything, if you cannot banish two frightful things from this world—interest and ambition." [12] "Frightful" though it was, the king did not believe that interest could be banished, from the minds of men or from their politics. The only alternative, therefore, if one was not to be taken advantage of, was to pursue one's interest more skillfully than anyone else. "The interest of the *State*," Frederick wrote in 1775, "must serve as a rule for those who are governing. . . . This law is sacred." Still, while the ruler was to be the "slave" of state interest, this master was more than self-indulgence or unchecked ambition; it was, again, the product of prudential calculation. Thus did Frederick distinguish between the wars undertaken in pursuit of French "interests" and those occasioned by French "vanity."

Leading the eighteenth century in his insistence that knowledge of one's true interest required reason and a lack of passion, Frederick was not exempt from the tendency of the era to underestimate the irrational in politics. He displayed this confidence in his *Histoire de mon temps*. In his enumeration of influences—"bad policy, prejudices, false calculations, corruptions in the ministers"—that could cloud the ruler's vision of where his state's interest lay, Frederick echoed the words of Rohan. Yet where the earlier author had said only that the concept of interest could not be mistaken, regardless of whether the ruler grasped the idea, the later statesman seemed to conclude that the ruler could not mistake where his state's interest lay, because the rationality of true interest would soon impress itself on his mind.

How mistaken this confidence was, Frederick learned to his cost during the Seven Years' War, when anger over Frederick's actions brought France and Austria to lay aside their conflicting interests and ally against him. He protested in 1757, "Who could have imagined that an inexplicable change of mind and the intrigues of a few gossiping women could have alienated [France] from her true interest, and from the only system that really suited her?" State interest had proved less self-evident than Frederick had believed.

Still, despite this limitation in his thought, the Prussian king in his writings did confirm two further advances in the understanding of interest. One was the rejection of the older form of the interest of the prince in favor of the interest of the state. Frederick, describing himself as "the first servant of the people," firmly refused to countenance the influence of dynastic or per-

---

12. All quotations from Frederick's writings are taken from Meinecke, *Machiavellism*, 272–339 *passim*.

sonal considerations; for him, interest was understood by the purely intellectual light of *raison d'état*. The second advance was an occasional hint—it
can hardly be called more than this—that he accepted the idea alluded to
by Thucydides that great powers, in defining their interests, had an obligation to think of the needs of the system in which they held a position of
leadership. Certainly he felt that the great absolutist monarchies of his day
were more admirable than the minor Italian states of Machiavelli's. "The
policy of petty rulers is a tissue of villainy: the policy of great rulers has in
it more of wisdom, dissimulation and the love of glory," he asserted in 1752.
Large states might indeed be more tempted to misuse their greater power,
but being free of the immediately pressing fears for their security suffered by
small states, they might also display more magnanimity. At a minimum,
large states were under a particular obligation to support their claimed interests with reasoned arguments that would be convincing to other actors
in the system.

Meanwhile, across the Atlantic, a remarkable group of men were leading an effort to remove the American people from that system. While they
rejected political ties to the Old World, they did not forget the political
maxims that European experience had taught. They saw that the American
interest would be served by aloofness from Europe's troubles, but they did
not discard the concept of interest itself. A dispatch written by Washington
in 1778, as commander of the American forces in the Revolution, was as
somber and unflinching as anything penned by Frederick: "A small knowledge of human nature will convince us, that, with far the greatest part of
mankind, interest is the governing principle; and that almost every man is
more or less, under its influence. . . . It is vain to exclaim against the depravity of human nature on this account; the fact is so, the experience of
every age and nation has proved it and we must in a great measure, change
the constitution of man, before we can make it otherwise. No institution,
not built on the presumptive truth of these maxims can succeed." That the
influence of selfish advantage was as ubiquitous among states as among
individuals, and even less softened by other, more generous feelings, was
repeatedly attested to by Washington and others. In the first draft of his
Farewell Address, the president warned, "Whatever may be their professions, be assured fellow Citizens and the event will (as it always has) invari-
ably prove, that Nations as well as individuals, act for their own benefit,
and not for the benefit of others, unless both interests happen to be assimi-

lated." Likewise, in the Constitutional Convention, John Rutledge had told his fellow delegates, "Interest alone is the governing principle with nations," and Charles Pinckney, referring to commercial advantages in general, had echoed the words of his South Carolina colleague: "States pursue their interests with less scruple than individuals." [13]

If the Americans followed European convention in believing that one side of human nature was inevitably self-seeking, they also accepted the counterbalancing thesis that man's rational faculties could temper and shape the selfish passions, forging them into calculated interest. Restraint was essential if the statesman was to follow his true interest, Hamilton argued in the "Pacificus-Helvidius" debate: "True honor is a rational thing. . . . [W]hen it is asserted that war is preferable to the sacrifice of our rights and interests, this, to be true, to be rational, must be understood of such rights and interests as are certain, as are important, such as regard the honor, security, and prosperity of our country. It is not a right disputable, or of small consequence, it is not an interest temporary, partial, and inconsiderable, which will justify, in our condition, an appeal to arms." One fundamental test of whether a leader's definition of state interest was indeed rational lay in the opinion of other states. The Americans might be striving to escape European domination, but for some of them at any rate, the general opinion of international—in this age, European—society remained a measure of the rationality of the objectives of policy. If one had correctly grasped one's true interest, one could make a reasoned case for it before the courts and council chambers of other countries. [14]

Finally, just as the Founders accepted the existence of an international society above the state, which conducted an ongoing review of the reasonableness of its aims, so did they delve below the level of the prince. By their adoption of popular government—including, though it was less complete here than in domestic politics, control over foreign policy—and by their insistence that that government was established to secure the rights of the

13. John C. Fitzpatrick, ed., *The Writings of George Washington* (37 vols.; Washington, D.C., 1933), X, 363, XXXV, 57; Max Farrand, ed., *The Records of the Federal Convention of 1787* (4 vols.; New Haven, 1911), II, 364, 449.

14. Arnold Wolfers and Laurence W. Martin, eds., *The Anglo-American Tradition in Foreign Affairs: Readings from Thomas More to Woodrow Wilson* (New Haven, 1956), 150–51; *Federalist* 63, in Alexander Hamilton, John Jay, and James Madison, *The Federalist* (New York, 1937).

governed, those who founded the American Republic brought closer the day when "state interest" would be relabeled "national interest." Their construction of the institutions of republican government also reflected the belief that a well-ordered domestic regime would display a desirable combination of spirit, generosity in recognizing the rights of others, prudence, and rationality.[15]

Nationalism was set in opposition to the eighteenth-century view of interest, for the short run at least, during the turbulence of the Napoleonic Wars. From 1795 to 1815, wherever the French army marched, it carried the ideology of nationalism, which Napoleon used skillfully against the traditional monarchies he conquered and often effaced. Eventually, the states of the *ancien régime* had to employ the nationalist spirit they feared in order to dislodge French occupying forces and defeat Napoleon.

While nationalism was spreading across Europe, the concept of interest was being severely battered. Far from accepting the European framework within which France found herself, Napoleon set out to overturn it and achieve objectives that were the antithesis of moderate and limited. There was no need to present a reasoned case for French desires before the other powers of Europe; instead, it was for them to accommodate themselves as best they could to the new world created by the *Grande Armée*. Interest was wrenched back to the pure self-assertion of Machiavelli's experience, but with the difference that the egoism was that, not of the small Italian states, but of the greatest power on the Continent.

Following the final defeat of Napoleon in 1815, the representatives of the victorious powers gathered in Vienna with the aim of recreating this system. Considering the destruction that had gone before, they succeeded to a surprising degree.[16] The peace imposed on France was not a vengeful one, and the gains achieved by each of the victors were limited by all the others to what was consistent with an equilibrium of power. In fact, the limitation of state interest to what was considered reasonable by other actors in the system now received new formal, institutional expression in the

15. Nathan Tarcov, "Principle, Prudence, and the Constitutional Division of Foreign Policy," in *Foreign Policy and the Constitution,* ed. Robert A. Goldwin and Robert A. Licht (Washington, D.C., 1990), 20–39.

16. See Gulick, *Europe's Classical Balance of Power;* Henry A. Kissinger, *A World Restored: Metternich, Castlereagh and the Problems of Peace, 1812–1822* (Boston, 1973); C. K. Webster, *The Congress of Vienna, 1814–15* (London, 1919).

series of European congresses held between 1815 and 1822 and in the looser but still effective Concert of Europe that followed. The statesmen who recalled with a shudder the difficulty with which the Napoleonic aim of dominion was blunted had, of course, a special reason to limit all individual objectives and preserve equilibrium, but their system outlived them. As late as the Congress of Berlin in 1878, the other powers could by their united efforts persuade Russia to accept less in the Balkans than it had wanted. What had been restored in 1815 was more than the traditional rulers of the prerevolutionary period or the system of national borders through which France had burst: it was the idea that "Europe" constituted the bar before which the claims of European states were to be brought. Its decisions were not always definitive, but its very existence served to restrain the claims of all appellants. Its spirit was summarized by the man whose name was attached to the age, Prince Metternich: "*Politics* is the science of the vital interests of States in its widest meaning. Since, however, an isolated state no longer exists, and is found only in the annals of the heathen world . . . we must always view the *society* of states as the essential condition of the modern world. . . . The great axioms of political science proceed from the knowledge of the true political interests of *all states;* it is upon these general interests that rests the guarantee of their existence." [17]

While Europeans were restoring an international society constructed along these lines, Americans were turning from that society. As the generation of leaders who had seen the country through the Revolutionary and Napoleonic wars passed from the scene, and as the opportunity of settling a new continent beckoned, Americans paid less attention to international affairs and their leaders disparaged the rules of conduct, such as the balance of power, that underlay the European states-system and the conception of its interest by each member of that system.

Given this isolation, it is the more striking that in their domestic politics Americans inculcated a doctrine with distinct similarities to Metternich's portrayal of state interest. This doctrine—which Tocqueville, in *Democracy in America,* labeled "self-interest rightly understood"—saw the individual citizen pursuing his private interests within the framework of a larger system that allowed all citizens to do the same. Like the theories of Frederick, Metternich, and others on the international level, this doctrine did not attempt

17. Gulick, *Europe's Classical Balance of Power,* 32.

what it saw as the futile task of persuading citizens to set aside their personal interests and devote themselves wholly to the common good. Instead, it sought to convince them of two things: (1) that diverting some of their resources to maintaining the system that gave them the freedom to pursue their own interest was itself in the long run also in their interest; and (2) that the preservation of the system depended to some extent on their willingness to moderate the demands of their private interests and to compromise their claims with those of others. The preservation of liberty did not comport with the fixation on private affairs by "serious" people who had no time for politics: "These people think they are following the principle of self-interest, but the idea they entertain of that principle is a very rude one; and the better to look after what they call their business, they neglect their chief business, which is to remain their own masters." Yet in a liberal regime citizens could not be asked to sacrifice their private interests entirely to the state. Tocqueville aimed for something less demanding, the recognition that the assertion of private interests had to be limited by the need to protect the liberal regime that made such assertion possible. "Regularity, temperance, moderation, foresight, self-command"—these were the qualities urged upon states by the classical doctrine of rational, restrained state interest; they were also the product, Tocqueville was convinced, of the "daily small acts of self-denial" that interest, rightly understood, would counsel.[18]

Tocqueville, of course, was speaking of an established polity with a charter laying out its basic consensus on political conduct—the Constitution—and a sovereign government wielding the authority to use force against those who pressed their interests so far as to break the bounds set by the community. Metternich and the others were referring to what was at best a confederation of sovereignties with no charter but the basic similarities of their cultures and no governing mechanism except the operation of the balance of power. The common interest was noticeably more tangible in the one case than in the other.

It is perhaps not surprising, then, that whereas the American regime could call on a sense of common interest, as well as its military power, to defeat an attempt at secession when the governing consensus broke down

18. Alexis de Tocqueville, *Democracy in America,* trans. Henry Reeve (2 vols., 1840; rpr. New York, 1961), II, 167, 147, xx.

and afterward to recreate one people, the European conception of rational, limited state interest decayed during the advance of the nineteenth century and finally collapsed in World War I. Some scholars have seen the breakdown of restraint in the failure of Bismarck's successors to manage the alliances he had created; others have traced it to his own contemptuous question when reminded that all the great powers had a European responsibility: "Who is Europe?" The old illusion that Nature always supplied an ultimate harmony of interests was replaced by the new illusion that Nature supplied the example of the survival of the fittest and countenanced the destruction of "inferior" systems of social organization.[19]

It may be, as Frederich Kratochwil argues, that German leaders went furthest in turning their backs on the older expectation that only those claims would be put forward that could be validated before Europe's international society. Berlin's diplomacy increasingly seemed to recognize no rights but its own and to accept no goal but its unrestrained power. Certainly, Germany suffered greatly after the war from the collapse of the European consensus on how far states could go in defining their interests. The Allies at Versailles recognized no obligation to justify their terms to the vanquished. As E. H. Carr has said: "One reason for the unprecedented vindictiveness of the peace treaties, and in particular of their economic causes, was that practical men no longer believed—as they had done fifty or a hundred years earlier—in an underlying harmony of interests between victors and defeated. The object was now to eliminate a competitor, a revival of whose prosperity might menace your own."[20] The events of the following decades and the unrestrained ambition of communism, fascism, and what Hans Morgenthau called "nationalistic universalism" only further confirmed the destruction of the limits that interest had once placed on the aims of states.

Meanwhile, in the United States, the unfolding years of the twentieth century were witness both to the most vigorous denunciations of national interest from those in high office and to a reawakened attention to the concept in academic circles. The tone for the former was set by Woodrow Wil-

19. George F. Kennan, *The Decline of Bismarck's European Order: Franco-Russian Relations, 1875–1890* (Princeton, 1979); Kratochwil, "On the Notion of 'Interest,'" 21–23.
20. See E. H. Carr, *The Twenty Years' Crisis, 1919–1939* (1939; rpr. New York, 1964), 22–62.

son in an address on Latin American policy delivered in the first year of his presidency: "Interest does not tie nations together; it sometimes separates them. But sympathy and understanding do unite them. . . . It is a very perilous thing to determine the foreign policy of a nation in the terms of material interest. It not only is unfair to those with whom you are dealing, but it is degrading as regards your own actions." Wilson's criticism overbore the earlier emphasis on interest by turn-of-the-century analysts such as Admiral Alfred T. Mahan and continued to dominate the public comments of American leaders through the Second World War, even as their actions groped for an accommodation between the ideals and interests that Wilson set up as opposites.[21]

Academic scholarship on national interest blossomed in the 1930s with Charles A. Beard's publication of *The Idea of National Interest* in 1934 and, later that same year, of a companion volume, *The Open Door at Home*.[22] As with so much of Beard's writings, however, these studies emphasized purely economic motives to the near-exclusion of all others. Thus, the great increase in attention to national interests came with the early postwar years and the growth of the "realist" school of political analysis, led by Hans J. Morgenthau.[23]

21. Arthur S. Link, ed., *The Papers of Woodrow Wilson* (46 vols. to date; Princeton, 1978), XXVIII, 448–50. Wilson's disparagement of national interests is all the more striking when one considers that much of the regulatory legislation of the Progressive period and of Wilson's own New Freedom rested on the ability of executive agencies and the courts to give reasonably specific definition to the related concept, "the public interest." See also Robert E. Osgood, *Ideals and Self-Interest in America's Foreign Relations: The Great Transformation of the Twentieth Century* (Chicago, 1953).

22. Charles A. Beard, *The Open Door at Home: A Trial Philosophy of National Interest* (New York, 1934).

23. Morgenthau's writings were voluminous. Among the most important on this subject were *In Defense of the National Interest: A Critical Examination of American Foreign Policy* (New York, 1951); "The Primacy of the National Interest," *American Scholar*, XVIII (Spring, 1949), 207–212; "The Mainsprings of American Foreign Policy: The National Interest vs. Moral Abstractions," *American Political Science Review*, XLIV (December, 1950), 833–45; "Another 'Great Debate': The National Interest of the United States," *American Political Science Review*, XLVI (December, 1952), 961–88; "What Is the National Interest of the United States?," *Annals of the American Academy of Political and Social Science*, CCLXXXII (July, 1952), 1–7; and "The Yardstick of National Interest," *Annals of the American Academy of Political and Social Science*, CCXCVI (November, 1954), 77–84.

Like the eighteenth-century statesmen, Morgenthau defined national interests in terms of the protection or expansion of the power of the state; like them, he believed that these interests could be apprehended through the exercise of the statesman's rationality. He feared that in abandoning the concept of interest in the late nineteenth and early twentieth centuries, national leaders, especially those in the United States, had thrown aside their surest guide to action, and his writings on the subject constituted as much a persuasive effort—designed to draw the attention of statesmen back to their lodestar—as a didactic or analytical one, meant to explore the various facets of the concept for scholarly understanding. Thus, when he compared national interest to the law of gravity, he did not mean, as critics charged, that leaders, regardless of their inclinations, were led as if by some invisible hand always and inevitably to act in accordance with their interest. If this had been so, there would have been no need to advocate following national interests. Instead, he was saying that if leaders ignored interest in their foreign policies they and their states would pay a price, just as one could defy the law of gravity and leap from a cliff but would incur a penalty for it. When he stated that interest should be the sole guide to state action, he was not being amoral. Rather, in his role as advocate, he was arguing that because interests could be compromised, while abstract moral or legal principles could not, a world directed by interest would be one characterized by moderate, limited state goals and actions—precisely the kind of world in which ethics would be most likely to survive. Against the breakdown of international order in the twentieth century, Morgenthau proposed revivifying national interest as a means of limiting state ambitions and restraining state actions.

The views of Morgenthau's opponents and other critics of analysis or policy founded on national interest will constitute the following chapter. Between them, the realists and the idealists conducted the "great debate" over moral principles and state actions until the behavioralist revolution of the 1960s condemned them both as sterile and unscientific. After a period of disuse in the 1970s, the concept of national interest has recently sparked renewed attention, particularly as debates over interdependence and ethics have raised once again old questions about the sources and limitations of state action. One can today subscribe to a foreign-policy journal entitled *The National Interest;* one can read a popular novel in the title of which the term appears.[24] It seems a propitious time to try to discover what national interest might say to the international politics of the 1990s. But first one ought to explore with the critics those limitations with which they have charged the idea and policies based on it.

24. See Marvin Kalb and Ted Koppel, *In the National Interest* (New York, 1978); Joseph Frankel, *National Interest* (New York, 1970); Donald E. Nuechterlein, *United States National Interests in a Changing World* (Lexington, Ky., 1973); Nuechterlein, *National Interests and Presidential Leadership: The Setting of Priorities* (Boulder, 1978); Stephen D. Krasner, *Defending the National Interest: Raw Materials Investments and U.S. Foreign Policy* (Princeton, 1978); Charles R. Beitz, *Political Theory and International Relations* (Princeton, 1979); Robert C. Johansen, *The National Interest and the Human Interest: An Analysis of U.S. Foreign Policy* (Princeton, 1980); Donald E. Nuechterlein, *America Overcommitted: United States National Interests in the 1980s* (Lexington, Ky., 1985); Karl von Vorys, *American National Interest: Virtue and Power in Foreign Policy* (New York, 1990).

II Debunking the National Interest

ANY DEFENSE OF the national interest bears a heavy burden of proof, for the charges against the concept are serious. The indictments consist of two main charges, each composed of several counts. The first is that *the national interest* is an ambiguous or even meaningless term, both because of the difficulty of defining an interest and because of uncertainty over the relationship between particular interests and the national interest. The second is that the national interest is an undesirable and even dangerous guide to thought and action, because it fails to reflect accurately the contending voices of a pluralistic society, and because it encourages an attitude of narrow nationalism that is unsuited to an interdependent world and is morally insupportable when judged by broader standards of ethics.[1]

THE AMBIGUITY OF THE NATIONAL INTEREST

A first group of observers questions the usefulness of *the national interest* because they find its meaning or meanings vague, uncertain, and even mutually contradictory. In the judgment of Cecil Crabb, for instance, "The concept of national interest . . . suffers acutely from imprecision and ambiguity. It is one thing to assert that America and all other nations *have* diplomatic interests; it is quite another thing to *define* these interests." Nevertheless, Crabb finds, "Not infrequently, among realists concepts like the 'national interest' degenerate into a kind of incantation or nostrum of foreign policy, as though intoning it often enough provides a sufficient guide to sound foreign policy formulation and execution." Similarly, Philip W. Quigg

1. Cf. Carl J. Friedrich, ed., *The Public Interest* (New York, 1962); Glendon Schubert, *The Public Interest: A Critique of the Theory of a Political Concept* (Glencoe, Ill., 1960).

argues, "People often speak of the national interest as though it were a sort of Rosetta Stone, providing answers to all the most perplexing questions of foreign policy. For some critics it is enough to assert that a particular policy is not in our national interest to establish that the policy is bad." And yet, "if it were self-evident what the national interest was and how it could be attained, Congress could complete its annual business in a few months and the Washington bureaucracy could be cut in half."[2] An incantation, a Rosetta Stone—these are terms more suited to the mystic or the antiquarian than to the analyst of the diplomatic conduct of states.

What is an interest?

Many of the doubts voiced by these writers and others concerning the value of the concept of national interest can be traced to uncertainties over the meaning of the term *interest,* whether of a national or any other kind. The problem is not that *interest* has no meaning, but that it has acquired too many, and that writers employing the term are not always consistent in the meaning they have chosen, nor do they make clear to their readers which meaning they are using at any one point. A phrase that is made to signify everything may eventually signify nothing, and interest, say some, has already followed *system* down this murky and treacherous path.[3]

The term has undeniably been used in a number of different ways. First, an interest may be a group that shares a particular goal or a common characteristic. In this sense, it is often joined with other terms to form such phrases as the neutral "interest group," the pejorative "special interest," or the still less desirable "selfish interest." Madison employed *interest* in this first manner in *Federalist* 10 when he referred to a "landed interest, manufacturing interest, a moneyed interest [and] many lesser interests" and said that "regulation of these various and interfering interests forms the principal task of modern legislation." Second, an interest has been defined as a pattern

2. Cecil V. Crabb, Jr., *American Foreign Policy in the Nuclear Age* (New York, 1972); Cecil V. Crabb, Jr., and June Savoy, "Hans J. Morgenthau's Version of *Realpolitik*," *Political Science Reviewer,* V (1975), 226; Philip W. Quigg, *America the Dutiful: An Assessment of U.S. Foreign Policy* (New York, 1971), 107, 108.

3. See Samuel Krislov, "What Is an Interest? The Rival Answers of Bentley, Pound, and MacIver," *Western Political Quarterly,* XVI (December, 1963), 831.

of action, or "any policy or course of action which an individual (or group of individuals) thinks will increase his chances to get what he wants, irrespective of what it is that he wants." This "interpolation from the actual activity of the group" was the meaning attached by Arthur Bentley, one of the early proponents of the group, or interest, theory of politics. In Bentley's view, observable actions, the only reliable data in the empirical study of politics, were an accurate reflector of the wishes of individuals and groups, which in turn constituted the fundamentals of politics. "The interest I put forward is a specific group interest in some definite course of conduct or activity," he asserted. "Group and group activity are equivalent terms."[4]

If *interest* may be taken to mean (1) a group with a common goal, or (2) the pattern of conduct members of the group display in attempting to reach that goal, it may also signify the object of their efforts or the goal itself. *Interest* defined as an objective or as a desirable state of affairs encompasses several other meanings. One is (3) *interest* as something that is desired or sought after. *Interest* in this sense is purely subjective, since it is defined solely by the preferences of the actor. It may be questioned on other grounds, but it cannot be said not to be his interest; if he wants it, then it *is* his interest. Warner R. Schilling is employing *interest* in this sense when he contends that no author "presumably intends to burden the reader with the conception of a self acting against its interests."[5] So was the Maryland state legislator who, when asked whether his sponsorship of a bill dealing with a retail trade in which he himself was involved did not constitute a conflict of interest, replied, "How does this conflict with my interest?"

Fourth, an interest may be more than a simple want or desire; it may be the object of a reasoned claim. Virginia Held has expressed this meaning in symbolic terms, explaining that the statement "x is in the interest of Ii" may mean that "a claim by or in behalf of Ii for x is asserted as justifiable," and gives supporting reasons in its defense. *Interest* in this sense is thus a mixture of simple want and moral or legal justification (which may or may not be valid, depending on its logic and its congruence with an accepted set of

4. Clarke E. Cochran, "The Politics of Interest: Philosophy and the Limitations of the Science of Politics," *American Journal of Political Science,* XVII (November, 1973), 751; Bentley quoted in Krislov, "What Is an Interest?," 832; Grenville Wall, "The Concept of Interest in Politics," *Politics and Society,* V (1975), 490.

5. Warner R. Schilling, "The Clarification of Ends: Or, Which Interest Is the National?," *World Politics,* VII (July, 1956), 576.

overarching norms to which all claims are appealed). This meaning of *interest* is closest to that employed by Kratochwil in his discussion of interest in eighteenth- and early nineteenth-century international politics.[6] It is also the first of the definitions of *interest* surveyed here to postulate the existence of politically relevant standards of conduct beyond groups and their assertions of desire.

Finally, one can find usages of *interest* that rest entirely on these regulatory standards, to the exclusion of preferences or wants. In this sense, one's interest constitutes that which is good or beneficial for one, regardless of whether it is what one wishes. An adherent of this view of *interest* would respond to Schilling's statement by saying that it is certainly possible for a self to act against its interest, since it may well have been led, through ignorance or vice, to desire what is not good for it. "A child may want to drink from a bottle of cleaning fluid, but it would be strange indeed to say that it was in his interest to do so," Cochran has asserted. "The phenomenon of 'mistaking one's interest' is, unfortunately, not rare." In this, he is following the view laid down by Lord Halifax more than three centuries ago:

> I will not deny but that *interest will not lie* is a right maxim, wherever it is sure to be understood; else one had as good affirm that no man in particular, or mankind in general, can ever be mistaken. [But] a nation is a great while before they can see, and generally must feel first before their sight is quite cleared. This maketh it so long before they can see their interest, that for the most part it is too late for them to pursue it. If men must be supposed always to follow their true interests, it must be meant of a new manufactory of mankind by God Almighty; there must be some new clay; the old stuff never yet made any such infallible creature.[7]

In this sense, interest, when it is correctly perceived, may well be a restraint on, rather than a reflection of, one's wants, preferences, or desires.

6. Virginia Held, *The Public Interest and Individual Interests* (New York, 1970), 31; Friedrich Kratochwil, "On the Notion of 'Interest' in International Relations," *International Organization,* XXXVI (Winter, 1982), 1–30.

7. Clarke E. Cochran, "Political Science and 'the Public Interest,'" *Journal of Politics,* XXXVI (May, 1974), 335; J. P. Kenyon, ed., *Halifax: Complete Works* (Baltimore, 1969), 158.

It will be seen that this fifth meaning of *interest* stands in direct contrast to the third meaning, resting precisely on wants, which may be irrelevant to the question of one's long-term good. Both meanings may be differentiated from the notion of interest as a claim advanced with justifications, and none of the three can be equated with *interest* defined as a group or as a course of action. One is frequently hard-pressed to know which of the meanings is being used by authors who fail to define the term. When Secretary of State Alexander Haig warned, "The dictates of self-interests cannot be ignored forever," in which sense was he employing it?[8] The diversity of meanings can mislead the unwary writer or speaker into unconsciously sliding from one usage to another within the same work, disseminating confusion rather than enlightenment. It is this confusion engendered by the variable and uncertain meanings of interest that forms the first count in the charge of ambiguity against national interest.

What is the national interest?

Confusion is unlikely to be resolved simply by modifying the noun *interest* with the adjective *national*. How is the national interest arrived at? What is its relation to particular interests, of individuals or of other social groups? Crabb has called for answers to these questions in decrying "inadequate attention to the process by which the national interest of the United States and other countries is formulated, continually reformulated, and translated into national policies and programs."[9] The problem, once again, is not that those concerned with the national interest have given no thought and provided no responses to these questions, but that they have returned a number of differing answers, each of which has been subjected to further objections from the critics.

Like the term *interest*, the term *national interest* has been given more than its share of mutually inconsistent meanings. One is that the national interest or the public interest (the two are often assumed to be synonymous) is nothing more than the sum of all the particular subnational interests found within the society in question. As a vector sum may be calculated

8. U.S. Department of State, *Bulletin,* LXXXI (August, 1981), 86, LXXXIII (March, 1983), 82.
9. Crabb and Savoy, "Morgenthau's Version of *Realpolitik,*" 226.

from the various forces acting on a body according to the laws of physics, so the overall interest of the society is a resultant of the various contending interests comprising it. These interests make their demands upon the political system, bargain and compete within it, and—assuming that the rules governing political action are fairly drawn and administered—arrive at the common good. Bentley supplied the classic statement of this first view in dismissing serious notions of a "public interest": "We shall never find a group interest of the society as a whole . . . [T]he society itself is nothing other than the complex of the groups that compose it." Beard found the same thinking applied to the national interest—"an aggregation of particularities assembled like eggs in a basket."[10] Under this definition, there was no need to prove that Beard's particularities were in the national interest; their success in imposing themselves on the political system meant by definition that they were a part of the common good. Nor is there in fact any means of such a demonstration, since there exists no standard by which policy may be judged except political success.

This argument is fairly standard pluralist doctrine, and it should therefore not be surprising that Thomas Cook and Malcolm Moos, in their attempt to break the link between national interest and traditional concepts of *raison d'état* and make it compatible with the diversity of American society, should have come closest to adopting this first definition. They praise "the normal pursuit of individual interests, ideally held to constitute in their sum the more appropriate long-term interest of the nation," and hold that the objective of diplomacy "must be to render viable and to harmonize, in a coherent and dynamic pattern of policy, the diverse elements which in their sum comprise the national interest of the American social order." This "new and slowly evolved American contribution by example to a better world order" is "most suited to attain the dominance of a societal, rather than a statist, concept of national interest." Cook and Moos do say, "A national interest, it is true, is not merely a sum of individual interests, which, in part by very reason of their divergencies, cannot be added or averaged." Nevertheless, their concept of the national interest is of "an interest which is molded and shaped by the more finite interests." "The national interest is at most a continuous and quasi-organic outcome and synthesis of an interplay of forces, in which varied concepts of the national role and function

10. Arthur Bentley, *The Process of Government*, ed. Peter Odegard (1908; rpr. Cambridge, Mass., 1967), 222; Charles A. Beard, *The Idea of National Interest: An Analytical Study in American Foreign Policy* (New York, 1934), 167.

and of the relationship of particular interests to the nation are an inherent part."[11] The national interest remains subsequent, rather than prior, to the existence of less inclusive interests.

James Rosenau, a severe critic of the national interest however it is defined, points out that adherents of the first definition—whom he calls "subjectivists"—must eschew any idea that the national interest is necessarily stable for extended periods of time. It is, instead, "a pluralist set of subjective preferences that change whenever the requirements and aspirations of the nation's members change."[12] As such, it loses all power to guide policy. If the national interest has no reality other than as a reflection of the struggles of less inclusive interests, it is incapable of performing one of the primary functions its defenders reserve for it—serving as a standard of judgment for the formulation and execution of policy. It is rather an epiphenomenon, a scorecard of the success or failure of other, smaller collectivities.

Indeed, under the first definition there is, properly speaking, no nation at all, but a congeries of economic, regional, and other interest groups operating within a common institutional framework. This definition has been criticized as resting on an atomistic picture of individuals in society that gives too little weight to shared values and mutual attachments from which patriotism and nationalism derive their continuing force in world politics. Robert Paul Wolff has identified problems of conservation, public order, and the cultivation of the arts as examples of public goods, or concerns "of the society as a whole, not of any particular groups," and has gone on to point out, "To deal with such problems, there must be some way of constituting the whole society a genuine group with a group purpose and a conception of the common good."[13] Wolff could have added foreign policy as another concern that affects the whole of society and not simply unconnected groups within society.

Feeling the necessity of giving the common good somewhat more sub-

11. Thomas Cook and Malcolm Moos, "The American Idea of International Interest," *American Political Science Review*, XLVII (March, 1953), 31–42 *passim*; Cook and Moos, "Foreign Policy: The Realism of Idealism," *American Political Science Review*, XLVI (June, 1952), 345. Cook and Moos further develop these ideas in their "Hindrances to Foreign Policy: Individualism and Legalism," *Journal of Politics*, XV (February, 1953), 114–39, and in *Power Through Purpose: The Realism of Idealism as a Basis for Foreign Policy* (Baltimore, 1954), esp. 86–138.

12. "National Interest," in *International Encyclopedia of the Social Sciences*, XI, 35–36.

13. Robert Paul Wolff, *The Poverty of Liberalism* (Boston, 1968), 159.

stance than the first definition allows it, yet reluctant to grant that the nation as a whole might have views distinct from those advocated by groups within it, some observers have argued that the nation does have an interest in remaining the holder of the ring in political competition. This is the second meaning attached to the national or public interest—that it consists solely in the public's maintenance of an arena open to the free and fair competition of all interest groups. The nation is no longer a mirror, but a referee, who holds no opinions of his own on the desirable outcome of the contest but is concerned that the rules be followed while it is being played.

For support of this definition of *the national interest,* one may turn to Bernard Crick and the early Walter Lippmann. Crick has defined politics itself as the willingness to settle questions by means of free elections, negotiation, and other methods characteristic of liberal political systems, and he has identified the public interest with the preservation of this method of decisionmaking: "The plain truth is that what holds a free state together is neither general will nor a common interest, but simply politics itself. . . . In a political system the 'public interest', 'the common good', and 'the general will' are simply pretentious or partisan ways of describing the common interest in preserving the means of making public decisions politically." Likewise, in a passage striking because of its contrast with the better-known opinion he was to express thirty years later, Lippmann advocated a restrictive conception of the public interest that would concern itself with rules, not results: "The interest of the public is not in the rules and contracts and customs themselves but in the maintenance of a regime of rules, contract and custom. The public is interested in law, not in the laws; in the method of law, not in the substance; in the sanctity of contract, not in a particular contract; in understanding based on custom, not in this custom or that. . . . For there is only one common interest: that all special interests shall act according to settled rule." [14]

This endeavor to give the public or national interest a procedural rather than a substantive content has been subjected to the same criticisms raised against the first definition. By its own terms the national interest, under this definition, lacks a starting point other than the rules and the preservation of fair competition. Yet without an underlying sense

14. Bernard Crick, *In Defence of Politics* (2nd ed.; Chicago, 1972), 22, 124, 181; Walter Lippmann, *The Phantom Public: A Sequel to "Public Opinion"* (New York, 1922), 104–106.

of the common good, where do the rules originate, and how does one decide what is "fair"? The national interest can serve as a standard of judgment, but only of the methods utilized by participants in the political struggle, never of their ends; and it has no response when the rules themselves are challenged. It remains a variable dependent on the balance of forces struck within each country and the rules governing its political system; it is unavailable for the comparisons of foreign policies across national boundaries and across time in which many of its proponents have hoped to employ it. (There is also a school of thought that combines the first and second definitions and sees the public or national interest in both the point of equilibrium reached in the struggle among interest groups and the set of rules under which struggle is to be carried on. This double-barreled conception of national interest remains open to the objections laid against its constituent parts.) [15]

Among recent writers on the national interest, Stephen Krasner has come closest to adopting a third usage: "the preferences of central decision-makers." Espousing what he calls the "statist approach" to the study of foreign policy, he also notes, "This approach to the national interest . . . has no normative compenent. Policy-makers may define the national interest in ways that most observers would find abhorrent or stupid." And Donald Nuechterlein has defined the national interest as "*the perceived needs and desires* of some sovereign state comprising its external environment." [16] Like all definitions based on preferences, *national interest* in this meaning cannot be regarded as unchanging. It will vary with the wishes and desires of those occupying positions of influence in the state's policy-making apparatus. Thus Kenneth Boulding's injunction: "One thing we must learn is that the national interest is a variable and not a constant. . . . Within wide limits,

15. See Anthony Downs, "The Public Interest: Its Meaning in a Democracy," *Social Research*, XXIX (Spring, 1962), 1–36; Frank J. Sorauf, "The Public Interest Reconsidered," *Journal of Politics*, XIX (November, 1957), 616–39.

16. Stephen D. Krasner, *Defending the National Interest: Raw Materials Investments and U.S. Foreign Policy* (Princeton, 1978), 10, 43, 54*n*; Donald E. Nuechterlein, *National Interests and Presidential Leadership: The Setting of Priorities* (Boulder, 1978), 3. Krasner does add, however, that policy makers' preferences can accurately be called the national interest only "if they meet two desiderata: first, they are concerned with the general interests of the society (they do not persistently benefit some groups or classes and harm others); second, they maintain the same transitive ordering over time" (53). Thus, Krasner's position also draws on some elements of the fifth definition of national interest, discussed below.

this is a subjective variable."[17] Leaving aside for the moment the question of the source of the "wide limits," one can see that as policy makers are replaced from time to time, those assuming authority will bring with them their own ideas on the proper ends of policy, and the national interest will be altered according to these new preferences. No unvarying yardstick exists by which their validity may be tested, opening the way for the abuses described in the second section of this chapter.

A fourth meaning of *national interest* does provide such a yardstick, though not a single, universal one. Here, national interest is defined by the type of regime in place. Different regimes have different ends and require different foreign policies to promote those ends; a democracy will not have the same diplomatic goals as an aristocracy. The national interest, far from being the set of personal preferences of those in control of the state, is determined by the good of the type of government and society in question and, once settled in this manner, stands as a fixed point of reference according to which wishes, desires, and policy alternatives may be said to advance or retard the national good. A democracy cannot have the same ends, or national interest, as a dictatorship, nor a status-quo power as a revolutionary regime; societies of similar types, on the other hand, may share a conception of the national interest, by which the policies followed by any of them may be guided. Any state therefore has a set of standards alongside which its own attempt to follow the national interest can be placed, though not all states will be held to the same standards.

Raymond Aron in particular denied "that the national interest might, can or should be defined apart from the internal regime, the aspirations characteristic of the different classes, the political idea of the state." Granting that "the collectivity does not always change objectives when it changes its constitution, historical idea or ruling elite," he asked, "But how can the political units maintain, through revolutions, the same ambitions and the same methods?" In this opinion, Aron stood with writers, before and since, who have seen in "the political idea of the state" one of the primary determinants of state action in international affairs and, therefore, a gauge of the success or failure of such action.[18] The regime is the lock into which the key

17. In Erwin Knoll and Judith Nies McFadden, eds., *American Militarism, 1970: A Dialogue on the Distortion of Our National Priorities and the Need to Reassert Control over the Defense Establishment* (New York, 1969), 90.

18. Raymond Aron, *Peace and War: A Theory of International Relations*, trans. Rich-

of individual policies fits. Unless the key matches the lock, the door will not open; and different types of doors are equipped with different types of locks. Without this knowledge, neither the analyst nor the statesman will gain admittance to an understanding of the sources of diplomatic success.

In opposition to this view stood the figure perhaps most closely associated with study of the national interest in the past generation, Hans Morgenthau. Like Aron, Morgenthau employed the lessons of history; but unlike his French contemporary, he drew lessons entirely incompatible with the idea that national interest was dependent on and could be discerned from the nature of a political regime. His disagreement was fundamental with those who "assume that the kind of foreign policy a nation pursues is determined by the kind of domestic institutions it possesses and the kind of political philosophy to which it adheres. All of recorded history militates against that assumption. The national interest of great powers and, in good measure, the methods by which it is to be secured are impervious to ideological or institutional changes." [19]

Morgenthau adhered to a different conception of national interest, one that saw the goals of states as unaffected by the type of regime they possessed. National interest was the common currency of international relations and, as such, had to be applicable to all states, whatever their form of social organization. If it were held to vary among regimes, they would no longer speak the same language—that of interest. If their aims were incommensurate, two consequences, both of them unfortunate, would follow: statesmen would lose the common ground of national interest on which they might otherwise compromise their differences; and analysts would be left with no fixed point of reference by which they could measure the success or

---

ard Howard Fox and Annette Baker Fox (Abridged version; Garden City, N.Y., 1973), 83; Richard D. Sears, "The Classical Understanding of International Politics," in *Power, Principles and Interests: A Reader in World Politics*, ed. Jeffrey Salmon *et al.* (Lexington, Mass., 1985), 10–12; Kenneth N. Waltz, *Man, the State and War: A Theoretical Analysis* (New York, 1959), 80–158; Arthur Schlesinger, Jr., "Foreign Policy and the American Character," *Foreign Affairs*, LXII (Fall, 1983), 1–16; Aron, "What Is a Theory of International Relations?," *Journal of International Affairs*, XXI (1967), 194; Stanley Hoffmann, "Notes on the Limits of 'Realism,'" *Social Research*, XLVIII (Winter, 1981), 653–59; Michael Joseph Smith, "Hans Morgenthau and the American National Interest in the Early Cold War," *Social Research*, XLVIII (Winter, 1981), 766–85.

19. Hans J. Morgenthau, *The Restoration of American Politics* (Chicago, 1962), 199.

failure of the policies they studied. Policy and analysis would not be left *completely* at sea, as they would if national interest were nothing more than individual preferences, but they would still lack a single plane on which the foreign policies of all states might meet. The diplomatic ends of diverse regimes would lie in different dimensions, so to speak, with no point at which they could be seen to intersect.

Morgenthau and others have instead favored a fifth definition of *national interest,* one which is independent of (or, more accurately, encompasses) subnational interests and is common to all states, regardless or their reigning philosophy. Here, the "key concept of interest defined as power is an objective category which is universally valid." Hostage to an international environment made threatening by the aggressive urges intrinsic to human nature and by the absence of any effective protecting world government, states seek, by maintaining or augmenting their power, to protect their national interest, which means, first and foremost, their independence. "National security, then," is the cornerstone of the nation's interest, which "diplomacy must defend with adequate power without compromise."[20]

All states, if they are to be successful in preserving their security, must be guided by their national interest when they enter the arena of international politics. Not all international actions are political actions, but insofar as states are engaged in politics, their strategies and their actions may be judged according to the standard, derived "by rational political analysis," of national interest.

> Any rational approach to foreign policy requires the assumption that there exists a national interest as an objective datum, by which thought and action can orient themselves. Without that assumption, we could not speak of truth with regard to matters of foreign policy but only of opinion. People would take a stand according to their individual preferences, and there would be no possibility of distinguishing between correct and false opinion. One man's opinion would be as good as the next one's, and power to make one opinion prevail over the others in the contest of the marketplace would be the only applicable criterion.

20. Hans J. Morgenthau, *Politics Among Nations: The Struggle for Power and Peace* (5th ed.; New York, 1978), 8, 553; Morgenthau, "Another 'Great Debate': The National Interest of the United States," *American Political Science Review,* XLVI (December, 1952), 973.

It is obvious that nobody seriously concerned with foreign policy shares these sophist assumptions. We all assume implicitly that there exists a truth about matters political which is accessible to human reason. History bears that assumption out.[21]

Furthermore, this standard is timeless and universal.

But here the proponents of the other usages of *national interest* return the criticisms made of their preferred formulations, arguing the inadequacies of this overarching and ubiquitous national interest. If a national interest formed by conflicting particular interests is analytically unsatisfactory, they say, one that stands above those other interests is empirically insupportable. Here, one may cite Aron: "The plurality of concrete objectives and of ultimate objectives forbids a rational definition of 'national interest.' . . . Collectivities are composed of individuals and groups, each of which seeks its own objectives. . . . The interests of these individuals or of these groups, as they express themselves in actual behavior, are not spontaneously in accord with each other, and added together they do not constitute a general interest."[22]

Critics also charge that this conception of *national interest,* in postulating power as the goal of all states, ignores the reality that different states do in fact pursue different ends. National goals may vary from the expansionism of Napoleonic France to the isolationism of contemporary Myanmar, and only when facing the most immediate of threats will most states react in a similar way. Even when a state's independence—the preservation of which lies at the heart of its national interest—is threatened, it may choose, as did Czechoslovakia in 1938, to surrender rather than incur the deaths and destruction that would accompany resistance. The multitudinous objectives of states cannot fit the Procrustean bed of a single goal—power—into which this last definition of *national interest* tries to force them; no matter how elegant the theory, a messy world refuses to be bound by it.[23]

21. Hans J. Morgenthau and Noam Chomsky, "The National Interest and the Pentagon Papers," *Partisan Review,* XXXIX (1972), 362; Morgenthau, "The Reality of the National Interest," *Partisan Review,* XLVII (1980), 578.

22. Aron, *Peace and War,* 83. See also David B. Truman, *The Governmental Process: Political Interests and Public Opinion* (New York, 1951), 50–51.

23. See Arnold Wolfers' discussion of the lack of uniformity in national goals in his *Discord and Collaboration: Essays on International Politics* (Baltimore, 1962), 67–102, 147–66.

Finally, this definition is said to be open to manipulation and abuse on the part of those who are granted or arrogate to themselves the power to discern and transform into concrete policy a national interest that does not depend on the interplay of specific interests in an open political process. The danger of irresponsible power inherent in national interest will be treated below: let it suffice for now to record the conviction of Cook and Moos that "the theory and practice of a democratic society and culture are incompatible with an interpretation of the nation which pursues a super-interest according to which the interests of groups and persons are defined and determined, rather than an interest which is molded and shaped by the more finite interests." [24]

Conclusion: The ambiguity of the national interest

It seems, then, that the first defect of *the national interest* in the eyes of its critics is that it is a meaningless term with little or no substantive content. It cannot be defined—or, rather, it has too many definitions, all of them mutually incompatible. Analysts who have employed the concept in their work, including those who have found it a useful tool in the study of politics, have been unable to agree on what *the national interest* means; and the definition proposed by each camp has been attacked by the others on both normative and empirical grounds. How, it is asked, can a concept that is itself the subject of so much dispute prove useful in analyzing the disputes of international relations? Rather than a means of explaining events, it is a curious oddity in the history of political ideas, which should be studied as the political equivalent of alchemy or spontaneous generation. Its ambiguity makes it "a kind of UFO—an unidentified flying object." [25]

This ambiguity means that "the national interest" is adequate to neither

---

Also see Hedley Bull's dismissal of national interest, for this reason, as "an empty or vacuous guide," in *The Anarchical Society: A Study of Order in World Politics* (New York, 1977), 66–67. *Cf.* Vernon Van Dyke, "Values and Interests," *American Political Science Review,* LVI (September, 1962), 569; Felix Oppenheim, "Instrumental Values and Ultimate Goals," *American Political Science Review,* LVI (December, 1962), 975–76.

24. Cook and Moos, "The Realism of Idealism," 345.

25. Thomas L. Hughes, "On the Causes of Our Discontents," *Foreign Affairs,* XLVII (July, 1969), 666.

of the two functions envisaged for it by its proponents: the analytical function of an unvarying standard against which particular foreign-policy actions may be set in order to be explained, and the commendatory function of an ideal toward which the actions of statesmen *ought* to be directed.[26] If "the national interest" is the name attached to the outcome of the struggle for control over policy among various subnational actors, clearly it can have no power in determining whether what was done was in fact the correct course of action. It cannot be used as a measure of the policies of all nations, since it varies from state to state. It is itself "a variable and not a constant." Lacking even minimal consensus among scholars on what it means, it leaves unanswered a central question in international politics; whence derive the aims of states? If there is no single set of goals, together labeled "the national interest," which all states pursue, can the foreign policies of states be compared in any way? An ambiguous national interest is no guide; in fact, it is a hindrance, since it may easily become tautological. "Unless the national interest is precisely defined," P. D. Marchant has warned, "it would be easy, but unenlightening, to see it always informing the policy of the successful statesmen and quite absent from the minds of the unsuccessful."[27] How does one know when a statesman has followed the national interest? When he has been successful. How does one know when he has been successful? When he has followed the national interest.

THE DANGER OF THE NATIONAL INTEREST

If the first group of critics sees the national interest as a UFO, the second believes that it comes from a distinctly unfriendly planet. The burden of the second charge is that reference to "the national interest" by scholars and policy makers carries undesirable and even dangerous consequences for the country and the world. This charge, like the first, is made up of two counts. The first is that the national interest does not serve the nation well enough. Because of its ambiguity, "the national interest" can be a high-minded slogan lending respectability to policies that may have been arrived at in un-

26. See Richard E. Flathman, *The Public Interest: An Essay Concerning the Normative Discourse of Politics* (New York, 1966).

27. P. D. Marchant, "Realism and Foreign Policy," *International Relations*, I (April, 1959), 561.

democratic, unrepresentative ways and may have little to do with what are in fact the real needs of most members of the society. Employed as a cloak for policies determined by particular subnational groups, the term *national interest* may subvert the whole nation's true interest. Alternatively, for those who accept the pluralist competition of interests as the best approximation of rational policy-making that beings of finite intelligence can achieve, "the national interest" threatens to lure officials into abandoning the partial rationality of incrementalism for the false hope of complete rationality. Such hubris can deprive policy of whatever rationality it might achieve. The second count, by contrast, is that the national interest serves the nation only too well and too exclusively. While policies directed to the national good may have been justified when states were the most effective agents for solving human problems, the national interest is obsolescent in an age in which interdependence and the complexity and scope of global challenges make entities more inclusive than the state the proper ones to look to for the satisfaction of human wants. Moreover, excessive attention to national advantage can mean neglect of the broader human good, leading to a foreign policy that is at least grasping and uncompromising and may be wholly egoistic and aggressive. It is on these largely normative grounds that the second panel of witnesses against the national interest (who, of course, include many of the same figures as the first) present their evidence. Here, "the national interest" is "a questionable concept,"[28] not so much because it is analytically flawed as because it promotes policies that are unwise, unfair—in a word, dangerous.

The undemocratic national interest

This objection to the national interest derives its force both from the concept's vagueness and from its commendatory function: no one seems to know what *the national interest* means, yet everyone is in favor of it. Under these circumstances, one runs the "risk that national interest is retroactively read into public policies in the formulation of which it may have played no, or at best only a marginal, role." The term may be appropriated by subna-

28. The phrase is David Reisman's. See Carl Marcy, ed., *Common Sense in U.S.-Soviet Relations* (Washington, D.C., 1978), 50.

tional groups and its widespread appeal among the general public used to cover these groups' own aims, which, if they were to be revealed for what they were—the desires of "special interests," not the "national interest"—would be far less likely to obtain public support.[29]

Because of its vagueness, the national interest gives special-interest groups the opportunity to advertise their goals as something more than what they really are; because of its commendatory function, it gives them the motive to do so. If "the national interest" were not part of political discourse, particular interests would be forced to compete on equal terms and to make their case stand on its own merits when they submitted their claims to the political process. Since "the national interest" *is* widely, if not always thoughtfully, employed, political debate is often replaced by a rush by each group to drape its goals in the mantle of national interest.[30]

One should not assume that this is a tactic only of pressure groups—economic, ethnic, or ideological—outside the government. The bureaucratic-politics school, in interpreting policy as the result of pulling and hauling by intragovernmental actors and in attacking Morgenthau and others for their reliance on the "rational-actor model," makes it clear that, far from being the end of policy or a guide to it, the national interest serves as a weapon wielded in the bureaucratic struggle by public officials. Career personnel, political appointees, and elected officials, like nongovernmental pressure groups, all seek to identify their aims with the national interest in order to persuade their peers and superiors to embody those aims in policy. Thus Morton Halperin writes on the purposes of the arguments that accompany a proposal through the bureaucracy: "one purpose of arguments is to demonstrate to [senior] players that something can be supported on national interest grounds. The national interest arguments need not be totally persuasive or irrefutable; they simply must demonstrate that it is possible to support a certain outcome on national interest grounds."[31] Players in these

29. Fred A. Sondermann, "The Concept of the National Interest," *Orbis*, XXI (Spring, 1977), 133. See also Truman, *The Governmental Process*, 51; Charles P. Kindleberger, *Power and Money: The Economics of International Politics and the Politics of International Economics* (New York, 1970), 21–22.

30. See "National Interest," in *International Encyclopedia of the Social Sciences*, XI, 36–37.

31. Morton Halperin, *Bureaucratic Politics and Foreign Policy* (Washington, D.C., 1974), 136–37. The national-interest argument can make its influence felt downward as well

intragovernmental games may be pursuing aims designed to promote their personal advancement, to increase the authority and resources of their organizations, or to advance domestic goals unrelated to foreign policy. The national interest serves as a convenient cover for actions taken with one or more of these goals in mind, justifying them to the desired audience, inside government or out.

However the policies have been arrived at and whoever the particular interests that have been influential in the decision-making process, the result is a course of action that may bear only an accidental resemblance to any valid common good. Despite this fact, or more likely because of it, national-interest rhetoric may then be employed to stifle dissent by painting opponents as unpatriotic. In this sense, national interest "can turn into a weapon that saps democratic processes. There has probably never been a tyrant in history who did not justify himself with the excuse of the national interest, and probably very few who did not succeed in believing that they were the living embodiment of the national interest." [32]

It is this *ex post facto* application of the "national interest" label by decision makers to actions that may have actually been taken with very little thought given to the good of the entire nation that strikes some observers as undemocratic: "Just as tranquilizers quiet the inner agitation of the individual, so do slogans like 'national interest' mask the inner agitations of the body politic by obscuring and concealing the ideas, motives and interests of those who occupy the seats of power. In a very real sense 'national interest' is the opiate of twentieth century masses." Drugged by this meretricious slogan with its sugar coating of patriotism, the people may submit to a soulless *raison d'état* that sacrifices their rights in the name of the national interest and "leads to the ultimate enthronement of the organic nation state, with statism as its present-day corollary." [33]

---

as upward through the chain of command. See Halperin's assertion that "one of the President's most important assets is his ability to persuade his principal associates that something he wishes to do is in the national interest" (281–82).

32. David Wood, "In National Interest," London *Times*, June 9, 1969, p. 9. See also Crabb, *American Foreign Policy,* 473; Gerhard Colm, "In Defense of the Public Interest," *Social Research,* XXVII (Autumn, 1960), 306–307.

33. Eugene David Weinstein, "The Ignoble Lie—National Interest Ideology in American Civilization" (Ph.D. dissertation, University of Minnesota, 1967), 280; Cook and Moos, "The American Idea of International Interest," 36.

The fear has even been expressed that the national interest may justify the violent suppression of minorities. Bernard Crick has attacked the idea of a common good or of "some allegedly objective 'general will' or public interest" on these grounds: "These are misleading and pretentious explanations of how a community holds together; worse, they can even be justifications for the sudden destruction of some elements in the community in favour of others—there is no right to obstruct the general will, it is said."[34] Here one finds the complete degradation of the national interest—from an aspiration for the common good to a rationalization for the elimination of unwelcome members of the society.

The irrational national interest

The first explication of the dangers presented by the national interest rested on the charge that participants in the policy-making process make decisions on grounds other than a reasoned conception of the common good, and then draw on the loyalty evoked by that common good to smother opposition to their self-interested actions. The second argues that policy makers, whatever their intentions, cannot in fact achieve full rationality in their decisions, and says that they would be more dangerous if they tried. The first criticism questioned the motives of political actors; the second doubts their capacities. The rational political analysis demanded by Morgenthau is, in this view, beyond the ability of human beings, and any serious attempt to achieve it would imperil personal freedom.

This imposing standard of rational conduct is propounded by Herbert Simon, who has sought to demonstrate that for a choice among alternative actions to be considered wholly rational, there must be complete awareness of all possible choices, complete knowledge of all their consequences, and complete comparisons among all possible sets of consequences. In fact, none of these conditions is fulfilled in the decisions that officials make in the course of their duties. "I can testify from personal experience," George F. Kennan has said, "that not only can one never know, when one takes a farreaching decision in foreign policy, precisely what the consequences are going to be, but almost never do these consequences fully coincide with

34. Crick, *In Defence of Politics*, 24.

what one intended or expected." Statesmen are always under the gun, forced to make important choices in hurried circumstances on the basis of incomplete information. In a crisis-prone world of imperfect communication and frequent intentional deception, diplomacy cannot proceed otherwise. Even if they were granted more time, decisions makers could not achieve full rationality because of the limitations of human foresight and intelligence. Instead, in Simon's terms, human beings are capable only of "bounded rationality." [35]

Lippmann has defined the national or public interest as "what men would choose if they saw clearly, thought rationally, acted disinterestedly and benevolently." If rational deliberation and choice for the common good are made impossible by human limitations, what is to take their place? Kennan has advocated that the statesman be "guided by firm and sound principle instead of depending exclusively on his own farsightedness and powers of calculation." By contrast, for Charles E. Lindblom, an acceptable substitute is to be found in the pluralist competition of particular interests discussed above: "disjointed incrementalism—partisan mutual adjustment" will settle questions one by one, at different locations scattered throughout the political system, on the basis of the interplay of contending groups, in a way that is "good enough." The terms on which any issue is resolved will bear no necessary relation to those governing the resolution of others, and "stable long-term aspirations" that, taken together, might form an approximation of the national interest "will not appear as dominant values in the eyes of the analyst." [36]

Any attempt to substitute for this incremental approach a rational consideration of the broad lines of policy as a whole would be both impractical and hazardous. An approach to true rationality would require a system of information gathering, decision making, and implementation oversight so vast and highly centralized that it is highly unlikely to be attempted and, if

35. Herbert Simon, *Administrative Behavior: A Study in Decision-Making Processes in Administrative Organization* (New York, 1945), 67; George F. Kennan, "Foreign Policy and Christian Conscience," *Atlantic*, CCIII (May, 1959), 44; Herbert Simon, *Models of Man* (New York, 1957), xxiv, 198.

36. Walter Lippmann, *Essays in the Public Philosophy* (New York, 1955), 40; Kennan, "Foreign Policy and Christian Conscience," 44; Charles E. Lindblom, *The Intelligence of Democracy: Decision Making Through Mutual Adjustment* (New York, 1965); David Braybrooke and Charles Lindblom, *A Strategy of Decision: Policy Evaluation as a Social Process* (New York, 1963), 102.

attempted, would constitute a danger to liberty.[37] The demands the national interest makes on human rationality are incompatible with the limitations of the real world; any determined effort to overcome those limitations would be incompatible with a free society and would succeed merely in depriving the country of the incomplete but attainable rationality found in disjointed incrementalism—partisan mutual adjustment. Here, as elsewhere in political life, the best is the enemy of the good.

The obsolescent national interest

One of the sharpest attacks on the value of the national interest as a means of interpreting world politics has come from those who argue that nations themselves are obsolescent and their "interests" illusory. The advance of onrushing technological change, symbolized by the awesome capabilities of modern nuclear weapons and the intercontinental ballistic missiles that carry them, has made the idea of the front line of battle meaningless. All citizens, combatant and noncombatant alike, would be in the trenches in the event of a nuclear exchange, vulnerable to destruction by enemy weapons from which their own government is unable to protect them, as it is unable to protect itself. For some three hundred years (taking the Treaty of Westphalia as a somewhat arbitrary starting point) states were generally able to shelter their citizens from attack behind an impenetrable shield of frontier fortifications through which invaders had to pass. In today's age of insecurity and "permeability," they can no longer promise such safety to their peoples. Security, if it is obtainable at all, must be sought in agreements and institutional devices that transcend the state, which is rapidly losing its usefulness, though broader measures for assuring security have not yet superceded it. If not yet obsolete (because no fully effective replacement for it is in place), the state is undoubtedly obsolescent. It has lost its *raison d'être*, the protection of its inhabitants. If the national state is becoming a thing of the past, then so is that bundle of state goals known as "the national interest."[38]

37. Lindblom, *The Intelligence of Democracy*, 283, 285.

38. John H. Herz, "Rise and Demise of the Territorial State," in Herz, *The Nation-State and the Crisis of World Politics: Essays on International Politics in the Twentieth Century* (New York, 1976), 122. *Cf.* pp. 226–52.

Still, the indictment continues, one need not reach for the apocalyptic horrors of nuclear war to demonstrate the irrelevant and misleading nature of the national interest: the evidence is to be seen in the marketplace every day. Economic interdependence has hampered the ability of nation-states to chart their own course in matters of fiscal and monetary policies affecting inflation and unemployment, in the level of taxation and stringency of environmental regulation that have a significant impact on foreign trade, and in the rules under which economic activities outside one's own national borders—from satellite communications to mining the resources of the ocean floor—may be conducted. Writing more than a quarter of a century ago, an observer discerned in the early manifestation of these trends "an interdependence of people from antipodes to antipodes for all values, an interdependence which makes any conception of 'national interest' apart from the interest of most of the people of the world, the sheerest of illusions." [39]

As reliance on interpretations of "international" politics that make states the center of analysis has declined, interest in the power and objectives of other participants in "world" politics has increased. On one hand are those entities, including formal, structured organizations and informal groupings drawn together by mutual identification, that span geographical areas and populations far broader than those encompassed by any state. At most they lay claim to the loyalties, at least they figure in the calculations, of national elites and national publics. [40]

On the other hand are those subnational forces that in a world of increased interdependence see less and less utility in subordinating their goals to a hierarchical national interest defined by others and more and more advantages to be gained from alliances with like-minded forces in other states. This bargaining, carried on directly among such subnational groups without regard to national boundaries, tends to devalue the national interest because it bypasses and undercuts the coordination of those who presumably are to define the national interest, the central policy-makers. [41] Thus,

39. Myres S. McDougal, "Law and Power," *American Journal of International Law,* XLVII (January, 1952), 109.

40. See Joseph Frankel, "National Interest: A Vindication," *International Journal,* XXIV (Autumn, 1969), 718.

41. See J. Martin Rochester, "The 'National Interest' and Contemporary World Politics," *Review of Politics,* XL (January, 1978), 77–96; Robert Keohane and Joseph Nye, *Power and Interdependence: World Politics in Transition* (Boston, 1976); Stanley Hoffmann, *Primacy or World Order: American Foreign Policy Since the Cold War* (New York, 1980), 111–14.

squeezed from above and below by the impact of transnationalism, national decision-makers, and by extension the national interest, find themselves playing an increasingly marginal role in the world's political process. In such a world, say the critics, the national interest is both parochial and passé.

The exclusivist national interest

One further accusation against "the national interest" remains: that it is an inadequate and unappealing guide to foreign policy because, by positing the good of a single state as an acceptable rationale for diplomatic action, it excludes consideration of the rights and interests of most of mankind. National interest gives a superficially plausible justification to national egotism and to a grasping and perhaps aggressive foreign policy. The population of every state constitutes a minority of the world's inhabitants; even China can claim no more than a quarter of humanity. Even if the national interest is formulated to benefit, not simply an elite, but the whole of the national community, that national community forms only a small part of the world community. Because it ignores the world community, the national interest is too narrow a foundation on which to construct an enlightened international policy.

The criticism of the national interest as exclusivist takes two forms, which might be called the "soft" and the "hard" rejection. The soft rejection of the national interest accepts the national good as a valid goal of foreign policy but argues that the wise statesman will always seek communities of interest shared with like-minded states faced with the same problem or recognizing the same opportunity; talk of national interest creates competition and division of interest within this community where harmony would otherwise exist and impedes mutually beneficial cooperation. The hard rejection goes further and says that the preference for a national group defined by national interest is incompatible with any comprehensive system of ethics; conduct that was ethically valid would treat each person equally, regardless of his or her place of residence or nationality.

Those identified with the first, soft version of the exclusivist critique fear that use of concepts like the national interest brings out the worst in national leaders. A foreign minister who would otherwise be willing to compromise on a matter of interest to an alliance partner is instead persuaded to strike an obstructionist posture, popular at home, in defense of purely national interests; a president retreats from challenging but possibly productive international involvement into a crabbed isolationism that ignores events outside the national boundaries. Such an outlook is ultimately self-defeating, since policy defined solely in terms of its benefits for one nation instantly forfeits the useful collaboration of other nations. Concentration on national interest places blinders on decision makers; it cuts off the broader vision that is necessary to enlightened statesmanship.

John J. McCloy, for example, feared in 1953 that a policy couched in terms of national interest would widen the national fissures in, and thereby weaken, the necessary coalition against Soviet expansionism: "In a free world faced with the divisive forces unleashed by the Soviet Union, in a world whose salvation from all points of view—political, economic and military—is dependent upon a sense of community, what hope would there be of building such a community if the United States could present only a calculated policy of United States national interest to bind nations together?"[42] By comparison, in 1969 Thomas L. Hughes saw in national interest "things which do not readily lend themselves to a more inspiring description." "By definition," he argued, "national interest, whatever it is, lacks primary interest to others."[43] Hughes and McCloy differed in their immediate foreign-policy objectives, but they agreed that whatever its goal, if the United States wished to work with others, it would find that cloaking its words and actions in garments cut to fit the cloth of national interest would attract the notice of many but the sympathy of none. No nation that needed and wanted the goodwill of others could afford to rely on national interest.

McCloy, Hughes, and the other soft-exclusivist critics have based their arguments on instrumental objections to the national interest; they doubt its utility. The hard-exclusivist critics go further and ground their rejection of national interest on ethical issues; they doubt its justice. This second camp starts from the premise that any valid system of justice is universal, that it prescribes equal treatment of all human beings, unless there are intel-

42. John J. McCloy, *The Challenge to American Foreign Policy* (Cambridge, Mass., 1953), 23–26. McCloy expands on his definition of a "community of interest" on p. 65.

43. Hughes, "On the Causes of Our Discontents," 665–66. See also William Y. Elliott, ed., *United States Foreign Policy: Its Organization and Control* (New York, 1952), 21–23; and Elliott, *Prospect for America: The Rockefeller Panel Reports* (Garden City, N.Y., 1961), 20–21, 26.

lectually compelling and morally acceptable grounds for discriminating among individuals or classes of individuals. Prior conduct of individuals can supply such a ground: one can justify depriving criminals, but not others, of their freedom by sending them to prison as punishment directly related to their crimes. The simple fact of birth on one spot of the earth's surface as opposed to another, however, does not provide an acceptable reason for discrimination. Yet this differential treatment is precisely what national interest, with its focus on the good of a territorially defined portion of the human family, attempts to protect.

Charles R. Beitz has set forth the view that the proper unit for the ethical analysis of world politics is the individual, not the state. He concludes that "to clarify the issues involved in debates regarding foreign policy choices, it would seem preferable to dispense with the idea of the national interest altogether and instead appeal directly to the rights and interests of all persons affected by the choice."[44] Robert C. Johansen, emphasizing the argument of the "tragedy of the commons," under which rationally self-interested conduct by each actor results in degrading the system as a whole to the ultimate harm of all, has put forward an even sharper expression of the hard exclusivist criticism. He finds the "operational definition given to the national interest by the superpowers," for example, in "the temptation . . . to secure resources and power for one national or regional segment of the species while letting other segments of the species suffer or die." Those policy makers who pursue the national interest "are agents of the past and subverters of a more humane future," and their nationalism "will eventually be understood to be as morally outrageous as racism is viewed today."[45]

Finally, Robert W. Tucker sought in 1952 to demonstrate that once the national interest is accepted as the guide to national action, no harm to those outside the national community—no matter how severe in absolute terms or how great in proportion to the benefit derived by the national community—can count as an argument against a state action. "It must be understood," he says, "that once we deny the binding character of interna-

44. Charles R. Beitz, *Political Theory and International Relations* (Princeton, 1979), 55. Beitz relies heavily on an application in the international realm of the principles in John Rawls's *A Theory of Justice* (Cambridge, Mass., 1971).

45. Robert C. Johansen, *The National Interest and the Human Interest: An Analysis of U.S. Foreign Policy* (Princeton, 1980), 391–93.

tional moral obligations and assert the moral supremacy of the national interest, no action on the part of the state can be considered—from the viewpoint, of course, of that particular state's national interest—to be immoral. Thus the logical consequence of asserting the moral supremacy of the national interest is to assert the moral inferiority of all other national interests."[46]

Conclusion: the danger of the national interest

The national interest has been said to be dangerous in a number of ways. The first of these, that it is undemocratic, follows directly from its ambiguity. Because one can pin it down to no one specific meaning, it is easily used to mask the narrow self-interest of groups, inside or outside government, that may dominate the policy process. Although the common good in reality plays little part in the development of policy in such circumstances, the rhetoric of national interest can shroud the maneuvers of particular interests and stifle or even crush the objections of outsiders, thereby vitiating democratic control of the state's actions. The commendatory label of national interest is too easily hijacked by special interests.

By contrast, those who attack the national interest as irrational advocate a policy-making process in which various subunits press their particular demands and policy emerges from the outcomes of a series of discrete contests over individual issues. Trying to see policy as a whole and determine it in a comprehensively rational way is beyond the capacities of human intelligence and information-gathering capabilities, the argument runs; policy arrived at incrementally through the interplay of "selfish" groups is the closest approximation of rationality one can realistically achieve. The wholly rational ideal would be beyond man's grasp. It might endanger liberty because of the centralized political system it would require; it would almost certainly fail to achieve comprehensive rationality and might well produce policy that was more irrational, since, deprived of the power of self-interested groups to push them into the decision process, many factors

46. Robert W. Tucker, "Professor Morgenthau's Theory of Political 'Realism,'" *American Political Science Review*, XLVI (March, 1952), 223. See also McDougal, "Law and Power"; Paul Seabury, *Power, Freedom, and Diplomacy: The Foreign Policy of the United States of America* (New York, 1963), 141–46; Louis Rene Beres, *Reason and Realpolitik: U.S. Foreign Policy and World Order* (Lexington, Mass., 1984).

would never be examined. Where the first group distrusts the interplay of interests and fears that national-interest *language* will mask and thus protect it, the second relies on the interplay of interests and fears that national-interest *thinking* will tempt officials to abandon it.

Despite their differences, these first two camps of the "national-interest-as-dangerous" school clearly adhere to a vision of the common good: for the first, it is policy that is democratically arrived at; for the second, comprehensive rationality. What they suspect is that talk of a national interest endangers that common good; it screens the machinations of interest groups from public scrutiny and tars as unpatriotic the critics who wish to democratize the operations of government; or it tempts political actors to go beyond the limited rationality of which they are capable in a vain quest for perfection likely to destroy what rationality the process does have. Democrats think that the process of decision will be more open and tolerant of dissent without references to the national interest; pluralists and incrementalists, that it will be more rational. Both camps believe that use of the *term* national interest endangers their *concept* of national interest. In that, they are critics to only a limited extent.

The two groups are also at one in limiting their criticism in another respect: they both recognize that the term will continue to be used by some—though, not, they hope, by all. The first group harbors no illusions that actors in the political process will relinquish a rhetorical device that has proved so effective. Members of the first group affirm that scholars can profitably study the national interest as a political tactic—this is the "political significance in assertions of a totally inclusive interest within a nation" of which David Truman has written—but they hope that scholars will not fall prey to the attractions of the national interest themselves. For impartial outside analysis, Sondermann has said, the national interest raises "the problem of attempting to use a phrase so serviceable in public rhetoric as a concept of scholarly inquiry which is supposed to rise above debaters' ploys." "The national interest exists subjectively for those involved in politics; it does not exist objectively for those who wish to analyze politics," John H. Kautsky has added. "It ought to follow that the political scientist should leave the concept to the politician and policy-maker."[47]

47. Sondermann, "The Concept of the National Interest," 133; John H. Kautsky, "The National Interest: The Entomologist and the Beetle," *Midwest Journal of Political Science*, X (May, 1966), 224. See also Werner Levi, "National Interest," *American Political Science Re-*

On the other hand, scholars in the second group continue to employ an implicit concept of the national interest (or its equivalent). When they endeavor to demonstrate how a pluralist-incrementalist policy process produces the most nearly rational, "best" result, they have in mind an idea of the common good that is best served by this approach, even when they would reject explicit reference to a common interest.[48] It is too dangerous, however, for actors in that process to think and act in terms of the national interest, for to do so encourages them to confuse their own partial objectives with the overall good of society and to make unrealistically high demands on the rationality of the political system.

Against these two criticisms of the danger posed by the national interest one may set the second two critiques: that the national interest is obsolescent and that it is exclusivist. These two counts against the concept see no value, implicit or explicit, in it, nor do they hold that anyone—scholar or statesman—can profitably guide his actions by the national interest. The "obsolescent" school, it is true, does concede that in the past, states had to be led by their national interests, for self-preservation; and the soft exclusivists contend that thinking in terms of broader community interests will serve the national good as well. But in present circumstances, with interdependence fast becoming the dominant fact of world politics, both these groups fear that a policy constructed and couched in terms of national interest will inevitably be cast along lines so narrow that it will repel other states instead of attracting their sympathy and cooperation—and success in the face of modern challenges requires cooperation.

The most sweeping criticism of the national interest, that of the hard exclusivists, adopts a cosmopolitan standard of justice and denies that any system of thought that makes its goal the good of only a part of mankind could possibly meet that standard. It takes the indictment of unconstrained pluralism made by the national interest—that there is no guarantee that the unregulated interplay of the self-interested parts will result in the good of the whole—and applies it to the national interest itself. Self-interested actions by states are likely to produce only the destruction of

---

view, LXV (June, 1971), 487–88; "National Interest," in *International Encyclopedia of the Social Sciences,* XI, 34.

48. See Aaron Wildavsky, *The Politics of the Budgetary Process* (Boston, 1964), for a work employing incrementalist analysis along with an implicit idea of the common good.

the common goods of the world (*e.g.*, the environment), which it is no one's responsibility to protect. National-interest thinking creates an impenetrable barrier to concern for the suffering of other human beings—on one side (within the state), charity and a sense of common responsibility; on the other, utter indifference. Such a standard, say the critics, is condemned by any comprehensive system of ethics; so, too, should the national interest be condemned.

III   Defining the National Interest

GIVEN THE CASE laid out in the preceding chapter, it might be thought that *the national interest* should be retired from the vocabulary of scholar and statesman alike. If this is not to happen, a successful defense of *the national interest* must first demonstrate that it is not unacceptably vague by giving it a consistent, coherent meaning. Only then can we discover whether this definition meets the objections of the critics who say that the national interest is dangerous. The arguments against the concept may lead to an improved understanding of it through its reformulation and clarification, but do they mean that it cannot be formulated and clarified in the first instance?

THE NATIONAL INTEREST AND THE COMMON GOOD

The definition of *national interest* proposed here rejects the view that society is simply a framework for the interaction—sometimes cooperative, more often competitive—of smaller interest groups, which form the real data of politics. Society is that, certainly, but it is also a large group itself, with common standards of political ethics, with ties of mutual respect and appreciation (not only coinciding interests) binding its members together, and with a real common good that in the long run benefits all those within the group, in their role as members of the whole, if not always in their capacity of members of a subgroup. Individuals in society join together for purposes broader than convenience and the promotion of their own unshared aims; the society, in the words of Yves R. Simon, is more than a "partnership." Instead, it is a "community," or a "fellowship of common norms and common life . . . which gives meaning to human existence." Or if society can be seen as a partnership, it is in the sense of Burke's famous passage: "It is a partnership in all science; a partnership in all art; a partnership in every virtue and in all perfection. As the ends of such a partnership cannot be obtained in many generations, it becomes a partnership not only between those who are living, but between those who are living, those who are dead, and those who are to be born."[1]

The ties that bind us to a wider community may be seen in the career of every self-made individual, even in societies far removed from the historic, organic setting of which Burke spoke. The values of society, inherited from the past and constantly renewed and changed among those who share the present, promote, for example, the very approval of individual self-reliance or personal freedom that is sometimes said to be stifled by an emphasis placed on the common good. We cannot escape history, as Lincoln said, and the legacy of the past informs its inheritors, not singly but together.

If the society as a whole is granted a reality other than that of the sum of its contending parts, then it becomes difficult to deny that the group defined by the society has its "interest" just as the smaller, more particular groups have theirs. As they have their goals, so society has its own, more inclusive end: its preservation and improvement as the expression of the common life of its citizens and the means for promoting their common norms. Society's interest is the common good, which is determined neither by the interaction of interest groups nor by the answers given by a majority of respondents to public-opinion polls, but by an assessment of what will benefit this community in its aim of providing the best possible shared life for those who grow together within its bounds. In a true community, this shared experience does not threaten individual conscience, but recognizes an important but frequently neglected facet of it. The individual person lives and works in several roles, including family member, economic producer or consumer, adherent of a political party—and citizen. The notion of the common good argues that this last role cannot be reduced to any of the others or to some combination of them, and that acknowledgment of the autonomy of the role of citizen enriches individual lives rather than impoverishes them.[2]

1. Clarke E. Cochran, "Yves R. Simon and 'the Common Good': A Note on the Concept," *Ethics*, LXXXVIII (April, 1978), 229–39; Edmund Burke, *Reflections on the Revolution in France*, in *The Works of Edmund Burke* (8 vols.; London, 1910), II, 368. See also Cochran, "Political Science and 'The Public Interest,'" *Journal of Politics*, XXXVI (May, 1974), 327–55.

2. See Brian Barry, "The Public Interest," in *The Bias of Pluralism*, ed. William E. Con-

The common good or common interest, then, is an end that is defined by rational consideration of what leads to the benefit of the society, and by ✓ a normative choice of where the good of the whole lies. This exercise of rationality begins from the defining principles of the regime and works toward the public policy choices that will most effectively advance those principles. It assumes that norms have meaning, that some goals are inherently more worthy than others, and that society need not maintain the sort of value neutrality that precludes an autonomous public good and makes public policy a resultant of the collision of private interests.

Many different agencies within the society can be means of expressing the public good and attempting to bring this goal closer to reality. Recognition of the common good does not rule out diversity or make scattered centers of power within the society illegitimate or subject to state control. However, the political arena is perhaps the most important location for efforts to comprehend and further the common good. The public interest or the national interest lies in the obligation to protect and promote the good of the society. (This is far from saying that the public interest is always served by increasing the power of the state, or by siding with claims of state authority against individual rights or the traditions of groups within the society. Sometimes the state is better fitted to advance the public interest by having the scope of its authority limited.)

In the international realm, safeguarding the good of the society includes the ability to protect the society from outside threats: hence the emphasis, in much thinking on international relations, on the power that is necessary to deter or defeat outside interference with the society's never-realized but ever-continuing striving after the common good. A foreign policy guided by the national interest would seek to advance this common good by recognizing opportunities that foreign affairs may open; at a minimum, it would ward off foreign dangers to allow the society to continue its search for the public interest unhindered by extra-community threats. S. I. Benn, citing "the force of Mill's insistence on liberty and self-determination in character-building," has contended that "anything which is a condition necessary to the development of an individual into a person capable of making respon-

nolly (New York, 1969), 173–74; Walter Lippmann, *Essays in the Public Philosophy* (New York, 1955), 123–38; Mark Lilla, "What Is the Civic Interest?," *Public Interest*, no. 81 (Fall, 1985), 64–81.

sible decisions in his own interest, is both in his and in the public interest."
In a similar fashion, a nation's interest lies in that which allows it to develop
an understanding of its own needs and its common good, so that it can make
responsible decisions—an act that requires autonomy. Although he speaks
the language of morality and not of interest, Michael Walzer refers to the
same sort of shield, behind which a deliberative evolution takes place, when
he writes, "Over a long period of time, shared experiences and cooperative
activity of many different kinds shape a common life," or "a process of
association and mutuality, the ongoing character of which the state claims
to protect against external encroachment." George Kennan has applied this
definition to the national interest of the United States, for example: "The
fundamental interest of our Government in international affairs is . . . to
assure that we should be permitted, as a people, to continue this Pilgrim's
Progress toward a better America under the most favorable possible conditions, with a minimum of foreign interference, and also with a minimum of
inconvenience or provocation to the interests of other nations."[3]

This end of the community should not be reduced to the goals pursued
by policy makers. Nor can it be equated with a consensus in public opinion.
The common good is autonomous and forms the standard by which one
may judge official actions and popular opinion and assess the arguments
that officials use to justify their preferred policies. In the goals they set,
statesmen and other citizens may attempt to approximate the common
good, sometimes with success. Still, the complex set of aims they define by
their decisions and actions is only an estimation of the common interest; the
interest is itself an objective reality that does not depend on the aims selected
by policy makers. If these officials are skillful and wise, the national interest
they define will be quite close to the objective national good. But the two
are not the same. When I speak of redefining the national interest, therefore,
I refer to this set of goals in which leaders approach the national interest—their *perceptions* of the national interest—rather than the common
good itself. Without recourse to the underlying common good, however, it
is difficult to see how the actions of policy makers may be judged or the
terms in which a national debate can be carried on. Not every wish of po-

3. S. I. Benn, "'Interests' in Politics," in *Proceedings of the Aristotelian Society* (Lon-
don, 1960), n.s., LX, 139; Michael Walzer, *Just and Unjust Wars: A Moral Argument with
Historical Illustrations* (New York, 1977), 54; George F. Kennan, "Lectures on Foreign
Policy," *Illinois Law Review*, XLV (January–February, 1951), 734.

litical actors is in accord with the common good, and leaders should try, through precept and example, to distinguish between a widespread desire and the common interest, and to persuade their fellow citizens to prefer the latter.

With this background, one can compare "the national interest" and "the public interest," two phrases that are often treated as if they are synonymous. Nuechterlein identifies one significant difference when he suggests that "the way in which a government deals with the internal environment of the state is usually referred to as the *public interest,* but the way it deals with the external environment is the *national interest.*" The fact that the national interest and the public interest operate in different spheres leads to another distinction concerning their ethical legitimacy, a distinction perhaps most cogently expressed by Paul Seabury when he noted that the public interest referred to the whole of the society to which it was ascribed, while the national interest was always "engaged . . . in tension, conflict and co-operation" with the national interest of other members of the society of states, no one of which was superior to the others.[4] The public interest justifies public-spirited policy as a means to an end, the end being the good of that moral and political community found within national societies; national interest derives from the lack of community in international society and the consequent necessity for self-serving policies. The public interest forms the highest good in a society whose common good is defined by disinterested consideration of the legitimate well-being of all its members. The national interest serves the highest good in any one society; but looked at on the international level, it is one of a number of contending goods, each of which accords no deference to the others, because the common purposes of international society are few and weak.[5]

The national interest, even in a limited, constitutional state, may well be a narrower concept than the public interest. The latter may call for large positive goals to be carried out by government or other agencies for the betterment of the whole society; again, varying with the regime, it lays on the political realm a number of injunctions beginning "Thou shalt," as ex-

4. Donald E. Nuechterlein, *National Interests and Presidential Leadership: The Setting of Priorities* (Boulder, 1978), 4; Paul Seabury, *Power, Freedom, and Diplomacy: The Foreign Policy of the United States of America* (New York, 1963), 71–72, 8.

5. See Hans J. Morgenthau, *In Defense of the National Interest: A Critical Examination of American Foreign Policy* (New York, 1951), 47–50.

pressions of its positive obligations. The latter enjoins a negative duty in general: "Thou shalt not" allow forces originating outside the society to interfere with its domestic search for its common good. If the threats to the public interest from the international environment are large and immediate—as in a semi-anarchical states-system they may well be—the consequent policies demanded by the national interest may be expensive and intrusive upon the lives of citizens. But once the society meets its requirements of security and absence of outside interference, then other international questions may be said to be less than vital to the national interest and may much more safely be left to be affected by other forces, such as the interplay of private interests. Just where the limits of the national interest extend depends on the security position of the state in question, but for most states the national interest sets only the broad guidelines of what will allow the domestic debate to continue without undue outside interference. Thus, it does not pretend to give detailed answers to every dispute over specific issues.

"THE NATIONAL INTEREST" AND "NATIONAL INTERESTS"

The anarchical nature of the outside world sets limits on what a national society, acting through its state, can do consistent with its own safety. As the arena of competing sovereignties, the international realm brings us from discussions of a common society and its accompanying institutional framework to reflections on the interactions of contending units that recognize comparatively little society among them and no finally authoritative institutions over them. We go from the national *interest* to many national *interests*, and the difference in the possibilities for effective governance is profound.

The change from the singular *interest* to the plural *interests* is significant not only in the sense that there is more than one state with its interest at stake in international politics, but also in the sense that each state presses many different claims, or interests, on that fragile international society. These "interests" are claims that each society, usually through the agency of its state, makes on the outside world. The hope is frequently stated that if its interests are satisfied, the society will be able to continue its internal search for its own overall national interest, but states can put forward claims for reasons that go well beyond the limited aim of warding off interference by outsiders. These claims may be for objectives that the state is able to gain for itself, either without the involvement or over the objections of other members of the states-system. Alternatively, the claims may require the co-operation, willing or unwilling, of other states, which may or may not share in the benefits their attainment will bring. They range, as Hans Morgenthau noted, over "the whole gamut of objectives any nation has ever pursued or might possibly pursue." If a state has its back to the wall and is fighting for its life, its national interest may contract to the single goal of survival; in less desperate circumstances, the national interest may allow a range of specific interests, within which leaders may make choices of which to pursue without derogating from the overall common good. When Secretary of State Alexander Haig described the Middle East as "that complex and unstable region in which we have so many important economic, political, strategic, and even spiritual interests," one could see that however significant the United States considered the region, America's existence was not at stake there. Instead, there were many potential claims, or interests, each of which might have been desirable, but no one of which was vital.[6]

Given the diversity of these asserted interests and the lack of infinite resources (of material goods, prestige, or any other means of attaining these ends), some ordering principle must be at work selecting among all potential interests. In addition to internal questions of regime and the personal choices of individuals in positions of authority, two external constraints may help to determine which claims the leaders of a state will feel themselves prudent in making on its behalf and which are likely to be satisfied.

One constraint will be the state's geopolitical position. The security of a state in a self-help system, the balance between its power and its commitments, goes far toward delimiting its "moral opportunity"—that is, the degree to which it is safe in trying to realize its domestic principles in its international actions.[7] Because of their circumstances, some states are safer than others and can devote more of their resources to the promotion of their ideals. (Examples might include Great Britain's role in the abolition of the

---

6. Hans J. Morgenthau, *Politics Among Nations: The Struggle for Power and Peace* (5th ed.; New York, 1978), 9; U.S. Department of State, Bureau of Public Affairs, Current Policy No. 312, "U.S. Strategy in the Middle East," 2.

7. See Arnold Wolfers and Laurence W. Martin, eds., *The Anglo-American Tradition in Foreign Affairs: Readings from Thomas More to Woodrow Wilson* (New Haven, 1956), xvi–xvii, xx–xxiii.

slave trade and the United States' intervention in Vietnam.) Others, in a less secure setting, may believe that they lack the luxury of participating in reformist efforts and must focus their attention solely on their material interests. An awareness of the limits on his country's freedom of action was apparent in the words of South Vietnamese president Nguyen Van Thieu when he rejected the terms for a peace agreement negotiated by Henry Kissinger with North Vietnam in October of 1972:

> You are a giant, Dr. Kissinger. So you can probably afford the luxury of being easy in this agreement. I cannot. A bad agreement means nothing to you. What is the loss of South Vietnam if you look at the world's map? Just a speck. The loss of South Vietnam may even be good for you. It may be good to contain China, good for your world strategy. But a little Vietnamese doesn't play with a strategic map of the world. For us, it isn't a question of choosing between Moscow and Peking. It is a question of choosing between life and death.[8]

A second constraint, less often noted than the first, can be found in an international consensus, to the extent that it exists, on the proper extent of each state's interests. Here we return to the distinction between *interest* on one hand and *desire* or *want* on the other. Whether one is an individual, a group, or a state, if an object is truly one's interest, one can say more than "I want this." One cay say, "This is an interest of mine, or is in my interest, because—" and give a reasoned explanation of why the object, if achieved, conduces to one's good. *Interest,* that is to say, implies a common conceptual framework, within which all the players have a similar understanding of what constitutes a reasonable argument for what is "good" for each player and accept that interest can be justified by argument and not simply imposed by force. Even though states are pursuing different objectives, their leaders can recognize the terms of a valid or convincing rationale put forward by others in justification of their own goals.[9]

8. Quoted in John G. Stoessinger, *Henry Kissinger: The Anguish of Power* (New York, 1976), 68. Stephen Krasner discusses the differences between idealistic and interested states, not always to the advantage of the former, in his *Defending the National Interest: Raw Materials Investments and U.S. Foreign Policy* (Princeton, 1978), 333–47.
9. See Richard E. Flathman, *The Public Interest: An Essay Concerning the Normative*

Within the framework of a states-system, individual states assert claims—to territory, to predominance in a specific region, to any of the possible external objectives of political entities—and present reasons supporting these claims, or interests, to other members of the system. Although there is no international sovereign to define, much less disallow, an excessive claim, there are sanctions against flouting the current consensus on what the system can stand, found in the possibility that states will combine against one of their number that they believe is overreaching itself. Short of provoking such a defensive alliance, states are deterred or dissuaded from pursuing unilaterally conceived national interests to their full realization by the countervailing benefits to be derived from remaining within the prevailing agreement on acceptable and mutually reconcilable demands. And that agreement in turn derives from calculations of the amount of power that it is safe to allow any one state to accumulate. Participants in the states-system do not agree on much. They do agree on the desirability of allowing the game to go on, and this consensus entails preventing any player from transforming the system of independent states into a universal empire under its control. A distribution of power sufficiently dispersed to disallow any such threat: this is the international standard of the "anarchical society" against which asserted national interests are judged.

Thus, when the governments of states must decide whether to oppose, acquiesce in, or support claims put forward by one of their number, they assess the justifications on three grounds. One is the asserting state's national interest: Can this claim be reasonably connected to the continued independence of that state and its ability to carry on its domestic search for its common good? The second is the national interest of the states that must respond: Is this claim likely to undermine *their* autonomy and their own quest for the unhindered development of their regimes? The third is the international distribution of power that safeguards the self-determination of the great body of states: Will this claim, if allowed, leave the way open to an unbalanced distribution of power that could ultimately threaten the in-

---

Discourse of Politics (New York, 1966), esp. 68–84; Benn, "'Interests' in Politics," 123–40. Analysis of these common standards makes up a good deal of the literature on the concept of "international society." See Hedley Bull, *The Anarchical Society: A Study of Order in World Politics* (New York, 1977); Evan Luard, *International Society* (London, 1990); and James Mayall, *Nationalism and International Society* (Cambridge, Eng., 1990).

dependence that characterizes the states-system? These questions set the terms of the arguments that the public statements by those speaking for the asserting state must make as they explain the rationale for their interests.

The goals that the state asserts in its external relationships—these national interests, or, to distinguish them from the common good, these "state interests"—may vary almost without limit among states and, within one state, across time. Circumstances may make almost any aim a state interest of some state at some point. Yet, while these state interests display tremendous variety, they form a common thread that runs through much of international politics. On the basis of trade-offs among these interests, compromises can be struck and diplomacy carried on. Two states need not have the same interests to reach a settlement; in fact, they may more readily strike a bargain if they do not need or want the same thing. Despite their differences of regime, states can find in these interests a common language in which they may carry on diplomatic discourse. As Tocqueville told his fellow members of the Chamber of Deputies in his report on Algeria in 1847, "It would be unwise to believe that we could succeed in binding the indigenous peoples to ourselves through a community of ideas and habits, but we can hope to do so through a community of interests."[10]

On the other hand, because the overall common good in the care of each state depends so heavily on the society's constitutive principles, it is unique to each society (though different societies may have regimes that are more or less similar, giving the national interest of one a greater or lesser resemblance to the national interest of another). There is no unanimity among the citizens on the exact dimensions of the common good, but the debate over public policy is carried on in mutually comprehensible terms and in reference to shared principles. The national interest of a community sets that community apart from the outside world; it necessarily looks to those bonds that are shared by the members of the community among themselves but not with others. The national interest of one society may be incomprehensible to a society of another type.

Individual state interests, having almost infinite variety and particularity, can nevertheless form the common ground on which states may meet to compose or at least confine their differences through self-interested bar-

10. Alexis de Tocqueville, *Ecrits et Discours Politiques*, ed. J. P. Mayer (Paris, 1962), 329, Vol. III, Pt. 2 of Tocqueville, *Oeuvres Complètes*, 18 vols. projected.

ter. The much more constant overall national interest, going to the heart of a society's self-definition and resting on what makes it distinctive as a national community, reminds states of their differences on questions of transcendent importance. An international politics of interest focuses on the bargains states can strike and pushes into the background basic questions on which they will probably never be able to agree; it picks and chooses among a laundry list of particular interests and leaves unargued the fundamental issues of the national purpose that items on the list are intended to serve. Insofar as the United States and the Soviet Union reached agreement in their uneasy common history, they did so by concentrating on particular state interests—weapons systems, geographically defined spheres of influence, trading compacts—and not by debating their two overarching national interests, which were grounded in opposing conceptions of the best regime and the place of the individual. As the domestic changes let loose in the Soviet Union by Mikhail Gorbachev have altered the face of Soviet society, Americans have recognized more points of likeness in aspects of the two regimes and overall relations have become far less tense, but diplomatic haggling has continued to revolve around particular interests as they clash and coincide.

LINKS BETWEEN THE TWO REALMS

Thus, a state may be guided by an overall national interest, defined by its internal institutions, which assumes a coherent society—indeed, within which its citizens cannot truly know themselves except through the life they share with other members of that society, and which it is the duty of government to shield from intervention by those beyond its borders. This overall national interest supplies a general, but potent, justification for organized political activity directed toward the common good. At the same time, the state may generate many different national or state interests, or asserted claims—claims that the state finds it necessary to make because there exists no comparable international society, though there may be an inchoate system that has a common definition of a rational, justifiable claim.

One should not confuse or equate these two usages of *national interest.* It is mistaken to argue that the national society is merely the framework for the clash of self-interested groups and individuals—or at least to offer this as a general rule, without looking at particular societies. Some political entities may indeed have lost the sense of national interest altogether; they may have so thoroughly disintegrated through internecine strife and the rise of competing loyalties that the word *citizen* has for their inhabitants ceased to carry any connotation of common loyalty, belief, or affection. Lebanon seems a clear example today of such an atomization of society, and the break-up of the Soviet Union into its component parts may prove to be another. Even those contemporary countries that are not engaged in civil war are in spirit far removed from the Aristotelean polis, the civic-minded small republic rejected by Madison in *Federalist* 10, and the organic society revered by Burke. Peaceful though their politics is, it often displays precious little disinterested devotion to an abstract common good.[11] The assumption that *all* politics is simply the clash of particular interests and nothing else, however, is probably even more misleading than the assertion that *no* politics is anything but the disinterested search for impartial justice. To deny the common good as an object of deliberation is to reduce the domestic polity to the harsher level of the international setting. A self-fulfilling prophecy, undiluted pluralism inculcates a narrow self-interestedness that weakens whatever degree of national community and fraternity might otherwise exist.

Nor should one succumb to the fallacy of an automatic harmony of interests in the international realm; this grants its community too much substance and ignores the large element of competitiveness and hostility that characterizes international life. "To make the harmonization of interests the goal of political action is not the same thing as to postulate that a natural harmony of interests exists; and it is this latter postulate which has caused so much confusion in international thinking," warned E. H. Carr. It causes confusion still. Rather, international society is, in the words of one recent writer, "not a purposive association constituted by a joint wish on the part of all states to pursue certain ends in concert" but "an association of independent and diverse political communities, each devoted to its own ends and its own conceptions of the good, often related to one another by nothing more than the fragile ties of a common tradition of diplomacy."[12] Thus, pluralism makes its reappearance, now on the larger international stage.

11. See "Officiously to Keep Alive," *Economist,* October 1, 1988, p. 15; Inis L. Claude, Jr., "Myths About the State," *Review of International Studies,* XII (1986), 3–4; Bennett M. Berger, "Disenchanting the Concept of Community," *Society,* XXV (September–October, 1988), 50–52.

12. E. H. Carr, *The Twenty Years' Crisis, 1919–1939* (1939; rpr. New York, 1964), 51; Terry Nardin, *Law, Morality, and the Relations of States* (Princeton, 1983), 19.

Although it is often overlooked, one of the practices that has restrained states and maintained some order among them even as they pursued different ends is the acceptance of national interests as a guide to policy.

While the overall national interest and particular national interests ought to be distinguished, there is an interplay between the domestic and the international political debates that define these two kinds of national interest. Indeed, the debates can rarely be kept hidden from each other, and the vital decisions of foreign policy are often the result of a kind of conversation between the internal and the external. How might they affect each other?

The external debate may intrude on the internal when it is argued that restraints must be placed on personal or other private interests to allow the state to compete in the world arena. If the state is to show that it is serious in asserting a claim in the international society or in restraining what it views as excessive claims made by other states, it may take a stronger hand in domestic society by increasing taxes or by imposing wartime censorship of speech and the press or other controls on individual liberties.[13] It is worth noting that in seventeenth-century England, *national interest* and *raison d'état*—two terms that we tend to think of as being intimately linked—were often placed in opposition. The national interest was said (by the champions of Parliament, at any rate) to lie in the freedom of individuals and corporate entities to pursue their own ends, free from impositions made on them by royal authority in the name of state necessity, or the "primacy of foreign policy."[14] The inability to reconcile this parliamentary definition of the national interest with the king's definition of what was required abroad to protect England's national interests led to interminable wrangles over taxing authority, to rival assertions of other prerogatives, and ultimately to civil war. Today, ironically, it is the national interest that is criticized as dangerously open to undemocratic abuse because of the ease with which it may be employed to justify suppressing minorities (or even majorities). Even if this charge is exaggerated, effective action in the international setting may require some degree of domestic conformity.

13. A failure to link internal and external policies in this way may lead to charges of bluffing and hypocrisy. See, for example, Stephen S. Rosenfeld, "Mixed Signals," Washington *Post*, January 22, 1982, Sec. A, p. 15.

14. See J. A. W. Gunn, "'Interest Will Not Lie': A Seventeenth-Century Political Maxim," *Journal of the History of Ideas*, XXIX (October–December, 1968), 551–64.

Likewise, participants in the internal debate may seek to influence it by appeals to world opinion. In this case, what is seen as the general international consensus on a particular state's interests and duties becomes a source of authority for those on the domestic scene who wish to move that state's definition of its national interest in the same direction. When domestic actors ask themselves and their opponents, "What does the world expect of us," even if only in a cynical way, they are calling in the external world's judgment to redress the internal balance. Secretary of State Dean Acheson spoke in this way in an address in 1952: "Our position of leadership in the world calls for responsibility, not only by officials, but by all of us. It requires that we take no narrow view of our interests but that we conceive them in a broad and understanding way so that they include the interests of those joined with us in the defense of freedom. It requires that we do not do reckless things which impair these interests. We cannot dictate, we cannot be irresponsible, if we are to fulfill the mission of leadership among free peoples." [15] Here, Acheson was using what he believed was the existing pattern of expectations among Western nations on the proper role of the United States (its interests and its duties) to convince the American electorate to define the national interest so as to include an open and generous leadership abroad.

International actors may at times undertake to influence the internal debate in other states as well. Here the outside restraints on a state's definition of its interests are not being pulled into that state's domestic politics but are pushing themselves in, usually in an effort to persuade policy makers in the state that is made the object of such attention to conceive of their national interest in a modest way that does not entail putting unacceptable claims on the international society. George Kennan intended his original policy of containment to have this effect: as the leaders of the Soviet Union were confronted by the international community's continued successful resistance to their asserted demands for Soviet influence and power, the political climate within the Kremlin would change. Frustrated ideological fervor would diminish; the considerable domestic problems of the USSR would force their way to the head of the government's agenda; the regime would "mellow" and, over time, would come to accept a definition of its national interest that did not demand unconstrained hostility toward any center of

15. U.S. Department of State, *Bulletin*, XXVI (September 22, 1952), 427.

power the Kremlin did not control. For Kennan, "the main thing" was to "keep clearly in mind the image of what we would like to see in the personality of Russia as an actor on the world stage," and to derive from that definition of international behavior the domestic changes in Soviet governmental practice that the West could realistically and legitimately hope to encourage.[16] Skeptical of talk about the convergence of widely different social systems, uncomfortable with calls from foreigners for basic reforms in cultures that bore little resemblance to their own, anxious to fix the attention of policy makers primarily on international stability and the management of power, Kennan nevertheless believed that if a tacit, but lasting, international understanding was to be achieved on the acceptable limits within which the Soviet state might assert its national interests, the worst features of Soviet internal totalitarianism had to be eased.

On the other hand, *the internal debate may influence the external.* The external consensus on a state's proper national interests may be altered when the outside world "overhears" that state's internal debates. What other states might be willing to allow to a country whose domestic political process is dominated by those who are fundamentally satisfied with their nation's present status in the international order and evince little desire for conquest or other expansion of its power, they may resist ceding to a state in whose councils they hear prominent voices calling for further gains at someone else's expense. Is the state in question a status-quo power, or is it not? "Our notions of interest," noted Hume, "are much warped by our affections," including either the fear or the confidence that domestic statements on the requirements of a country's national interest inspire among decision makers abroad. "Though nations, in the main, are governed by what they suppose their interest," Alexander Hamilton recognized, "he must be imperfectly versed in human nature who thinks it indifferent whether the maxims of a State tend to excite kind or unkind dispositions in others, or who does not know that these dispositions may insensibly mould or bias the views of self-interest."[17]

Likewise, in attacking the agreement reached at Munich in 1938, Winston Churchill made the argument that what might have been conceded to

16. George F. Kennan, "America and the Russian Future," *Foreign Affairs*, XXIX (April, 1951), 368,

17. David Hume, *The History of England* (6 vols.; Philadelphia, n.d.), VI, 128; Wolfers and Martin, eds., *The Anglo-American Tradition*, 149.

the Weimar Republic could not safely be granted to the much more brutal and belligerent Nazi regime:

> You have to consider the character of the Nazi movement and the rule which it implies. The Prime Minister desires to see cordial relations between this country and Germany. There is no difficulty at all in having cordial relations with the German people. Our hearts go out to them. But they have no power. You must have diplomatic and correct relations, but there can never be friendship between the British democracy and the Nazi Power, that Power which spurns Christian ethics, which cheers its onward course by a barbarous paganism, which vaunts the spirit of aggression and conquest, which derives strength and perverted pleasure from persecution, and uses, as we have seen, with pitiless brutality the threat of murderous force. That Power cannot ever be the trusted friend of the British democracy.

Such assessments from the outside may be mistaken. Foreign observers tend to perceive more self-partiality in others' policies, more altruism in their own. Still, whatever its accuracy, a general sense that a state conceives of its national good in a way that makes it aggressive or dangerously expansionist can cause other states to close ranks against it and to narrow their view of its justifiable interests, in their own self-defense.[18]

To expect that the society of states will respond in this way to internal developments in one of its members, one must assume that leaders are paying attention to domestic events elsewhere and will act on what they see. It is possible, however, that those who are formally participants in the diplomatic game, accorded all the rights and duties that international law grants to the government of any sovereign state, may in fact be so preoccupied with the internal debate that they quite ignore the external. Polities that have recently undergone a revolutionary upheaval may be consumed in working out the terms of the radically revised conception of their common good that their change of regime has given them. In such cases, membership in a states-

18. Joel H. Weiner, ed., *Great Britain: Foreign Policy and the Span of Empire, 1689–1971—A Documentary History* (4 vols.; New York, 1972), II, 1030–31. See also Stephen M. Walt, "Alliance Formation and the Balance of World Power," *International Security*, IX (Spring, 1985), 3–43.

system of watchful players, who check excessive claims of interest on the part of any one of them, may be seen as a distraction. Lenin, confronted with the necessity of coping with an international system that the Bolshevik Revolution had quickly proved incapable of overthrowing, responded with the startled question, "What, are we going to have foreign relations?"[19]

Alternatively, states, particularly new states, may be solely concerned with the internal definition of their national interest through the fostering of a sense of nationhood, the creation of effective institutions of government, and the weakening of other foci of loyalty, such as the tribe, the region, the caste, or the religious group. In these cases, when the national interest in the sense of a common good cannot be said to exist and the national interest in the sense of a process for accommodating society's politically important actors (which can be either relatively egalitarian or more or less hierarchical) is still being worked out, socialization into an external consensus on the safe limits of state interests may be the last thing on the minds of policy makers. When the primacy of domestic policy is a fact of political life, even those charged with the conduct of foreign affairs may desire nothing more than to be left alone. Isolationism, neutrality, or neutralism has frequently been the response of state leaders who do not wish to have to make the choices and take the actions necessary to set multilateral bounds to the asserted interests of other states. Since these states are often small, weak, and fragile, while effective countermeasures (whether diplomatic, military, or otherwise) to potentially hegemonic states must generally be taken by those with a measure of size, strength, and resilience, this desire to opt out may not have very serious consequences for international stability. Kenneth Waltz has said that the result of interstate inequality in a bipolar setting is that in many cases "the two big states do the work while the small ones have the fun." Still, to the extent that domestic preoccupations with creating, redefining, or preserving the regime's idea of its national interest restrict participation in the ongoing international assessment of states' asserted claims, the internal debate over the national interest impinges on the collective external judgment of national interests.[20]

Finally, those who would ameliorate the conflicts of international rela-

19. Gordon A. Craig and Felix Gilbert, eds., *The Twenties* (1953; rpr. New York, 1967), 235, Vol. I of Craig and Gilbert, eds., *The Diplomats, 1919–1939*, 2 vols.

20. Claude, "Myths About the State"; Kenneth N. Waltz, *Theory of International Politics* (Reading, Mass., 1979), 185.

tions have sometimes hoped that democratization of the domestic political process would lead to greater respect for the interests of others abroad. Acceptance of the principles of national self-determination and nonintervention, and a general attitude of peaceableness, would be the result when the control of foreign affairs was given over to those who paid the costs of conflict, rather than those who benefited from it. Reasoning from a belief that the great mass of people were everywhere pacific, Woodrow Wilson and others have held that if the participants in the internal political debate were changed, the country's position in the external debate would change as well. If democracy had this effect in enough countries, the international standards on allowable interests would shift in a more cooperative, humane direction.[21]

THE CHANGING NATIONAL INTEREST

Different patterns of interaction between the internal debate over the requirements of the national interest, on one hand, and the international debate over any state's asserted national interests, on the other, may appear concurrently over different issues. In the 1980s the United States and other countries provided assistance Afghan rebels in order to compel the Soviet Union to withdraw the claim implicit in Moscow's occupation of Afghanistan, and by 1992 this external pressure, coupled with an internal change of leadership, was apparently succeeding. At the same time, restructuring of the Soviet domestic economy to replace some state enterprises with cooperative or individual ones and to encourage joint ventures with foreign firms indicated a reduction in Soviet economic autarchy, which in turn could explain Moscow's renewed expressions of interest in membership in the International Monetary Fund. These patterns inevitably change over time as well, as do the specific interests asserted by the government of any state.

One sees here the difference among the public interest (the society's common good, "a form or a final end"), which, though it is "not perfectly or wholly attainable," remains fairly constant unless there is a marked change of regime; the overall national interest (the retention by society of

21. Kenneth N. Waltz, *Man, the State, and War: A Theoretical Analysis* (New York, 1959), 117–19.

autonomy as it seeks its final end), which changes even less often; and specific national interests, which may indeed change, gaining or losing in importance and "justifiability" to others as circumstances alter. Analysts who forget this distinction run the risk of meriting Voltaire's rebuke: "Puffendorf, and those who write like him on the interests of princes, make almanacs, which are defective even for the current year, and which next year are absolutely good for nothing."[22] Statesmen of every era, working toward their society's public interest even though they never reach it, have the opportunity and the responsibility to reexamine the catalog of state interests or claims bequeathed to them by their predecessors. It is all too easy, as Admiral Mahan reminded his readers at the turn of the century, for a given set of asserted interests to congeal and thus persist in policy long after events have rendered them outdated. Mahan saw in the Monroe Doctrine an adaptability to different situations that marked a truly basic and long-lasting state interest—"an enduring principle of necessary self-interest"—because it lay at the heart of "not merely the interests of individual citizens, but the interests of the United States as a nation." Yet it was mistaken to assume that every interest was so important or that asserted claims never needed to be adjusted to "the ebb and flow of mundane things." The greatest statesmen, Martin Needler has more recently observed, may be "those whose vision extended to the creation of new roads for policy to take, and indeed the perception of national interests previously only dimly comprehended."[23]

Dean Acheson took this line of reasoning to what is perhaps its logical conclusion when, in an address on June 29, 1951, he raised the possibility that the country could acquire interests of which it was not even aware: "What we must do is to be conscious of our national interests. A commitment is a national vital interest of which we have become conscious and for which we have made provision, but we may have national interests, which are just as valid, of which we have not become conscious and for which we have not made provision—about which we should immediately become conscious and about which we should immediately make provision."[24] In

22. Cochran, "Political Science and 'the Public Interest,'" 355; *The Works of Voltaire: A Contemporary Version*, trans. William F. Fleming (42 vols.; rpr. New York, 1927), Vol. XIX, Pt. 2, p. 226.

23. Alfred T. Mahan, *The Interest of America in Sea Power, Present and Future* (Boston, 1911), 155–56; Mahan, *The Problem of Asia and Its Effects upon International Policies* (Boston, 1905), 16; Martin C. Needler, *Understanding Foreign Policy* (New York, 1966), 13.

24. U.S. Department of State, *Bulletin.* XXV (July 23, 1951), 126.

this statement, Acheson was putting his fellow citizens and other states on notice that there were interests the United States might soon assert for the first time. It was clear that he believed these claims could be justified with reasons—within the national community, reasons appealing to the need to serve the common good; in the more limited society of the international realm, reasons appealing to the desire to preserve the system of independent states by preventing the accumulation of a preponderance of power in the hands of any state that might overturn the system. But the country had yet to show that it would defend its emerging interests with diplomacy and, if need be, force. If Acheson lost the internal debate—if the United States failed to provide for the interests that in his view the international situation gave it good reasons for asserting—then an increasingly threatening environment would impair the ability of Americans to discuss, search out, and move toward their society's common good.

DEFINITIONS AND DELIBERATION

To sum up, if one were asked to decide whether national interest is, in James Rosenau's terms, an objective or a subjective concept, I suggest that one's proper answer would be, without equivocation, "Both." The public interest, properly understood, is the object of policy makers' discussions, not the outcome of their decisions. It is the goal they ought to have in mind as they deliberate; it is the standard that gives them some ground for choosing one policy over another. Without it, they are reduced to saying that they "like" one alternative, without being able to give reasons for their choice, or asserting that they advocate a position because it will redound to their narrow personal advantage. The public interest, the shared good of the national community, gives politics the character of a debate (even if politics also comprises a struggle for power), and it provides decision makers with a framework setting the terms of the debate—one standing between the interest of an individual or a group, on one hand, and an insubstantial universal community or general moral principles on the other. Thus one can begin to interpret President Reagan's statement in 1986, in response to a reporter's question, "Anything we do is in our national security interest." [25] If the na-

---

25. "National Interest," in *International Encyclopedia of the Social Sciences,* XI, 35–39; Washington *Post,* July 21, 1986, Sec. A, p. 2.

tional interest is considered a pleasing euphemism for "what I (or my advisers) want to do," then the comment is a truism: whatever is the outcome of the policy process is *always* in the national interest. But if the protection of this debate from outside interference is a standard against which specific actions can be measured, then the president's statement becomes a meaningful contention, and others may logically present evidence to sustain or disprove it.

While this national interest prompts leaders to make policy by asking themselves certain questions, it does not guarantee that they will all arrive at a single answer. They may press a variety of claims, or asserted national interests, on the society of states. If these interests are to be distinguished from simple wishes or desires, they can be justified with reference both to the common good of the national community in the name of which they are pressed, and to the basic "charter" of the states-system, which lacks the concern for others found in a living national community but does disallow the accumulation of excessive power by any state potentially capable of overthrowing the system. Subjective in the sense that they are claims put forward at decision makers' discretion, these interests may nevertheless be labeled harmful or mistaken (not merely the products of a different but equally valid opinion) if their sponsors cannot produce arguments to overcome objections that the policies they entail will undermine the national common good or transgress the (admittedly generous) limits imposed by the society of states.

Identifying these two meanings of *national interest* does not exhaust the list of reasons for which officials may act—others would include personal profit or advancement within an organizational hierarchy, electoral concerns, bureaucratic routines, and transcendent moral obligations. Nor should one assume that interest is always one of the factors considered in the decision-making process: atomized political systems may lack any conception of the common good to use as a reference point; aggressive states may ignore the justifiability of their own or others' interests if the web of interests acts as a restraint. Gaining a conceptual grasp on such a central term in international relations is, however, a prerequisite to deciding whether explanations based on these other influences do not leave a gap in our understanding of the states-system that only national interest can fill.

IV Defending the National Interest

IF THE PRECEDING pages have done anything to make "the national interest" less ambiguous, there still remains the task of demonstrating that the concept is not dangerous, or at least of sketching out ways in which it could be rendered less dangerous. This chapter will take up the four counts in this charge against the national interest—that it is undemocratic, that it is irrational, that it is obsolescent, and that it is exclusivist—and deal with them in turn, though most attention will be devoted to a response to the fourth count, which I consider the most substantial.

It is all the more important to sort out and respond to the four objections because of their various and conflicting perspectives. The undemocratic critique suspects the struggle among self-interested groups and fears that the national interest will be used to conceal it; the irrational critique relies on the groups' struggle to make policy and fears that the national interest will be used to interfere with it. The undemocratic critique holds that the nation still has a grip on popular loyalties, which can be abused; the obsolescent critique holds that the nation is being increasingly bypassed and neglected as other loyalties are developed. Those who consider the national interest irrational argue that the free interplay of self-interested forces will produce the best result for the whole; those who believe the national interest exclusivist deny that the interplay of self-interested policies—by states—will lead to the global coordination that is necessary for the good of the human race. The exclusivist objection argues that the good of individual national communities is too narrow a focus for policy; the undemocratic objection argues that the national good is precisely what decision makers should aim at. Observers who feel that the national interest is obsolescent are confident that the state is giving way to functional and supranational bodies more competent to deal with contemporary crises; observers who feel that the national interest is exclusivist fear that the state is all too adept at hanging on in the face of challenges, thereby endangering the "human interest." While one or more of the charges the national interest could be valid, it is logically impossible for all of them to be so, since they contradict one another. A successful response to the four charges must pick its way carefully through this minefield if it is to distinguish erroneous objections from legitimate questions raised about the national interest.

RESPONDING TO THE FOUR CHARGES

The undemocratic national interest

term vs. concept

It should be admitted at once that the term *national interest* can be used as a convenient and often convincing cover for the machinations of self-interested subnational groups and even as a rationalization for the suppression of dissenting groups. Many a pressure group has sailed under the false colors of the common good; many a tyrant has done the same. At other times, *national interest* sanctifies a policy that is not venal or vicious, but is still mistaken and costly. In 1989, when the British government, acting on the asserted grounds of national security, forced the Kuwait Investment Office to sell two-thirds of its shares in British Petroleum to the corporation's management at a cost to BP of 2.4 billion pounds, the *Economist* drily commented, "The Kuwaitis got a profit of about £120m on their investment; other BP shareholders had the honour of protecting the national interest."[1] The question remains, however, whether this misuse of the concept justifies its abandonment. Any tool may be used wrongly. It is difficult to think of a political concept in the name of which crimes have not been committed—whether freedom, democracy, nationalism, justice, or, indeed, pluralism. Politics seems inseparable from sophistry—the desire to twist words to serve one's immediate ends. If this count against the national interest were applied consistently, political discourse would soon be left with no language at all.

Of course, it might be objected that "the national interest," because of its potent emotional content, is a particularly effective disguise for special interests and therefore particularly dangerous. Yet if one seeks the reason for the power of the concept, one also finds its strongest defense. Members

1. *Economist*, January 7, 1989, p. 53.

72

of the community are drawn to the national interest because it stands for the protection of what holds them together as a community; without this overarching community and its larger good, what ground does one have for resisting the pressures of special interests and opposing actions by some members of the community that may threaten the rights of other members?[2] The view that says politics is simply the asserting and counterasserting of power by unconnected groups gives no grounds for complaint when groups do exactly that. A belief in the national interest can justify a principled opposition to group demands; an understanding of the national interest can give one the insight to know when group aims can safely be granted and when they should be unmasked as having gone too far. The *term* national interest may be twisted to undemocratic purposes, but the *concept* of national interest forms a bulwark protecting a free regime against disintegration and collapse.

The irrational national interest

The most convincing reason for believing that the national interest is not irrational as a guide to policy and analysis is the implausibility of the alternative. In defining *rationality* as the ability to identify all possible options, to foresee all their direct and indirect consequences, and to compare every set of consequences with every other—all before making a decision and taking any action—Herbert Simon is erecting something of a straw man. Omniscience is an impossible demand; "the craving for this sort of mistake-proof certainty," in the words of Michael Oakeshott, "may be regarded as, in some respects, the relic of a belief in magic." If adhered to strictly, it would in fact preclude all action as the policy maker pursued an endless chain of ever-more-remote effects, in the process becoming, as Herbert Storing has said, "a candidate for the psychiatrist's couch."[3]

2. Gerhard Colm, "In Defense of the Public Interest," *Social Research*, XXVII (Autumn, 1960), 306–307.

3. Michael Oakeshott, *Rationalism in Politics* (New York, 1962), 93; Herbert Storing, *Essays on the Scientific Study of Politics* (New York, 1962), 76. See also Storing's argument on this point in "The Crucial Link: Public Administration, Responsibility, and the Public Interest," *Public Administration Review*, XXIV (March, 1964), 39–46, and in "American Statesmanship: Old and New," in *Bureaucrats, Policy Analysts, Statesmen: Who Leads?*, ed. Robert Goldwin (Washington, D.C., 1980), 88–113.

Having erected this imposing edifice only to pull it down again, Simon looks to the real world for an alternative. One would be the idea of statesmanship, which views rationality as "the sort of 'intelligence' appropriate to the idiom of activity concerned," and practical wisdom as the attempt to derive from native intelligence, tradition, and historical experience the best means for serving the community's proper ends. Frederick the Great, writing near the end of a long career, endorsed this deeper conception of statesmanship that came closer to the traditional and commonsense view: "One starts out from the most certain point one knows of; one combines this, as well as one can, with completely unknown things, and out of all this one draws conclusions that are as correct as possible."[4] Washington acted under a similar understanding that there was "no better guide than upright intentions and a close investigation," and that it was vain to seek "the standard of infallibility in political opinions."[5]

Simon means to concern himself with facts, not with values, and opts for "satisficing"—the selection of what is "good enough" from a limited range of choices, instead of the selection of the ideal from an infinite range. But does this strategy really solve the problem? How does the policy maker define the range from which he will choose? On what basis does he select one alternative over another, and how does he know that it is "good enough" to serve its intended purposes? Values have made a surreptitious reentry through the back door. It would seem more sensible to admit that the chosen means are inseparable from the ends. In foreign policy this means that the importance of particular state interests and the justifications for the policies designed to pursue them are derived from their usefulness in protecting the overall national interest, which cannot be understood apart from the country's notion of a good society.

Both Oakeshott and Storing have noted that Simon's conception of rationality portrays political conduct as a series of discrete choices rather than as the continuous application of practical wisdom to the ongoing needs of

4. Oakeshott, *Rationalism in Politics*, 110; Friedrich Meinecke, *Machiavellism: The Doctrine of Raison d'Etat and Its Place in Modern History,* trans. Douglas Scott (London, 1957), 321. Thirty-four years earlier, Frederick, speaking with youthful bravado, had voiced an understanding of rationality closer to Simon's: "It is a matter of wisdom to be able to know everything, to judge everything and to foresee everything" (Meinecke, *Machiavellism,* 286).

5. Cited in Norman J. Small, *Some Presidential Interpretations of the Presidency* (New York, 1970), 17.

the society. One can even more emphatically say the same thing of Lind-blom's extension of Simon's thought. The adherent of the "disjointed incre-mentalism—partisan mutual adjustment" approach is also convinced that the human mind is too limited to be capable of anything approaching com-plete rationality. Parceling policy out by leaving it to the interplay of groups at points all over the political system will presumably make action more rational, because each group will advance its own perspective and more factors will thereby be introduced into the process than could possibly be comprehended by any individual decision-maker. Policy emerges as a result of these disconnected choices, not from a prior guiding doctrine.

The argument seems to rest on extremes. If Simon's standard for ratio-nality asks too much of human wisdom, Lindblom's solution expects too little. It dismisses the possibility of the sort of statesmanship discussed here, without supplying any confidence that the operation of pressure groups and bureaucratic politics will result in policy that approximates the common good. Indeed, there appears to be little notion of a common good except the procedural one of economic efficiency and the fair competition of particular interests. (There may in fact be an underlying notion that goes beyond this, but it remains unarticulated.) Neither disjointed incrementalism—partisan mutual adjustment nor satisficing marks an advance in rationality on states-manship obligated to serve the national interest. Full rationality is insepa-rable from an understanding of the nation's ends and an overall view of policies designed to serve those ends. Political decentralization and eco-nomic free competition may well be very good things, but without attempt-ing to grasp the common interest that they further we have no way of decid-ing whether they are good or not.

The obsolescent national interest

Even realists, who make national interest one of the foundations of their conception of world politics, do not assume that the present multistate in-ternational system is destined to last forever. Morgenthau states explicitly that the organization of international politics that has existed since the sev-enteenth century holds no exemption from the mortality of all human in-stitutions: "While the realist indeed believes that interest is the perennial standard by which political action must be judged and directed, the contemporary connection between interest and the nation state is a product of history, and is therefore bound to disappear in the course of history."[6] It is always possible and indeed likely that states will lose their central position in political life at some point, and the importance and usefulness of understanding the national interest will then decline. Attention will shift to the interests of those geographically based institutions (whether they are larger or smaller than contemporary states) or those functionally organized bodies that will replace states at center stage. National interest will then join dynastic interest in the history of political ends and drop from the vocabulary of current political action, though the common good of these new groupings will continue to be a matter of concern.

When considering the merit of this charge against the national interest, the question arises, however, whether these events have in fact already taken place or are in the course of doing so. There is room for serious doubt that the state, despite the intractability of the problems facing it today, has been overtaken by history and is destined shortly to be superceded by more comprehensive or more efficient forms of social and political organization. The hardiness that the state has displayed over a history filled with challenges to its authority ought to induce caution in predicting its demise.

An observer relying on the sheer number of states could be forgiven for believing that the institution is in robust good health. From approximately fifty immediately after the Second World War, the total has climbed to over three times that in 1992. The whole trend of international politics during the contemporary period has been one of decentralization and secession, not the consolidation and merger that is said to be necessary to confront modern problems. With the breakup of the great colonial empires, more differentiation among ever-smaller units has been the defining characteristic of the age. The loosening of bipolarity and the collapse of the Communist bloc, and the Soviet Union itself, have also done much to increase the independence of individual states from alliance ties. One need not rehearse here the studies contending that the bonds of economic interdependence linking states are neither unprecedented nor, indeed, as tight as they have been at some periods in the past. The state appears to be, if not a permanent, at least a presently solid fixture on the international scene.[7]

6. Hans J. Morgenthau, *Politics Among Nations: The Struggle for Power and Peace* (5th ed.; New York, 1978), 10.

7. See Kenneth N. Waltz, "The Myth of National Interdependence," in *The Interna-*

Nor does it seem to be losing its grip on the domestic life of the society. Despite Marxist prognostications, the state is nowhere withering away. For more than a century, the state in every developed country has taken an increasing share of the society's resources for public purposes; the efforts of leaders like Prime Minister Thatcher and President Reagan to restrain the growth of government have been rewarded by a public sector that takes approximately the same proportion of gross national product today as when they assumed office. Many developing countries have relied on the state to speed the process of capital accumulation and industrialization that was accomplished in Europe and America over a longer period by private firms and entrepreneurs. Government is as omnipresent at home as governments are abroad.

What has driven both these broad trends is the continuing force of nationalism. Nationalist sentiment forced the separation of colonies from their metropoles; it went further and caused the breakup into their constituent parts of interstate organizations left behind by the Europeans, such as the links established by the British in East Africa and the Caribbean. State boundaries that diverged from ethnic ones only made political leaders more anxious to encourage "national" unity and to resist any infringement of their autonomy. Multinational corporations have not attained the control over small Third World countries that was expected (and feared) a decade and a half ago, because state leaders have been able to rely on the nationalist feelings of their citizens in resisting MNC threats and in driving hard bargains of their own.[8] The passing of the whip hand from the oil companies to the members of OPEC—demonstrated in the oil crisis of 1973 and 1974— is only the clearest example. The response of the British public to the hostilities over the Falkland Islands in 1982 shows that this reservoir of national feeling continues to exist in the industrialized countries as well. Every political leader who calls for government action to protect some deprived segment of the national community draws on it. Often this feeling can be relied on to override other political loyalties, a fact recognized by the Belgian statesman Paul-Henri Spaak when he remarked ruefully, speaking for his

---

tional Corporation: A Symposium, ed. Charles P. Kindleberger (Cambridge, Mass., 1970), 205–33.

8. Klaus Knorr, *The Power of the Nations: The Political Economy of International Relations* (New York, 1975), 256–84.

fellow West European socialists, "The thing we Socialists have nationalized most effectively is socialism!"

But, it may be objected, this discussion of the continuing hold of nationalist feeling misses the point in two ways. First, the very growth of the state apparatus has made coordination by leaders at the top increasingly difficult and side bargains between like-minded agencies or groups within different governments increasingly common. In these cases, the national interest, as defined by foreign ministries, is simply bypassed. Second, the loyalty of national publics to national governments says nothing about the erosion in the capacity of those governments to cope with present-day problems that are not confined within national boundaries. Here, the national interest is too narrow a perspective. The two objections may contradict each other—if problems are handed over to larger, supranational organizations, will those bodies not be even more ponderous and incapable of giving central direction?—but they deserve a response.

To the first objection one may reply that the obstacles to unified policy direction by central decision-makers are certainly very great. Differing objectives held by units within a government bureaucracy may frustrate attempts to impose coherence from above, as successive American presidents and secretaries of state have discovered to their cost. Still, the case that this inconsistency is inevitable has not been conclusively proved. Officials from Dean Acheson in his use of the State Department Policy Planning Staff to Henry Kissinger in his opening to China have found ways to escape the disintegration of policy. Efforts by their successors to do likewise are not aided by scholars' denials that there is a common good that policy makers ought to serve. Nor is it entirely clear that policy-making power is as widely dispersed in other countries as it is in the United States. The transformation of the foreign policy of the state into the foreign policies of its constituent units becomes a self-fulfilling prophecy if the analysis of diplomacy both legitimates this sort of breakup and denies there is any alternative.

Finally, do the issues making up an increasing part of the current diplomatic agenda overbear the ability of states to meet their challenges? If the question refers to individual states acting alone and unaided, the answer is definitely yes. Yet such isolation does not have to be the case. This possibility will be discussed at greater length in the following section. One can say now, however, that a policy guided by national interest in no way precludes cooperation among states in ways that serve their common interests by allowing them to cope together with problems that would defeat each state acting individually. The obsolescence of the national interest may some day be manifest, but it is not ensured by these current problems.

The exclusivist national interest

The accusation that it fails to take into account either the interests of others outside the nation or the transcendent rules of ethical conduct is perhaps the most serious made against the national interest. Going as it does to the heart of some of the ethical questions that have most troubled scholars and statesmen at least since the birth of the present states-system, the charge cannot be dismissed lightly. A tentative and partial answer may be all that is possible, but this should not make one shrink from the task of grappling with the issue.

In its soft form, the exclusivist critique undoubtedly has the value of reminding policy makers that policy propounded in terms of sheer national self-assertion is unlikely to attract the cooperation from others that may be essential to success. A diplomacy that gives little or no weight to the needs of others, as that of Wilhelmine Germany sometimes did before the First World War, may only alarm other members of the system. A state that always considers only its own interests is misusing the idea of national interest.

Nevertheless, a state that was led by the soft-exclusivist argument to portray itself as purely altruistic would also be adopting a risky course. Kennan, while endorsing a diplomacy that is "patient and conciliatory and understanding," has gone on to say that if the need to achieve one's goals sets a maximum limit on the frank admission of national interest in a policy, it also establishes a minimum. "Most foreign peoples do not believe that governments do things for selfless and altruistic motives," he has argued, "and if we do not reveal to them a good solid motive of self-interest for anything we do with regard to them, they are apt to invent one. This can be a more sinister one than we ever dreamed of, and their belief in it can cause serious confusion." The more clearly that American leaders could show their actions to be "a rational extrapolation of our own national interest," in other words, "the better understood and the more effective it is going to be abroad."[9] While the soft-exclusivist critics are correct in advising that a state should never abandon efforts to achieve communities of interest, then, their advice that "national interest" should be dropped entirely from the vocabulary of political leaders goes too far in the opposite direction. It leaves the official open to suspicions of hypocrisy, and it may well be unconvincing to its intended audience abroad. A prudent avowal of national interest and a willingness to allow the same to others avoids both a jarring insensitivity to the aims of other actors and a pretentious pose of being above the demands of self-preservation that is unconvincing in a setting that lacks the protection of law and government.

The hard-exclusivist critics are also partially correct. Compared with universal religious and other ethical systems, the national interest is limited and parochial as a guide to policy. Yet to say that national boundaries should be ignored and the national interest disregarded in the pursuit of a cosmopolitan standard of justice is to ignore the facts of power of which any effort to work toward a more humane world must take cognizance. In a system of world politics in which states control the main levers of power—power that can be used either to spread some measure of justice or to retreat from that goal—and give every sign of continuing that control in the foreseeable future, it is not at all clear that acting as if states did not exist would in fact promote justice. That course fails to take account of the measure of justice that states provide, which could be put at risk, and of the more limited but still important steps that states can take in the direction of reforms without putting their national interest at risk.

First, one ought not forget the justice that has been achieved because of the existence of states. Comparing the manner in which politics is carried on within states with its conduct among states, one could say that many states constitute islands of peace and stability in the midst of disorder. States have supplied the order that has allowed for the development of justice; national communities, when they live up to what is best within them, form cooperative endeavors to advance toward the principles of justice on which they are founded. While they do not embrace the whole of humankind, these national communities, when they rest on worthy ideals, have their own moral value. They awaken citizens to a selflessness and public spirit of

9. George F. Kennan, "Foreign Policy and Christian Conscience," *Atlantic,* CCIII (May, 1959), 44, 46. See also Wilton Dillon, *Gifts and Nations: The Obligation to Give, Receive, and Repay* (Hawthorne, N.Y., 1968).

which they might otherwise not be capable. Comparing the ties that undergird such communities to racism overlooks the fact that they produce effects that are good as well as bad.

Not all national ideals are worthy, of course. A regime like that of Nazi Germany may be founded on principles that are fundamentally vicious. It is straining the term to call such a nation a *community,* and it would be difficult to deny that the internal order it provided was outweighed by the injustice that it caused—indeed, that defined it. Only a great war prevented it from permanently expanding its principles to much of the rest of the world. The Hitlerian case raises the seemingly paradoxical example of a state that must be deprived of its national interest, or its autonomy, in order that its inhabitants might render themselves capable of making responsible decisions about their common public interest.[10] Yet, by disparaging the national interest, the hard-exclusivist critics are urging states that share their adherence to their ethical principles to risk their futures and trust the goodwill of such unscrupulous states that are unmoved by their appeals—a dubious way to increase respect for those principles.

Second, conceiving of international politics as an interplay among particular state interests may carry its own answer to the exclusivist charge. The picture is one of a broad but thin world community encompassing a number of much narrower but more potent national communities. When one moves to the international level, the idea of a common interest becomes vastly paler and weaker as the community becomes less solid. Enough of a community exists, however, to prevent the rulers in each state from being the sole judges in their own cause when they assert various state interests to support their common or national interest. Rather, the entire world community—frail and divided though it may be—has the last word, if it chooses, in defining the state's desire, either as a reasonable claim, supportable by justifying argument and compatible with prevailing ideas on the rights and duties of states, or as an unjustifiable grab for power. That many cases of juridically defined aggression succeed means that the international community's standards are loose, not that they are nonexistent. But they do supply some check on the excesses that can occur when the national interest of a particular state is invested with the aura of the highest good, from

10. See Michael Walzer, *Just and Unjust Wars: A Moral Argument with Historical Illustrations* (New York, 1977), 101–108; Walzer, "The Moral Standing of States: A Response to Four Critics," in *International Ethics,* ed. Charles R. Beitz *et al.* (Princeton, 1985), 217–37.

which there is no further appeal. And these standards may be strengthened when states act in a moderate, conservative way dictated by their state interests rather than attempting an ideological conversion of the world or acting on unlimited objectives that are said to serve "the national interest"— and nothing else.

Unadulterated self-assertion requires no concurrence from others; it depends only on one's strength and skill in imposing demands on them. Historically, however, this has not been an accurate description of interest-based stated policies. Particularly in the eighteenth and early nineteenth centuries, when acceptance of the doctrine of interests was at its height, seeking and defending state interests meant advancing them as claims within the framework of a larger interstate society—largely informal in the days of the *ancien régime,* given a name in devices like the Concert of Europe later, but always in the background as a judge of the compatibility of national desires with the order of the whole.[11] Powerful and daring states could flout the general expectations, but only at the cost of arousing the community and stimulating combinations against themselves.

The characteristic of the Napoleonic interlude that made it revolutionary was precisely that the emperor recognized no limits on his aims, that he did not bargain over interests but directly challenged European society in the name of liberty or nationalism. It takes two to bargain; it takes more to form a consensus on what constitutes an acceptable bargain; but Napoleon was not interested in the views of other parties, and he declined to content himself with the limited objectives dictated by "mere interests." The corresponding qualities of our own age—revolution, ideology—have fostered the tendency to misuse the language of national interests by breaking it out of its consensual setting and establishing it as a principle of ungoverned national egotism. Talleyrand acted on his understanding of interests within "Europe"; Hitler, only on desire and malevolence in an international realm that seemed to have returned to the state of nature.

The relationship between interest and international society worked both ways. The "diplomatic republic of Europe" gave or withheld its approval of assertions of interest by its member states and thereby moderated their demands on one another. But it was also the willingness of statesmen

11. Friedrich Kratochwil, "On the Notion of 'Interest' in International Relations," *International Organization,* XXXVI (Winter, 1982), 1–30.

to think and act in terms of interest that permitted the slow accumulation of customary expectations and norms that underlay the consensus. Had states continued to fight for the illimitable objectives of the wars of religion, a common cultural heritage would never have sufficed for the quasi society that Christendom formed. Kissinger was speaking of his hopes for both a more prudent American diplomacy and a more stable international order when he described his beliefs upon taking office: "Moral exuberance had inspired both overinvolvement and isolationism. It was my conviction that a concept of our fundamental national interests would provide a ballast of restraint and an assurance of continuity." [12]

Thus, the two meanings of *national interest* work to balance each other in ways that promote ethics in a world of power. The overall national interest is the statesman's prime responsibility, but conceiving his role as one of advancing narrower state interests reminds him that there are other players on the field with their own interests to protect, punctures undue tendencies toward national self-importance, may serve to restrain enthusiastic adventures, and calls attention to the shared framework of an international society within which the measured contest over interests can be carried out. Conversely, one's views of the interests grounding foreign policy is enlightened by keeping in mind that they serve the larger goal, the national interest, which is in turn shaped by more profound political and ethical considerations.

Calling on statesmen to scrap the national interest also ignores the opportunities they may seize to promote justice without abandoning the defense of the state and the national community. Ethical conduct and the national good are not necessarily in conflict. The following section discusses some steps that policy makers may take—not as simple or unalterable copybook maxims, but as general guidelines in dealing with immensely difficult problems—in search of these intersections of justice and prudence.

BROADENING AND NARROWING NATIONAL INTERESTS

The instances discussed above, often occasioned by crisis, when older conceptions of the best way to serve the national interest begin to seem inade-

12. Henry A. Kissinger, *White House Years* (Boston, 1979), 65.

quate and newer ones await their formulation, provide opportunities for creative statesmanship. When all about them seems in flux, wise policy-makers can seize the chance to remold their states' national interests, giving new emphasis to some elements in the picture of the world they received from their predecessors. They can be particularly vigilant in searching for ways in which to give more attention to two considerations likely to be slighted as governments formulate lists of their national interest: the inter-ests of other states and ethical principles.

Narrowing national interests

In their quest for accommodation, statesmen may be willing, for example, to narrow their conception of what the national interest requires through a readiness to compromise on claims not of the first rank. Governments can attempt to keep in mind those interests that other states are likely to regard as most important and refrain from trenching on these sensitive points whenever possible.

The process of narrowing may involve not only discrimination in the types of interest selected for emphasis but also modesty in their number. A prudently limited catalog of interests asserted overseas allows more atten-tion to be paid to those most deserving of it; more extended claims, on the other hand, may contribute, not to the state's well-being, but to distracting and unnecessary tensions with other states. The principle is illustrated by Walter Lippmann's oft-cited dictum that urges the "bringing into balance, with a comfortable surplus of power in reserve, [of] the nation's commit-ments and the nation's power." [13] The most striking example in our time of a narrowing of national interests has probably been the dissolution of the British Empire, in which, responding to altered circumstances, the British government divested itself of claims and responsibilities it had exercised for generations. It is an example from which the Soviet empire might profit. An intelligent pruning of a nation's conception of its interests may widen its margin of safety by increasing the ratio of the power it possesses to that amount of power required to fulfill its commitments.

Observers of international politics throughout American history have

13. Walter Lippmann, *U.S. Foreign Policy: Shield of the Republic* (Boston, 1943), 9–10.

recognized the wisdom of refusing to become overextended in one's appraisal of one's national interests, whether one is dealing with exposed geographical outposts, excessive legal claims, or pretentious moral poses. Hamilton advised as much when he cautioned a young, newly independent nation, inexperienced in the diplomatic arts, to be wary of stumbling into war with Great Britain over interests that were less than vital.[14] Washington's Farewell Address proclaimed the conviction, under which the succeeding century of American foreign policy was conducted, that the nation's true interest lay in avoiding the pitfalls of an overly assertive stance toward European nations superior in military power to the United States, thereby permitting the country to devote its growing energies to the discovery and development of the rich patrimony found on its own continent.

As the twentieth century dawned, the country was prepared to reap the benefits of that internal development by playing a more prominent role on the international stage. But Hamilton's philosophical descendant, Mahan, while supporting the larger concepts of national interests espoused by expansionists, cautioned the nation not to allow its reach to exceed its grasp. Fearing that the United States would be tempted into commitments that would spread its forces too thin, he called greatly dispersed interests "hostages to fortune," and spoke of "the military embarrassments that may attend widely extended political responsibility." "It is clearly the part of wisdom," he averred, "to retrench these where it can honorably be done, limiting minor activities, and concentrating purpose upon the necessary and greater external interests of the nation."[15]

With the country's return to isolationism in the interwar period, counsels of restraint were common, going well beyond what Mahan would have advocated. Perhaps the writer who was most insistent on restraining and cutting back American interests overseas during this time was Charles A.

14. For Hamilton's arguments defending Jay's Treaty, see "The Defence No. V" (August 5, 1795), in *The Papers of Alexander Hamilton,* ed. Harold C. Syrett (27 vols.; New York, 1973), XIX, 91–92. For a contrary view that "Hamilton's concept of the national interest, in fact, was grossly in error," while his great adversary, Thomas Jefferson, held a "view of the interest of the United States [that] has been vindicated by American history," see Albert H. Bowman, "Jefferson, Hamilton, and American Foreign Policy," *Political Science Quarterly,* LXXI (March, 1956), 18–41.

15. Alfred T. Mahan, *The Interest of America in Sea Power, Present and Future* (Boston, 1911), 212; Mahan, *The Problem of Asia and Its Effects upon International Policies* (Boston, 1905), 139.

Beard, whose advocacy of economic self-sufficiency led him to denounce any foreign commitments beyond those absolutely necessary to secure materials that could not be produced, or for which substitutes could not be found, at home. The overall national interest, in his view, was compromised by economic adventurers seeking to develop state interests in foreign lands where the national writ did not run. "In terms of economy," Beard said, "national interest involves stability and standard of life deliberately adjusted to each other in a long time perspective." This stability required "the utmost emancipation from dependence upon the economies, rivalries, revolutions, and wars of other nations" and "from dependence upon the course of international exchange." Beard's conception of the national interest, perhaps the most restrictive to be found in the twentieth century, defined almost all economic activity overseas by American domestic interests as a challenge to the United States' national interest.[16]

Beard's economic isolationism has attracted few disciples in the years since World War II. Yet, recognizing the continued merit of the general prescription of restraint in the Cold War era, scholars and statesmen alike have devoted their energies to applying it to contemporary conditions. In his four fundamental rules of diplomacy, Morgenthau identified a narrow set of national interests with the idea of spheres of influence: once states "have defined their national interests in terms of national security, they can draw back from their outlying positions, located close to, or within the sphere of national security on the other side, and retreat into their respective spheres, each self-contained within its orbit." Dean Acheson lamented the consequences of failing to follow Hamilton's example, Mahan's exhortation, and Morgenthau's advice. Speaking of the need "to comprehend, understand, and apportion our capabilities, the means at our disposal, to objectives which they can reach," and to recognize that the nation's means are not "unlimited," the former secretary of state warned that "the efficacy of the means may be vitally affected by the objective pursued. For instance—and the illustration is by no means theoretical—it may be possible to mobilize the force and consent capable of attaining a specific and limited objec-

16. Charles A. Beard, *The Open Door at Home: A Trial Philosophy of National Interest* (New York, 1934), 211–13. See also Beard's contention that "to encourage by State action American nationals to develop private interests in historic war zones beyond the effective control of American military and naval power is a betrayal of national interest conceived as supreme public interest" (*ibid.*, 269).

tive. The objective may be adequate but not all that one might wish. But extend the objective, and one is likely to find that consent is withdrawn and the force available is lessened. Even the limited objective may then be unobtainable."[17] More recently, the Carter administration—following a line of policy that could be traced through all administrations since Lyndon Johnson's—recognized and acted on a narrowed set of national interests when it concluded negotiations recognizing Panamanian sovereignty over the Panama Canal. Applying the tenets of the Monroe Doctrine in altered circumstances, the Carter administration accepted that control over the day-to-day operations of the canal had become less important to the United States and had dropped in the nation's hierarchy of interests since the turn of the century; it was willing to exchange this diminished state interest for the more significant aim of maintaining the continued operation of the canal in an atmosphere of reasonably harmonious cooperation with Panama and the other countries of Latin America.

These American proponents of narrowed national interests have not ignored the common good of the American national community. Nor have they been indifferent to the country's state interests. Instead, they stand squarely in the tradition of national-interest thought, which holds that the world is made up of many actors with legitimate interests. Indeed, it was precisely this willingness to accept the legitimacy of the goals of others and to bargain over the satisfaction of at least some of them—rather than to seek complete victory for oneself and the complete destruction of one's opponents—that marked the advance of an interest-directed world of international politics over the uncompromising religious conflict that had preceded it. A readiness to narrow one's conception of one's national interests is fully consistent with Morgenthau's advice "to judge other nations as we judge our own and, having judged them in this fashion, [to pursue] policies that respect the interests of other nations, while protecting and promoting those of our own."[18] A policy of narrowing national interests attempts to

17. Morgenthau, *Politics Among Nations*, 553–54. See also Morgenthau, *In Defense of the National Interest: A Critical Examination of American Foreign Policy* (New York, 1951), 137, 159, 242; Dean G. Acheson, Introduction to *Civilization and Foreign Policy: An Inquiry for Americans*, by Louis J. Halle (New York, 1955), xv.

18. Morgenthau, *Politics Among Nations*, 11. More recent scholarly works advocating a narrowed set of interests for the United States have included the following: David P. Calleo, *The Imperious Economy* (Cambridge, Mass., 1982); Calleo, *Beyond American Hegemony:*

respect the interests of other nations by recognizing practical limits to the interests of one's own nation.

Broadening national interests

If the list of national interests may be narrowed, it may also be broadened. States may forego what they see as their own immediate and particular interests in order to further different goals shared by other states as well. Such a redefinition of what the national interest requires, like that which narrows the concept, can be looked on as a matter of the allocation of finite resources—in this case, a decision to give higher priority to collective goods and, following Fred A. Sondermann's advice, to "make a conscious effort to frame [one's] interests and goals so as to include those of others as much as possible." [19]

This need not mean that a broadened set of national interests is synonymous with Arnold Wolfer's description of national self-abnegation: "goals transcending if not sacrificing the 'national interest' in any meaningful sense of the term." [20] To discover that some aspects of international politics do not constitute a zero-sum game is not to sacrifice the national interest; to establish aims and devise policies that benefit other nations as well as one's own is simply to become aware of another dimension of the national interest, one that might be overlooked in an over-hasty examination of immediate advantages. That some of these unshared advantages may be eschewed is undeniable. But the state does so in the expectation that the compensating benefits of cooperation will be at least as great. A policy that attempts to secure goods for several states need not be subversive of the national interest, so

---

The Future of the Western Alliance (New York, 1987); James Chace, Solvency: The Price of Survival (New York, 1982); Paul Kennedy, The Rise and Fall of the Great Powers: Economic Change and Military Conflict from 1500 to 2000 (New York, 1987); Alan Tonelson, "The Real National Interest," Foreign Policy, LXI (Winter, 1985–86), 49–72; and Christopher Layne, "The Real Conservative Agenda," Foreign Policy, LXI (Winter, 1985–86), 73–93.

19. Fred A. Sondermann, "The Concept of the National Interest," Orbis, XXI (Spring, 1977), 138.

20. Arnold Wolfers, Discord and Collaboration: Essays on International Politics (Baltimore, 1962), 93.

long as one's own state continues to share in the goods and one's relative position is not undermined.

Although they overlap, three examples of broadened national interests may be distinguished: the military alliance, the institutions of international law and organization, and cooperation in matters of nontraditional "low politics" like environmental protection. A nation may subsume its interests in an alliance against another nation or group of nations if it judges that by foregoing certain narrow advantages it strengthens its partners and bolsters the entire alliance. It thereby protects its more important or "deeper" interests, perhaps even the interest of national self-preservation.[21]

Another suggested example of broadened common interests is the slow accretion of international law. But the application of law to international disputes has been successful only when its proponents have recognized the force of interest in world politics and have made a convincing case for the proposition that bringing some particular aspects of the relations among nations under law would serve some important interest shared by all who would be bound by it. Rules of state behavior, "originating in the permanent interests of states to put their normal relations upon a stable basis by providing for predictable and enforceable conduct with respect to these relations," do serve the interest, shared by harried policy-makers in all states, of reducing the sources of uncertainty in their environment. Thus, this interest lies in process rather than in any substantive outcome, but it may be no less valuable to states for that, and whenever its benefits outweigh the transitory advantage to be gained by violating the procedures it establishes (which may not be infrequently), it may well be obeyed.[22] The situation in regard to international organization is similar. A forum such as the United Nations' General Assembly or the Security Council provides a convenient setting for the interplay and compromise of various interests, and its usefulness makes its continued existence itself an interest of the participating

21. See Philip W. Quigg, *America the Dutiful: An Assessment of U.S. Foreign Policy* (New York, 1971), 110.

22. Hans J. Morgenthau, "Positivism, Functionalism, and International Law," *American Journal of International Law*, XXXIV (April, 1940), 279. See James L. Brierly, *The Law of Nations: An Introduction to the International Law of Peace* (5th ed.; New York, 1955); Terry Nardin, *Law, Morality, and the Relations of States* (Princeton, 1983). The reasoning is the same in the case of the informal norms of cooperation in international regimes. See Robert O. Keohane, *After Hegemony: Cooperation and Discord in the World Political Economy* (Princeton, 1984), 49−132, 243−59.

nations.[23] Few states have not broadened their definitions of their national interests since World War II to include membership in the UN.

Alongside these broad political bodies stand the more narrowly focused technical or functional organs. Exemplified by the World Health Organization, the Food and Agriculture Organization, and the International Labor Organization, these social and humanitarian agencies make themselves useful to national interests by alleviating problems with which ordinary citizens, and therefore their governments, are immediately concerned: sickness and health, food, working conditions. Percy Corbett, while acknowledging "the impossibility of compensating with constitutional machinery for basic international conflicts between notions of both moral and material interest," found the technical agencies, because of the favorable ratio of the benefits they provide to the costs they impose, to be that form of international organization most compatible with the broadened interests of individual states, but only when they rested on "a firm conviction of national interest."[24]

These technical agencies of the UN introduce the third example of broadening national interests: states may undertake cooperative efforts—at some cost to themselves—against common problems. Unlike the first category, "alliances" under these circumstances are directed, not against other states, but against evils arising from the outside environment, such as economic depression, ecological degradation, or excessive population growth. Unlike the second, efforts made in this respect are not directed toward traditional diplomatic aims. Some may be tied to the UN; others, like the International Energy Agency, draw upon a smaller group of nations; and still other collective efforts may require no permanent organization at all. But regardless of the degree to which they are institutionalized and machinery for implementing them is established, they are all efforts meant to achieve what Wolfers has called "milieu goals," which by their very nature must be shared.[25]

23. Jiri Liska, "The Multiple Equilibrium and the American National Interest in International Organization," *Harvard Studies in International Affairs,* IV (February, 1954), 35–50; Hans J. Morgenthau, "The Yardstick of National Interest," *Annals of the American Academy of Political and Social Science,* CCXCVI (November, 1954), 77–84; Donald J. Puchala, "American Interests and the United Nations," *Political Science Quarterly,* XCVII (Winter, 1982–83), 571–88.

24. Percy Corbett, "National Interest, International Organization, and American Foreign Policy," *World Politics,* V (October, 1952), 64, 63.

25. Wolfers, *Discord and Collaboration,* 74. But see Inis L. Claude, Jr., "The United

Broadening and narrowing: limits and possibilities

One should not draw too sharp a differentiation between broadening and narrowing national interests: while separable in theory and exposition, they may often be inextricably linked in practice. The limiting aspects of a broadened national interest have long been recognized: "It has always been accepted that when states have common interests and common aims a more or less formalized machinery for international cooperation must be created. . . . But however complex the need and the organizational apparatus created to fulfill it, it is clear that some restriction on the freedom of the co-operating states to do as they please is necessarily involved."[26] In agreeing to cooperate, states forego their interest in that complete freedom of action that has been an important component of traditional conceptions of national sovereignty; in the act of broadening their national interests, they also narrow them. Similarly, when a state narrows its national interests by giving up some held or desired good, it may do so in the belief that it shares with the other states concerned a broadened national interest in relations amicable enough to prevent them from taking undue advantage of its sacrifice and to permit them to display a reciprocal respect for its interests in areas more important to it. Clearly, the United States hoped to obtain this sort of cooperation from the states of Central and South America when it turned the Canal Zone over to Panama.

Broadening and narrowing are frequently difficult to distinguish largely because they share two fundamental characteristics: both are attempts to take the interests of others into account; and neither can expect to achieve more than limited success in the endeavor. Because of the indeterminacy of international politics—the lack of hard knowledge about many of the problems faced by policy makers, the uncertainty over the precise consequences of one's actions—the range of choice for national action is considerable, and the number of occasions on which well-intentioned policy-makers may disagree is great. In these periods of doubt, the idea of broadened or narrowed national interest provides, first, a persistent reminder that there are

States and Great-Power Responsibilities," in *National Interest: Rhetoric, Leadership, and Policy*, ed. W. David Clinton (Lanham, Md., 1988), 84–85.

26. F. S. Northedge and M. J. Grieve, *A Hundred Years of International Relations* (New York, 1971), 345.

other players on the field whose interests may be as legitimate as one's own and, second, a beneficial source of that humility and generosity that are indispensable if the state's foreign policy is not to be reduced to the simple self-assertion that the exclusivist critics decry.

But one should not expect these attempts at cooperation and restraint to be met with complete success. In seeking these two routes to accommodation, states are not simply giving up things they prize; they are exchanging them for other things, possibly of greater value. It has not been assumed that states are capable of pure altruism, unmixed with any degree of self-interest, and therefore the question is not one of unhesitating self-sacrifice but one of the search for areas of mutual advantage.

Even this limited achievement often seems to be beyond the capacities of even the wisest state, as Reinhold Niebuhr has pointed out:

> Such is the social ignorance of peoples, that, far from doing justice to a foe or neighbor, they are as yet unable to conserve their own interests wisely. Since their ultimate interests are always protected best, by at least a measure of fairness toward their neighbors, the desire to gain an immediate selfish advantage always imperils their ultimate interests. . . .
>
> Perhaps the best that can be expected of nations is that they should justify their hypocrisies by a slight measure of real international achievement, and learn how to do justice to wider interests than their own, while they pursue their own.[27]

Self-interest enlightened by an understanding of the interests of others is self-interest nonetheless. National interests are flexible only to an extent. In fact, the word *flexible*, with its connotations of suppleness and easy adaptability, is probably less than appropriate. Interests may more properly be described as malleable: susceptible to alteration, but only slowly and reluctantly, in the heat of critical self-examination and under the pressure of competing values.

27. Reinhold Niebuhr, *Moral Man and Immoral Society: A Study in Ethics and Politics* (1932; rpr. New York, 1960), 86, 108. See also Kenneth W. Thompson, "Beyond National Interest: A Critical Evaluation of Reinhold Niebuhr's Theory of International Politics," *Review of Politics*, XVII (April, 1955), 167–88; and Russell F. Sizemore, "The Prudent Cold Warrior," *Ethics and International Affairs*, XI (1988), 199–217.

There is no magic in the phrases "narrowed" or "broadened" national interests. Leaders may redefine their states' interests in the pursuit of goals other than accommodation and conciliation: they may narrow their interests by rejecting opportunities for useful cooperation with others, preferring to seek ends that will benefit their states alone; they may broaden their interests by relying on self-assertion to gain a wider variety of advantages, regardless of whether all the goals declared to be in the national interest are warranted by the claims of justice or even simple utility. States may seek autarchy, heedless of the consequences for their neighbors, or they may pursue a course of aggression and exploitation. National interests narrowed or broadened in these ways may be less admirable, but they are no less common, and to harried decision-makers they may appear no less politic, than those altered for more just reasons. Even when the motives of statesmen are worthy, if they expand or contract their states' asserted interests without a proper appreciation of the consequences, they may bring disaster upon themselves, as Chamberlain did with his policy of appeasement.[28]

The problems derived from the coexistence of national interests in alliances are baffling and inescapable. No two states are ever in identical circumstances; no two sets of policy makers ever bring to their job exactly the same preconceptions and perceptions. The national interests of any pair of states, even those of close allies in very similar situations, will never be indistinguishable, and the points of divergence multiply as the number of allies grows. A continual process of mutual adjustment among their particular interests goes on as the price for the broadening by each partner of its national interests. As long as the benefits of common action (including the psychological benefit to decision makers of standing with old friends in familiar patterns) are seen to outweigh the costs to those interests that must be pinched in order to satisfy the needs of other partners, the alliance will remain intact. But it will not exist without strains. The reluctance of its members to make their response completely automatic in the event of an attack (a reluctance that was clearly in evidence during the United States Senate's debate over the North Atlantic Treaty in 1949, for example) reflects the fear that in some future crisis the national interests of the allies might

28. While not comparing the perils facing the United States in the late 1980s to those confronting Great Britain in the late 1930s, Paul Seabury charges American advocates of narrowed national interests with a similar failure to appreciate the likely results of their policies. See Seabury, "The Solvency Boys," *National Interest* (Fall, 1988), 100–105.

not coincide. The desire to preserve the freedom of action to protect one's interests that differ from those of other alliance partners sets the terms for Mahan's discussion of treaties: "the only certain foundation for harmony of action and continuance of relations is to be found in common interests and common habits of thought."[29]

It has frequently been argued that the avoidance of nuclear war is a common interest par excellence. Yet even (or perhaps especially) in dealing with this sensitive topic, statesmen are not willing to trust shared interests so far as to "pledge the unknown future" unconditionally. Article XIX, Paragraph 3, of the unratified SALT II agreement between the United States and the Soviet Union recognized that other interests may override the shared interest in arms control: "Each party shall, in exercising its national sovereignty, have the right to withdraw from this Treaty if it decides that extraordinary events related to the subject matter of this Treaty have jeopardized its supreme interests." The case is the same with international law and diplomatic practices. When the Iranian government decided that it was in its interest to support the militants who had seized the personnel of the American embassy in Tehran in late 1979 and taken them hostage, it was striking at the heart of the rules of diplomatic conduct; when the government ignored a subsequent order by the International Court of Justice for their release, it was flouting international law. The violations were unfortunately more sensational than unprecedented, and they illustrate why states are hesitant to proceed very far in subordinating their unshared interests to a broadened interest in international law. It is not sturdy enough to support the burdens that would be placed upon it if they did so.

Nor is the United Nations a broadened national interest so potent in its effects and so widely shared by its members that states can afford to place unlimited confidence in it. Morgenthau recognized the tentative nature of any commitment made by or to the international body: "To ask whether the United Nations is in the national interest of the United States is like asking whether negotiations or military alliances are in the national interest of the United States. The answer is bound to be that sometimes they are and sometimes they are not."[30] If the UN is no more than a tool for the diplomacy of states, then, while useful, it is to be valued no more than any other

---

29. Mahan, *The Problem of Asia*, 177–78.
30. Hans J. Morgenthau, *The Restoration of American Politics* (Chicago, 1962), 276.

implement. No carpenter would think of pledging himself always to do his work with a hammer; on many occasions he needs a saw or a plane instead. The UN is not an overriding national interest, but only one among many.

Cool calculation also characterizes the participation of states in the third kind of broadened national interest, that of cooperation in dealing with all the difficulties raised by economic, ecological, and social interdependence.[31] Because cooperation on these terms remains on the level of a bargain among self-interested players, it is peculiarly vulnerable to the temptation each faces to obtain the benefits of common action without paying the costs. Although collectively each of the parties to an international agreement to combat pollution of the air or sea has a shared interest in the success of the common endeavor, individually each can assume that his contribution will not determine its success or failure. Each, therefore, looking to his unshared interests, may decide to withhold his contribution and thereby reap the advantage obtained by the efforts of others at no expense to himself. When all parties reason in this way, collaboration founders on immediate self-interest. The resultant immobility in the face of serious challenges is a valid point made by those who are skeptical of national-interest thinking. The national interest gives no guarantee that cooperation necessary for the health of the planet will be achieved.

A broadened or narrowed national interest will not usher in the millennium. There are sacrifices that states dare not make; national interests are not infinitely malleable; any agreement, to be successful, must involve reciprocal benefits and be acceptable to both sides. When these conditions are not met, the attempt to establish a *modus vivendi* between two states through the broadening or narrowing of their national interests may well fail.

Furthermore, even in those instances when the attempt is successful, it can be expected to effect only a marginal improvement in the conditions of international affairs. The modest nature of what can be expected from nations reexamining their interests with the objectives and under the limitations that have been suggested may be illustrated by Tocqueville's previously cited description of the principle of "interest rightly understood." Tocqueville saw individual Americans pursuing their private interests within the

---

31. See John Gerard Ruggie, "Collective Goods and Future International Collaboration," *American Political Science Review*, LXVI (September, 1972), 874–93.

framework of a larger system that allowed all citizens to do the same. On the other hand, the spirit of a democratic age was inconsistent with expectations that the citizen would devote his complete attention to public and not private affairs (just as a system of sovereign states discourages an attitude of pure altruism on the part of any of them).[32] Tocqueville sought a compromise that would demonstrate that a measure of attention devoted to civic responsibilities would also serve self-interest while it mitigated against the self-absorption of complete devotion to unshared material gains: "If the principle of interest rightly understood were to sway the whole moral world, extraordinary virtues would doubtless be more rare; but I think that gross depravity would then also be less common."

Tocqueville may have underestimated the strength of community in even the individualistic American political culture and understated its ability to call forth self-sacrifice and the display of even "extraordinary virtues." But "interest rightly understood" accurately describes the comparative frailty of the international community and the limited extent of the demands it can make on its members. It entails a measure of self-restraint on private demands so that the realm in which they are made can continue to exist. A willingness to devote some of one's time to preserving the polity and its liberties on the national level corresponds to a willingness to act according to interest and not sheer cupidity on the international. A policy grounded in the protection of state interests is not a "lofty" doctrine, but if it teaches statesmen temperance, moderation, foresight, and self-command, it will have raised the ethical level of international behavior.

Interest rightly understood is applicable to international politics because it deals with citizens in their relations with one another, not with isolated individuals. Nor are states isolated from the outside world. A stable international order regarded by its members as legitimate can be sustained by national policies directed toward concrete interests—knowable claims

32. All quotations from Tocqueville are taken from *Democracy in America*, trans. Henry Reeve (2 vols., 1840; rpr. New York, 1961), II, Bk. 2, Chaps. 8, 14. See also John Stuart Mill, in his introduction to the first English translation, on the effect on the citizen of participation in public affairs: "He becomes acquainted with more varied business, and a larger range of considerations. He is made to feel that besides the interests which separate him from his fellow-citizens, he has interests which connect him with them; that not only the common weal is his weal, but that it partly depends upon his exertions" (*ibid.*, Vol. II, p. xx). Much the same could be said of statesmen in the eras in which international society is most fully developed.

conforming to the expectations held by all of how states will act. At the same time, this order is a prerequisite for an international community that widens the moral opportunity of its participants, permitting their policy to move beyond the pure self-aggrandizement of Machiavelli to an enlightened self-interest softened by the obligations imposed by membership in a community. The mutual expectations of states are not equivalent to universal moral duties. They are maxims of prudence and applied political ethics; their strength and comprehensiveness depend on the degree to which the members of the system share in a common ethical framework. A flawed vessel but a useful one, a broadened or narrowed national interest holds that measure of justice mixed with prudence that statesmen have found it safe to allow themselves.

Without the higher standard of morality, however, weighing self-interest against the interest of others may be insufficient to prod the state into acting with as much justice as it is capable of. Even when ideals are honored more in the breach than in the observance, they supply a goal; statesmen may aspire to the standard and through their aspirations may at least be prevented from being as selfish as they might otherwise be. States need a reason to be prudent, and this need is filled by ethical principles.[33] Diplomats admittedly face a situation of international anarchy that resists the easy application of moral maxims drawn from private life. Although ideals may comprise, as Winston Churchill said of the Atlantic Charter, "not a law, but a star"—not a body of rigidly enforceable rules, or even a set of clear directives, but a collection of standards to offer general guidance as circumstances permit—they are necessary nonetheless. They continually remind policy makers that interests and prudence are reliable and beneficial, but only relative, not ultimate, guides to action.

This discussion of broadening and narrowing national interest reveals both limits and possibilities. In particular, the differentiation between *national interest* and *national interests* is intended to accomplish two things. By recognizing the close link between the national interest and the common good, it avoids the sort of moral relativism that cuts the ground from under any attempt to join ethics with the analysis of international politics and restores the common good to a central place in the analysis of politics. However, by acknowledging the immediate goals or interests of states, which

33. See Mahan, *The Interest of America in Sea Power*, 230.

form a large part of the diplomacy of most states regardless of their regime, it supplies the currency in which all states may deal without being separated by their differences on the ultimate question of the nature of the good regime.

So, too, broadening and narrowing may give content to "enlightened national interest" by demonstrating how the statesman may attempt to infuse his country's interests with a concern for the interests of others and for ethical principles. The defense does not fully refute the objections of the exclusivist critics, for the kernel of their charges is undeniable: the national interest, because it looks to the good of a part of the human community and not the whole, falls short of a universal system of morality. These critics must ask themselves, however, (1) whether the national interest does not also lead to good results, by protecting national communities and their efforts toward justice, (2) whether there is any alternative to a reliance on the national interest, given the contemporary structure of world politics, and (3) whether an enlightened view of national interests may not go some way toward meeting their objections by recognizing at least a fragmentary society outside the national community. The exclusivists constitute the most formidable of the critics of national interest, for their questions go to the most fundamental issues of the relationship between national good and impartial justice. Nevertheless, the proper response to their charges is, not their preferred course of the abandonment of national interest, but instead a deeper understanding of it.

V The National Interest and the American Polity

As THE CRITICISMS outlined in Chapter II indicated, observers have frequently argued that American political culture is particularly inhospitable to any talk of, as well as to action grounded in, national interest. The assumption that organic ties bind the elements of society together and give them a shared overall interest apart from and professedly superior to their unique, unshared interests seems incompatible with an individualistic society that places more faith in progress than in tradition. A conception of politics that has never favored talk of "the state," that distrusts concentrated power, and that prefers to rely for the protection of liberty on opposed and contending interests rather than on professions of wisdom and goodwill be enlightened statesmen finds the implications of national interest too centralizing, too statist, for comfort. Likewise, a country that has remained aloof from the center of diplomatic activity for much of its history, whose idealism and inexperience have tempted it to divide the roster of states into "good" world citizens or "bad," driven either by moral impulses or by unalloyed greed—this sort of country would not naturally be drawn to an interpretation of world politics that posits a society of states that are at once self-interested and restrained by the need not to alarm other members of the states-system.

If these generalizations are correct, the United States would seem to be unpromising territory for a foreign policy based in national interest. The definition of *national interest* proposed here, and the ethos of this particular nation, do not appear to fit. This chapter will review some elements of the American political heritage in the belief that despite such skepticism, national interest is not so "un-American" as this dichotomy might suggest.

THE FOUNDERS AND THE NATIONAL INTEREST

Those who founded the American republic were well aware of the existence of subnational interests. Indeed, they were convinced that these varied particular interests were an inevitable feature of any liberal regime, as Madison asserted in *Federalist* 10: "The diversity in the faculties of men, from which the rights of property originate, is . . . an insuperable obstacle to a uniformity of interests. The protection of these faculties is the first object of government. From the protection of different and unequal faculties of acquiring property, the possession of different degrees and kinds of property immediately results; and from the influence of these on the sentiments and views of the respective proprietors, ensues a division of the society into different interests and parties." Differing interests "are thus sown in the nature of man," Madison went on, and it was the duty of a free government to protect the individual liberty that gave rise to these various groups within the national society.

The authors of the *Federalist Papers* understood *interest* to bear several different meanings. First, as Madison employed it in the passage cited above and in the quotation noted earlier concerning "a landed interest, a manufacturing interest, a mercantile interest, [and] a moneyed interest," the term could be used to mean a group of individuals possessing some common characteristic that gave them a common goal, often an economic one. At other points, *interest* is made synonymous with *desire* or *wish*. *Interest* in the sense of desire may well be opposed to the demands of justice, when the desire for gain leads one to unethical actions to satisfy that desire; "interested" groups or individuals sacrifice others to the pursuit of their own interests. *Federalist* 10 decries the fact that "measures are too often decided, not according to the rules of justice and the rights of the minor party, but by the superior force of an interested and overbearing majority"; *Federalist* 63 reminds the reader that popular opinion may be "misled by the artful representations of interested men."

Yet one also finds passages in which *interest* can be taken to mean that which one needs or ought to have. *Federalist* 35 distinguishes *interest* from *want* when Hamilton discusses the proposition "that all classes of citizens should have some of their own number in the representative body, in order that their feelings and interests may be the better understood and attended to." In *Federalist* 71 he is even clearer when he warns of the danger to the people from demagogues "who flatter their prejudices to betray their interests" and speaks of those occasions on which "the interests of the people are at variance with their inclinations." Finally, the disjunction between interest and desire can be present even when one sincerely believes one's wish to coincide with one's need. "The people can never wilfully betray their own interests," Madison grants in *Federalist* 63, but they may do so inadvertently through the selection of untrustworthy representatives. Hamilton distinguishes true interest from what one believes is in one's interest when, in concluding the case for the adoption of the Constitution, he states in *Federalist* 85 that in the framing of the document thirteen independent states had to be "accommodated in their interests or opinions of interests."

Despite their many references to these various kinds of subnational interests, however, the Founders also assume the existence of a common good or public interest distinct from more particular interests. *Federalist* 57 posits that the aim of every constitution should be "to obtain for rulers men who possess most wisdom to discern, and most virtue to pursue, the common good of the society." Madison in *Federalist* 62 refers to "the comprehensive interests" of the United States, and in the following paper, speaking directly to questions of foreign policy, points to the importance of farsighted policy "to the collective and permanent welfare of every country." The Articles of Confederation had proved wholly inadequate to the protection of the country's common interest; instead, Hamilton argues in *Federalist* 22, there had been "contemptible compromises of the public good," and "the faith, the reputation, the peace of the whole Union, are . . . continually at the mercies of the prejudices, the passions, and the interests of every member of which it is composed." The nation is faced with the "absurdity [of] . . . confiding to a government the direction of the most essential national interests, without daring to trust it to the authorities which are indispensable to their proper and efficient management," he says in *Federalist* 23. The common interest must instead be served by an effective common government. The proposed federal government would have its own "national interests, whether considered in relation to the several States or to foreign nations," Jay observes in *Federalist* 64, and the country's need would be for officials "who are best able to promote those interests."

The task that the Founders set themselves was to construct a government that would protect the vitality of the narrower, more particular subnational interests while defending the integrity of the overall national interest. The plan of government they devised relied on the interplay of interests for the preservation of the liberty of individuals and minorities against an unjust majority, while at the same time it sought institutional mechanisms likely to select and fortify officials who would pursue the common good and national safety even at the cost of defying domestic interests. In their "new science of politics," the Framers specifically abjured any attempt to eradicate these subnational interests by inculcating in the citizenry a purely public-spirited virtue; instead, they hoped to combine the freedom of self-interested pluralism with the fortitude of statesmen capable of defending the long-term good of the whole community at all times and not only when they were supported by a pluralist consensus.

Thus, in the well-known passage in *Federalist* 51, Madison points out the security to liberty to be gained from a variegated polity: "The society itself will be broken into so many parts, interests and classes of citizens, that the rights of individuals, or of the minority, will be in little danger from interested combinations of the majority. In a free government the security for civil rights must be the same as that for religious rights. It consists in the one case in the multiplicity of interests, and in the other in the multiplicity of sects. The degree of security in both cases will depend on the number of interests and sects." In his discussion of foreign affairs, Jay supports his colleague's argument by predicting that the new federal government will always be mindful of particular interests within the society; *Federalist* 64 contains the maxim that "the government must be a weak one indeed, if it should forget that the good of the whole can only be promoted by advancing the good of each of the parts or members which compose the whole."

At the same time, domestic interests are not the only ones to be considered. Madison in *Federalist* 14 pleads "the necessity of the Union, as our bulwark against foreign danger, as the conservator of peace among ourselves, as the guardian of our commerce and other common interests." Jay foresees in *Federalist* 64 that "in proportion as the United States assume a national form and a national character, so will the good of the whole be more and more an object of attention," and in *Federalist* 4 that "in the formation of treaties, [a unified federal government] will regard the interest of the whole and the particular interests of the parts as connected with that of the whole." We now find that subnational interests, far from defining by their sum the interest of the whole, are defined and delimited by their incorporation within the common good. The country's future demands a central political authority strong enough to pursue this common good effectively: "A government, the constitution of which renders it unfit to be trusted with all the powers which a free people *ought to delegate to any government,* would be an unsafe and improper depositary of the *National Interests,*" Hamilton declaims. "Wherever *these* can with propriety be confided, the coincident powers may safely accompany them."[1]

But how to grant officials the legitimate authority and the institutional strength to eschew a popular consensus in favor of a policy dictated by the greater knowledge and experience of leaders, without also opening the way to tyranny? The authors of the *Federalist Papers*—in their capacities as both pamphleteering advocates and political thinkers—recognize that great latitude given to public authorities sworn to serve the general good may conflict with, even destroy, the pluralist bargaining in which lies safety for individual rights. Hamilton in *Federalist* 59 distinguishes "the interest of the people" from "the interest of their . . . rulers." Madison in *Federalist* 51 warns that "creating a will in the community independent of the majority—that is, of the society itself[—] . . . is but a precarious security" against majority oppression of minorities, "because a power independent of the society may as well espouse the unjust views of the major, as the rightful interests of the minor party, and may possibly be turned against both parties." Distrust of rulers who extinguish liberty in the name of the national interest runs deep in these pages; one finds no sanguine hopes that responsibility to the national trust will free leaders from the tendency to aggrandizement that is the lot of all human nature. Madison could have said of leadership justified in the name of the public good what he does say in *Federalist* 41 of a standing military force—that it "is a dangerous, at the same time that it may be a necessary, provision."

The authors suggest two methods for safely combining the inevitably self-regarding presence of individual interests with a necessary but at times misused reliance on the common interest by leaders. One is to construct an institutional framework that will make the individual interest of officials coincident with the public interest. This course assumes little public spirit or selflessness on the part of rulers; it merely attempts to arrange incentives so that when an individual occupying high office acts to advance his own

1. *Federalist* 23, in Alexander Hamilton, John Jay, and James Madison, *The Federalist* (New York, 1937), emphasis in the original. All citations of individual *Federalist Papers* are to this edition.

interest—that is, either his wishes or that which is to his good in his capacity as a private person—he will, perhaps without realizing it, advance the good of the country as well.

Madison in *Federalist* 51 makes an argument supporting the separation of powers and, through it, limited government:

> The great security against a gradual concentration of the several powers in the same department, consists in giving to those who administer each department the necessary constitutional means and personal motives to resist encroachments of the others. . . . Ambition must be made to counteract ambition. The interest of the man must be connected with the constitutional rights of the place. . . .
>
> This policy of supplying, by opposite and rival interests, the defect of better motives, might be traced through the whole system of human affairs, private as well as public. We see it particularly displayed in all the subordinate distribution of power, where the constant aim is to divide and arrange the several offices in such a manner as that each may be a check on the other—that the private interest of every individual may be a sentinel over the public rights. These inventions of prudence cannot be less requisite in the distribution of the supreme powers of the State.

Because one cannot rely on those who govern to display the virtue to do so in the national interest, one must, out of "the defect of better motives," tempt them into desiring to do what they ought to do. Whatever the implied "reflection on human nature," security for the public interest, or shared good of the community, derives from its association with the private interest, or egotistic want, of the community's governors.

There is a second method for balancing the ubiquity of subnational interests with the necessity of protecting the nation's common interest. While it also requires the foresighted efforts of the framers of the institutions of state, it goes further than the first in the demands it places on the Founders' successors. It envisages a statesmanship that is willing to follow the public interest even when the personal interest of the officeholder or the outcome of the struggle among interest groups seems to dictate another course. This aspiration is itself to be gained in two ways: through further institutional safeguards and through a deeper understanding of what one's own interest requires.

At the Constitutional Convention in 1787, the delegates were not intent only on laying out a plan of government in which, to oppose aggrandizement by any component part, all were designed to check and balance one another. In addition, these men sought to write into the Constitution provisions that would (1) channel into the highest offices of the federal government those who would most clearly discern the public interest and, through it, the national interest, and (2) encourage them to act on their vision at all times when the good of the country required it, not merely on those occasions when the outcome of the pluralist bargaining process supported them. As far as they could, consistent with the spirit of a popular regime, the Founders reserved office and authority to those they felt would be best able to hold and exercise it with independent good judgment.

This determination lay behind constitutional directives concerning who was to be eligible for high office, how he was to make his way there and how long remain, and what the scope of his power was to be. Examining briefly the familiar sections of the Constitution dealing with the executive and the Senate, the two branches most intimately involved in the preservation of the national interest in foreign affairs, one sees that the authors were of the firm opinion that not all citizens were equally adept at serving the national interest. They meant, therefore, to discriminate among citizens— not in an invidious manner, but in the same way that they believed nature to have discriminated in the distribution of native character and ability, and circumstances in their cultivation.

Members of the Senate were to have attained at least thirty years of age and presidents thirty-five. This restriction—which, Abraham Baldwin reminded his fellow delegates at the convention, "all had concurred in the propriety of"[2]—was intended to confine the choice for these offices to those aspirants who possessed, in the words of *Federalist 62*, a "greater extent of information and stability of character." So, too, the requirements for citizenship (nine years for senators, fourteen years for presidents) were meant to limit the choice of the electors to men who had demonstrated that they were first attached to and knowledgeable of the interests of *this* country.

2. Max Farrand, ed., *The Records of the Federal Convention of 1787* (4 vols.; New Haven, 1911), II, 272.

Both senators and presidents were, in another filtering mechanism, to be indirectly elected. "The inference which naturally results from these considerations," according to Jay in *Federalist* 64, was "that the President and senators so chosen will always be of the number of those who best understand our national interests, whether considered in relation to the several States or to foreign nations, who are best able to promote those interests, and whose reputation for integrity inspires and merits confidence."

The president and senators thus selected would serve longer terms than the members of the most popular branch, the House of Representatives— the president for four years, the senators for six. This duration in office would grant to those who bore the primary responsibility for the conduct of the country's foreign relations, first, the experience to act wisely and, second, the firmness to act fearlessly in defense of the national interest. Those charged with pursuing such long-term aims should not only be "able and honest men, but also . . . should continue in place a sufficient time to become perfectly acquainted with our national concerns, and to form and introduce a system for the management of them." A "popular assembly, composed of members constantly coming and going in quick succession," would be inadequate for lack of prolonged exposure to the issues at hand.

Moreover, the opportunity to act without being forced to face an election in the immediate future would allow these leaders to employ their experience in ways that were in the long-term interest of the nation, even when such measures elicited no short-term popularity. Hamilton's passage on this subject, directed to the chief executive, could be applied to the Senate as well:

> The republican principle demands that the deliberate sense of the community should govern the conduct of those to whom they intrust the management of their affairs; but it does not require an unqualified complaisance to every sudden breeze of passion, or to every transient impulse which the people may receive from the arts of men, who flatter their prejudices to betray their interests. It is a just observation that the people commonly *intend* the PUBLIC GOOD. This often applies to their very errors. But their good sense would despise the adulator who should pretend that they always *reason* right about the *means* of promoting it. . . . When occasions present themselves, in which the interests of the people are at vari-

ance with their inclinations, it is the duty of the persons whom they have appointed to be the guardians of those interests, to withstand the temporary delusion, in order to give them time and opportunity for more cool and sedate reflection.[3]

Extended terms would, without removing these officials from ultimate democratic control, grant them some leeway to formulate and execute policies the benefits of which were not quickly apparent or immediately applauded.

To such custodians, then, the Constitution granted most of the direction of the country's foreign policy. The two branches did not possess a monopoly of control over foreign affairs. Nor were the extensive powers assigned to an individual and a small group, neither of whom was under direct democratic influence, agreed to without controversy; many of these provisions occasioned lively debate, both in the convention and afterward. Nor yet did even those who approved of this distribution of powers hold any blind faith in the ability and rectitude of the president and Senate under all circumstances; James Wilson reassured the Pennsylvania ratifying convention that "they are checks upon each other, and are so balanced as to produce security to the people."[4]

Nevertheless, almost all of the delegates to the Constitutional Convention and a majority of the delegates of the state ratifying conventions were persuaded that the Constitution went as far as possible in designing a system that would attract to its most responsible offices public servants likely to guide their actions by reference to the common good. Statements to the convention by Madison that the "Executive Magistrate [would] be considered as a national officer, acting for and equally sympathizing with every part of the [United] States," and by Gouverneur Morris of Pennsylvania that the president would be "the general Guardian of the National interests," were echoed by William Richardson Davie, who returned from Philadelphia to tell the North Carolina convention that the president, "being elected by the people of the United States at large, will have their general interest at

---

3. *Federalist* 71, emphasis in the original. See also *Federalist* 72.

4. See Farrand, ed., *Records of the Federal Convention*, II, 319, 639, III, 128, 166, 250, 358, 371–75, IV, 57. Elbridge Gerry, a delegate to the convention who refused to sign the finished document, called the powers of the president and Senate over foreign affairs one of his "principal objections to the plan."

heart." Madison's hope, expressed to the convention, that senators would be "the impartial umpires [and] Guardians of justice and General good"[5] was answered by Jay's confidence, noted in *Federalist 64*, that in general, membership in the Senate would be confined "to those men only who have become the most distinguished by their abilities and virtue, and in whom the people perceive just grounds for confidence."

Why were the Founders at such pains to draft the provisions of the Constitution dealing with foreign affairs in this way? What explains the care with which they attempted to fit together qualifications, length of term, and authority? Their own words at the time indicate that they acted thus because they believed that a public interest or common good did exist; that the pluralist competition among contending subnational interests was inadequate to the generation of policy to meet the national interest in the realm of diplomacy; and that officials, to be true to their trust, had to set aside the narrower interests of their constituents from time to time and follow the public interest. The Founders endeavored to construct a system most congenial to those who would accept this reasoning and most supportive of those who would act on it.

In all these ways, the authors of the *Federalist Papers* and their prominent contemporaries accepted that one's personal interest or the interest of one or more subnational groups might conflict with the interest of the entire community. They designed a selection system that they hoped would give an advantage in the competition for high office to those whose wisdom and patriotism would prompt them to prefer the more inclusive interest to the less. The passages cited above show them differentiating between the good of a class or association or of an individual acting in a private capacity and the good of the nation. Their efforts to reconcile a diverse, individualistic society with a common good did not stop here, however. They also sought to associate the lesser interests with the greater by arguing that each individual's and each group's true, long-run interest was dependent upon the well-being of the community of which he or it was a part. In essence, this was an effort to elevate the definition of one's interest and thereby to remove any conflict between it and the common good.[6]

5. *Ibid.*, I, 428, II, 81, 541, III, 348.

6. For an extended discussion of this point, see Paul Eidelberg, *A Discourse on Statesmanship: The Design and Transformation of the American Polity* (Urbana, Ill., 1974), 241–76.

More than once the Founders spoke in terms that indicated their hope that their fellow citizens would, given the proper education and example, be led to define their interests, not only as their own unshared material gain, but also as the preservation of the liberal republic that made it possible for them to seek their own goals. Madison wrote in a letter to James Monroe in 1786 of his belief that in order to be understood correctly, the term *interest* should be given the broader, more inclusive meaning.

> There is no maxim, in my opinion, which is more liable to be mis-applied, and which, therefore, more needs elucidation, than the current one, that the interest of the majority is the political standard of right and wrong. Taking the word "interest" as synonymous with "ultimate happiness," in which sense it is qualified with every necessary moral ingredient, the proposition is no doubt true. But taking it in the popular sense, as referring to immediate augmentation of property and wealth, nothing can be more false. In the latter sense, it would be in the interest of the majority . . . to despoil and enslave the minority.[7]

Despite the "immediate augmentation of property and wealth" that seizing the possessions of the minority would bring to the majority, it was in fact not in the interest of the majority to despoil and enslave the minority, because to do so would be to destroy the web of protections for individual rights against arbitrary government that also safeguarded the security of members of the majority. Part of the true interest of the majority was to preserve the system that sheltered the liberties of all.

For the Founders, recognition of this true interest required the establishment of a federal government secure and powerful enough to encompass the free interplay of groups and their narrower interests without being torn apart by them. Thus, in their letter to Congress transmitting the proposed Constitution, the delegates to the convention admitted that the arduousness of their labors had been increased "by a difference among the several States as to their situation, extent, habits, and particular interests." Nevertheless, the letter went on, "In our deliberations on this subject [of the extent of the

---

7. Robert A. Rutland and Charles F. Hobson, eds., *The Papers of James Madison* (16 vols. to date; Chicago, 1977), IX, 141.

powers of the new central government] we kept steadily in our view, that which appears to us the greatest interest of every true American, the consolidation of our union, in which is involved our prosperity, felicity, safety, perhaps our national existence." Likewise, in his Farewell Address of 1796 Washington gave pride of place to "interest" in his catalog of reasons for urging his fellow citizens not to let their unshared goals override the benefits they all derived from the safety and prosperity of the shared community.[8]

The Founders performed their educative task well. The sentiments expressed by Madison, by the convention delegates, and by Washington were those that, thirty-five years later, Tocqueville found expressed everywhere in American life: "The Americans . . . are fond of explaining almost all the actions of their lives by the principle of interest rightly understood; they show with complacency how an enlightened regard for themselves constantly prompts them to assist each other, and inclines them willingly to sacrifice a portion of their time and property for the welfare of the State."[9] For the French observer, as for the American statesmen, enlightened self-interest entailed a recognition of the dependence of subnational interest groups and individual wants on the continued vitality of the common good. Just as the interaction among these less inclusive interests prevented any one of them from gaining an unhealthy predominance and helped to preserve liberty—thereby serving the common interest—so a willingness to sacrifice for the common interest maintained the free community as a framework within which unshared interests could be elucidated and sought.

Madison, Washington, and the others did not confine the common interest to the maintenance of an open arena for the competition of particular interests groups; there was more to the common interest than the procedural virtues of unconfined pluralism.[10] Nevertheless, the inculcation of "self-interest rightly understood" by political leaders, and its acceptance by

8. Farrand, ed., *Records of the Federal Convention*, II, 666–67; John C. Fitzpatrick, ed., *The Writings of George Washington* (37 vols.; Washington, D.C., 1933), X, 220.

9. Alexis de Tocqueville, *Democracy in America*, trans. Henry Reeve (2 vols., 1840; rpr. New York, 1961), II, 146–47.

10. Eidelberg goes further and argues that, in the case of the country's republican rulers, a love of contemporary honor and lasting fame melds egotism and the common good. For the true statesman, defense of the common interest is not a means to the pursuit of his own selfish interest; the promise of glory means that service to the community *becomes* his end or his self-interest. Such a large-minded, though self-regarding, attitude is beyond the capacities of most citizens, however. See Eidelberg, *A Discourse on Statesmanship*, 257–63.

the polity at large, provides one important avenue marked by the Founders for combining their recognition of the strength and value of vigorous self-interested groups, on one hand, and their steadfast determination not to abandon the equally real and necessary concept of the common interest, on the other. Given the required capable officials, acting within the requisite sustaining institutions, guided by the proper wise outlook, the regime could blend the two.[11]

Bringing these considerations to the present opens several lines of thought. First of all, in the American regime it is expected that there will be competing visions of the best way to serve the public interest and protect the national interest. Despite the comparatively high degree of consensus on basic principles that characterizes the United States, it cannot be said too often that the national interest is not a license for the belief that "the president knows best." (Of course, it is equally true that dissenters from the policy of the chief executive should not be assumed to hold a monopoly on truth, either.) A willingness to engage in debate, and a faith in the beneficial effects of the clash of contending points of view, is at the heart of American politics—as Bernard Crick insists it is at the heart of all "politics," correctly understood. The question is what the debate is to be *about*. While recognizing personal and local interests, the American framework of government is intended to allow room as well for consideration of the common good and the desirability of checking outside interferences with Americans' search for—even their disagreements over—their public interest.[12]

Similarly, there are many institutional mechanisms that may translate the general duty to serve, and the useful belief in, the national interest into immediate decisions on policy. No one of them is always and everywhere valid. Often, conflicting "special interests" can be left to fight it out; only when their struggles begin to interfere with grand strategy do central decision-makers pull them up short. Their freedom to carry on the normal processes of pluralism most of the time only shows that the national interest

11. Needless to say, however, no guarantee of success existed. For an example of the disaster that resulted when the scheme of "opposite and rival interests," carried to extremes, was applied to foreign affairs in the War of 1812, see James S. Young, *The Washington Community, 1800–1828* (New York, 1966), 182–86. But see Arthur Maass, *Congress and the Common Good* (New York, 1983).

12. See Richard E. Flathman, *The Public Interest: An Essay Concerning the Normative Discourse of Politics* (New York, 1966), 72–73.

in foreign policy is concerned with securing the domestic debate from foreign threats, and that in the absence of a danger to security the national interest can leave a broad range within which choices may be made without bumping up against the overall common interest in national autonomy. Just as the ways of domestic politics are likely to be messy, and just as the Founders described no formula for recognizing who had been granted the best insight into the public interest, so there is no "one size fits all" process for translating the national interest into specific policy decisions. This is the rationality suitable to the prudential task of governing of which Oakeshott wrote. If officials or citizens deliberate seriously, keeping in mind even while they carry on their contests over immediate interests the larger necessity of preserving against outside threats the arena for their competition, they will be doing all the Framers asked of them.

DIPLOMACY AND NATIONAL INTERESTS

If one turns from the domestic community, with its creative tension between particular individual or group interests and the common interest of the country, to the international society, in which governments assert state interests and contend to have them recognized by the other members of the states-system, one finds a parallel record of American thought on the meaning and usefulness of the concept of "interest" in combining diversity and co-existence. While the record of diplomacy has not produced a work comparable to the *Federalist* that lays out in a concise but comprehensive way a coherent understanding of these issues (and neither has the diplomacy of any other country), it is possible to discern in the documentary history of statesmanship in the United States evidence that adds up to a partial substitute. Their public and private writings show that makers of American foreign policy have at times, both in the period immediately following the founding and afterwards, looked on national interests as claims upon the international society—claims for things intended to serve one's own national well-being, to be sure, but also claims that had to be supported by logical, persuasive argument. It is assuredly not true that such an understanding has governed American foreign policy on all issues at all times, as observers most supportive of a diplomacy founded on national interest have been quick to point out and decry. A brief examination of some representative documents in American diplomatic history will show, however, that an interest-based diplomacy does have roots in American soil and is more than a statist doctrine imported from or imposed by the Old World.

First, American leaders have on occasion employed the term *interest* in ways that demonstrated the distinction between a desire or a want, and a real benefit or interest. When Charles Pinckney took the floor of Congress on August 16, 1786, to criticize John Jay's proposed treaty with Spain, Pinckney argued that the position of the United States was more advantageous, and that of Spain more precarious, than Jay had asserted, and that therefore the new republic could obtain better terms than Congress was being asked to approve. In particular, Pinckney charged, Jay had misread the position of Great Britain, which, despite the ill-will remaining from the recent struggle with her former American colonies, would find weighty reasons not to side with Spain in any conflict in the New World: "Though the animosities of Great Britain are still warm, yet there is sufficient wisdom in her councils to make them yield to her interest. Though she loves us not, she hates France and Spain, and would avail herself of any opportunity, even upon less than equal terms, to strike a blow. With them she can never be in any other than a rival situation; with us, when the present differences shall have terminated, it will ever be her interest to be closely connected." [13] Pinckney pointed to the similarity of Anglo-American "language, governments, religion and policy" as a spur to their "alliance," and noted that the location of the United States would make it a desirable source of aid to London in any conflict with the Bourbon powers. Taken altogether, these considerations meant that far from fearing British participation in an opposing coalition, the United States could expect Britain's support "if she suffers her interest and her wishes to prevail."

The language is revealing: interest *and* wishes. Whether Pinckney was correct in his prediction need not detain us here. What is significant is that he clearly distinguished between what Britain, in the heat of anger, might wish to do, and what it was to her advantage to do. He identified the many factors, from the pressures of international rivalries to the correspondence

---

13. This and the following quotations illustrating the American diplomatic record are taken from two compilations: Ruhl J. Bartlett, ed., *The Record of American Diplomacy: Documents and Readings in the History of American Foreign Relations* (New York, 1947), and Norman A. Graebner, ed., *Ideas and Diplomacy: Readings in the Intellectual Tradition of American Foreign Policy* (New York, 1964).

of domestic regimes, that could mold a government's conception of its national interest. In the end, however, a state's asserted interests would have to be more than an arbitrary wish-list; they would be concrete objectives framed in terms comprehensible to other states in arguments similar to those Pinckney was presenting to his congressional colleagues.

If Pinckney distinguished between interests and wishes, a mid-nineteenth-century successor to Jay contended that interests were not equivalent to legal rights and duties. The occasion was an Anglo-French proposal that the United States join those two powers in a declaration opposing the attempt by any other power to obtain Cuba from Spain and forever renouncing any intention of gaining possession of the island themselves. In response, Secretary of State Edward Everett wrote to the French minister in Washington on December 1, 1852, that a treaty's terms—equal on parchment and in law—might be unequal in their substance because of differences in the interests of the states concerned. The proposed convention "assumes that the United States have no other or greater interest in the question than France or England; whereas it is necessary only to cast one's eye on the map to see how remote are the relations of Europe, and how intimate those of the United States, with this island."

Far distant from Cuba, London and Paris would only recognize the obvious by disclaiming all interest in it. Washington's situation was quite different. The island's location in relation to the approach to the Gulf of Mexico and America's five Gulf Coast states, to the mouth of the Mississippi, and to the isthmus route to California put it "at our doors." Everett asked what the Europeans' reaction would be "if an island like Cuba, belonging to the Spanish crown, guarded the entrance of the Thames and the Seine, and the United States should propose a convention like this to France and England." Here was national interest defined much more in geopolitical terms, much less on the grounds of domestic similarities of society, than in Pinckney's analysis. At the same time, such interests were part of "the natural order of things" and wholly unlike abstract legal principles, though they could be described in persuasive rational argument.

Such asserted interests, affected as they were by the ebb and flow of circumstances, did not rest on the cogency of supporting rationales alone, however, but also on the strength to back them up. Interests rely not simply on force of argument but, sometimes, on simple force. In his report to the House of Representatives on December 16, 1793, "on the privileges and restrictions on the commerce of the United States in foreign countries," Secretary of State Jefferson alluded to this face of national interests. Dubious of the utility of armed force, anxious to display "all the liberality and spirit of accommodation which the nature of the case will admit," Jefferson believed even so that the prospect of economic coercion could not be abandoned for a wholesale reliance on others' goodwill. "It is not to the moderation and justice of others we are to trust for fair and equal access to market with our productions, or for our due share in the transportation of them," he noted, "but to our own means of independence, and the firm will to use them." He assumed that states were in the main self-seeking, that this attribute strongly colored the ways they framed their interests, and that states' interests could clash. Faced with a states-system of this description, the United States should formulate its own interests (as Jefferson tried to do on questions of foreign trade in his report) and then prepare to reward or punish other states, economically, according to their willingness to accommodate themselves to this claim to a share of international trade.

At the same time, if a state is to go beyond a policy of unvarnished self-aggrandizement to a policy built on "interest," it will be able to make a case for the claims it puts forward. President Tyler's message to Congress of December 3, 1844, supporting the annexation of Texas, provides a good example of an attempt at this sort of buttressing argument. The Republic of Texas clearly desired admission to the Union, the president wrote, and such an act would "interfere in no respect with the rights of any other nation." The benefits to the United States—"the extension of our coastwise and foreign trade to an amount almost incalculable, the enlargement of the market for our manufactures, a constantly growing market for our agricultural productions, safety to our frontiers, and additional strength and stability to the Union"—meant that "every American interest would seem to require it." Even Mexico, Tyler averred, would find it in her "true interest" to end a costly, futile war to regain the lost province of Texas and enjoy the stability and prosperity of peace.

Mexico, to be sure, might not agree with the American president's estimation of its own true interest in Texas. Nor did Mexico agree with Secretary of State James Buchanan's assurance, in his instructions of November 10, 1845, to his special envoy to Mexico, John Slidell, that its interests no longer included possession of New Mexico: "It may hereafter, should it remain a Mexican province, become a subject of dispute and a source of bad feeling. . . . On the other hand, if, in adjusting the boundary, the province of New Mexico should be included within the limits of the United States, this would obviate the danger of future collisions. Mexico would part with a remote and detached province, the possession of which can never be advantageous to her; and she would be relieved from the trouble and expense of defending its inhabitants against the Indians." It would take a war with the United States to change Mexico's calculation of its interests. Nor was it clear that France would necessarily accept the case made by President Jefferson to the American minister in Paris, Robert Livingston, on April 18, 1802, that the French acquisition of New Orleans was not in *that* country's interest, despite Jefferson's careful instructions designed to refute any French arguments to the contrary. It was clear that Great Britain did *not* accept the assertion of an American interest in the Anglo-Venezuelan boundary dispute of 1895. Secretary of State Richard Olney's dispatch to the American ambassador in London, Thomas F. Bayard, on July 20 of that year, asserting that "the controversy is one in which both [the United States'] honor and its interests are involved," was met by Lord Salisbury's message to Sir Julian Pauncefote in Washington on November 26 that "it is a controversy with which the United States have no apparent practical concern."

Thus, the politics of interest gives no guarantee that states will agree, or that they will always be able to compose their differences with peaceful compromise. Washington may assert an interest, but London may reject it. Mexico or France may maintain a claim or interest, but the United States may argue that those states are mistaken and that their claims, if granted or allowed to stand, will not in fact conduce to their own benefit. One state may view the avowed interests of another as illegitimate: in a dispatch of August 6, 1785, from John Adams, then minister to London, to John Jay, Adams called British commercial policy "commercial hostilities" because "their direct objective is not so much the increase of their own wealth, ships, or sailors, as the diminution of ours." But all the disputes can be carried on in terms comprehensible to every participant and open to arguments framed in terms that recognize an international system in which all the players are expected to be self-interested but none can press its advantages too far.

Finally, a more demanding test of national-interest thinking would ask for evidence that a state has restrained its own desires. It is relatively easy to construct a case, even a disingenuous one, that supports one's claims for oneself. It is comparatively simple to find arguments that discredit the claims of another state, whether these are existing interests or interests newly asserted on its part. What is often more difficult is to constrain oneself by demonstrating that a prospective interest will in fact bring one no overall benefit, and it is harder yet to practice self-denial on the grounds that self-gratification would be incompatible with the stability and security of the other players or the system as a whole. Still, from time to time American leaders have done so, often as a way of criticizing assertions of an American interest by other Americans. In 1870, when President Grant sent to the Senate a treaty authorizing the annexation of Santo Domingo, advancing reasons having to do with commerce, defense, and the island's natural resources, Charles Sumner, in an address to the Senate on December 21, denounced the negotiations that had led to the proposed agreement, argued that the "ordinance of Nature," in the form of geography and climate, had guaranteed the independence of the Caribbean islands, and concluded that "we take counsel of our supposed interests rather than theirs, when we seek to remove them from the sphere in which they have been placed by Providence." In the same manner, the national debate over the possession of Oregon in the 1840s brought forth claims and denials of an American interest in the Pacific Northwest. Representative Robert Winthrop (like Sumner, from Massachusetts), in a speech to the House of Representatives on March 18, 1844, attacked the notion that control of the whole of the Oregon territory, as opposed to dividing the area with Great Britain, was a defensible interest of the United States or of any section of the country:

> Sir, I doubt whether the West has a particle of real interest in the possession of Oregon. It may have an interest—a momentary, seeming, delusive interest—in a war for Oregon. . . . But suppose the war were over, successfully over, and Oregon ours: what interest, let me ask—what real, substantial, permanent interest—would the West have in its possession? Are our western brethren straitened for elbow-room, or likely to be for a thousand years? Have they not too much land for their own advantage already? . . . What pretence have we for planting ourselves in our presumed rights at this late day, and for shutting our ears to all overtures of negotiation, and

all assertion or argument of the rights of others? None; none whatever. Such a course would subject us to the just reproach and scorn of the civilized world.

Winthrop, like Sumner, did not believe that a convincing case could be made for a claim that others had suggested the United States make on the states-system. While the territory in question might be something that this country could wish for, it was not an interest that Washington could reasonably expect London to yield.

In these examples of the rhetoric of public officials, one can see that the understanding of "national interests" as demands made on an international society with standards that were loose, but not too loose to make it possible for other states to judge the degree to which such demands might be allowed to succeed, was no more foreign to Americans than an understanding of "the national interest" that posited the existence of a common good that was usually compatible with, but distinguishable from, the demands of particular groups, and sought to protect it in an often-inhospitable international environment. The point of such an examination of the diplomatic record is not to spot the number of times American policy-makers used the word *interest* but to argue that this concept, used in these senses, was not simply a preoccupation of the Old World but has been employed, with some sophistication, on the western as well as the eastern shores of the North Atlantic. It is a part—not the whole, and not always even the most popular or the major portion, but a part—of the American diplomatic tradition, at least during the eighteenth and nineteenth centuries.[14] Whether it informed important actions of the United States after this country emerged from the Second World War a superpower is a question for the four succeeding chapters.

14. For the argument that this tradition had largely been lost by the end of the nineteenth century, see Robert E. Osgood, *Ideals and Self-Interest in America's Foreign Relations: The Great Transformation of the Twentieth Century* (Chicago, 1953), esp. 27–107; and Hans J. Morgenthau, *In Defense of the National Interest: A Critical Examination of American Foreign Policy* (New York, 1951), 13–28. For the contention that American efforts to define and secure interests differed from the European *Realpolitik* tradition, see Greg Russell, *Hans J. Morgenthau and the Ethics of American Statecraft* (Baton Rouge, 1990).

TWO National Interest in Practice

Foreign policies are not built upon abstractions. They are the result of practical conceptions of national interest arising from some immediate exigency or standing out vividly in historical perspective.

—Charles Evans Hughes, in
*Annals of the American Academy of
Political and Social Science*

Will springs from the two elements of moral sense and self-interest. Let us be brought to believe it is morally right, and, at the same time, favorable to, or, at least, not against, our interest, . . . and we shall find a way to do it, however great the task may be.

—Abraham Lincoln,
The Collected Works of Abraham Lincoln

VI   The Marshall Plan

THE EUROPEAN ECONOMY was not recovering from the shock it had received in the Second World War: by early 1947 that fact was becoming clear. This was more than a matter of wartime destruction, horrendous though that was. Inflation across the Continent made consumers skeptical of the value of money and anxious to withdraw from the normal money economy wherever possible; black markets flourished. Where economic activity remained aboveground, barter frequently replaced exchange tied to an untrustworthy currency. Barter in the domestic economy: the ties between city and country were increasingly frayed as farmers refused to continue growing surpluses for sale. Meanwhile, urban populations suffered and governments depleted their scarce currency reserves to pay for agricultural imports. Barter in the international economy: as the supply of foreign exchange dipped below the danger point, countries either swapped their meager goods for goods or negotiated bilateral agreements that did nothing to revive the multilateral economy. The International Monetary Fund had begun operation the previous year, but it was designed to deal with an already functioning monetary regime and could not cope with the problems of transition to that regime from the war's combination of chaos and rigid controls. No one knew what the "true" exchange rate between any two currencies should be, and no one had the capacity to produce goods for the American market that would earn the dollars to pay for the imports from the United States that everyone desperately needed. Beyond all this, the almost unprecedented harshness of the winter of 1946–1947 seriously disrupted recovery. Crops froze in the ground; transportation was halted; mines could not be worked. All these developments aggravated shortages, which worsened inflationary pressures and cut rations for already undernourished populations, further crippling productivity and widening the "dollar gap." Meanwhile, American goods were becoming more expensive.

With the removal of price controls in the United States in 1946, a spurt of inflation reduced the purchasing power of the Americans' 1946 loan of $3.75 billion to Great Britain by some 40 percent.

These problems were interconnected and mutually reinforcing; their combined effect was to put at risk Europe's economic future and, with it, the money Washington had already poured into the Old World through Lend-Lease, the United Nations Relief and Rehabilitation Administration, and the substantial postwar loans to Britain and France. In the early months of 1947, the conviction grew that more than economic well-being might be endangered if corrective measures were not taken. A transatlantic process of give and take ensued: growing disquiet within the American government over the economic plight in Europe, and the need to revive the western sectors of Germany as a motor for economic recovery elsewhere, prompted internal studies and several public speeches by Undersecretary of State Dean Acheson and others, leading up to Secretary Marshall's statement in June inviting a cooperative proposal for American aid. Over the summer and early fall, the Europeans consulted among themselves and, after the withdrawal from their talks of the Soviet Union and its allies, presented their version of a four-year multilateral plan for assistance. Meanwhile, the American administration was conducting its own studies of the United States' capacity to help and evolving its own ideas on an effective plan. In consultation with legislative leaders, it formulated a package and submitted it to Congress in December. After a dress-rehearsal discussion of the issues in the debate over a request for stopgap aid to tide some of the Europeans over until a decision could be taken on the full-scale European Recovery Program, and a further examination of the whole question in the spring of 1948, Congress passed and on April 3 President Truman signed into law the Marshall Plan. If any instance offered time for mature consideration of what the national interest required, it was this one; if states ever faced the opportunity and the obligation to make a case before others for their asserted interests, it was on this occasion. What does the record show they did?

THE MARSHALL PLAN AND THE COMMON GOOD

If one examines the year-long gestation of the European Recovery Program looking for evidence of some attention paid to the country's overall national interest, one's first reaction is to note the many instances in which the common good seemed to be the last thing on anyone's mind. Considerations of individual, group, or other subnational interests often drove the policy process. Agricultural and shipping interests wished to benefit from the tremendous resources that the United States government was expected to provide; other industries were anxious to reestablish their markets in Europe. Merely to list the individuals and organizations that testified or submitted written statements for the record in the Senate hearings on the European Recovery Program is to see the breadth of the interests that believed they would be affected: some eighty-nine groups, ranging from the National Association of Manufacturers, the American Federation of Labor, and the Federal Council of the Churches of Christ in America, to the North Carolina Federation of Women's Clubs, the American Turpentine Farmers Association Cooperative, and the Northwest Horticultural Council.[1]

In the hearings on interim aid, Secretary of Commerce Averell Harriman urged that the president be granted complete freedom to decide, case by case and month by month, whether goods obtained with aid monies should be purchased in the United States or abroad. Unconvinced by this argument, Congress leaned in favor of aiding domestic interests by encouraging the purchase of American goods for which domestic supply exceeded domestic demand. It provided that any commodity acquired by any government agency under any price support program, once it was determined by the president to be in excess of domestic requirements, could be used for foreign aid, even if the American government had to sell it to foreign buyers at a loss.

This provision would dispose of some commodities, but it did nothing for nonessential goods, which would not fall within a strict reading of the intention expressed in the legislation to provide only those goods that would "alleviate conditions of hunger and cold and prevent serious economic retrogression." In need of a device to help those commodities that could not be classified as necessities of life, members of Congress seized on the idea of "incentive goods"—consumer products that by making life more pleasant, could act as an incentive to labor and thereby increase productivity. A prime

---

1. See Hadley Arkes, *Bureaucracy, the Marshall Plan, and the National Interest* (Princeton, 1972), esp. 166–71, 328–29; Senate Committee on Foreign Relations, *European Recovery Program* (1948), Pt. 2, pp. iii–iv, Pt. 3, pp. iii–vi (hereinafter cited as Senate hearings, *European Recovery Program*).

example of an incentive good whose supporters sought its eligibility for interim aid funds was tobacco. Representative Virgil Chapman (Democrat, Kentucky) outlined to the House Committee on Foreign Affairs the benefits, both domestic and foreign, that he saw in allowing interim aid funds to be used to purchase tobacco: "Through this means we could begin its introduction as an incentive product and lead to more use of it in future plans. It would help to rehabilitate industry, break the black market, and give employment to people; it would become a source of revenue and, of course, would be a great morale builder for those people."[2] Senator Alben Barkley, the Democratic minority leader, was also from Kentucky and also interested in tobacco. As a result, incentive goods were added to the list of commodities that recipient countries were authorized to purchase with interim aid funds, though, in deference to the desire to hold down expenditures, only commodities not declared to be in short supply could be classified as incentive goods and no more than 5 percent of interim aid funds could be used to purchase such products. With the inclusion of this provision and the hope that similar purchases would be made under the much larger Marshall Plan, it is not surprising that Marshall later recalled, "I had good success in enlisting the cooperation of special interest groups."[3]

Commodities for which supply exceeded demand were only part of the ERP story, of course; those products for which demand exceeded supply aroused equally strong feelings. Consumers or purchasers of these goods wished to channel Marshall Plan purchases away from them, so as to avoid further bidding up their price in an already inflationary period. Here, the best example was petroleum, and the most forceful spokesmen were members of Congress representing New England states, where shortages of petroleum products were most severe. Senator Henry Cabot Lodge (Republican, Massachusetts) questioned the Harriman Committee's apparent desire to emphasize trucks over rail transport: "Why do we want to enlarge the use of petroleum-consuming methods of transportation in Europe? It seems

2. House Committee on Foreign Affairs, *Hearings before the House Committee on Foreign Affairs on proposed legislation to promote world peace and the general welfare, national interest, and foreign policy of the United States by providing interim aid to certain foreign countries* (1947), 118.

3. *Ibid.,* 353; General George C. Marshall, interview by Harry Price, October 30, 1952, p. 2, transcript in Oral History Interviews, Marshall Plan, folder for August–October, 1952, Harry S. Truman Library, Independence, Mo. (hereinafter cited as HSTL).

to me we ought to encourage the coal-consuming type. They have coal; they have not got petroleum. They either get petroleum from over here, where we have a problem, or else they get it from parts of the world [the Middle East] that are liable to be under the 'iron curtain.'" Representative John Davis Lodge (Republican, Connecticut) hoped for "repayment" of loans under the plan in the form of petroleum purchased by the Europeans from the Middle East, once Europe had attained economic recovery and the Middle East oil fields had achieved full production after 1951. The act authorizing interim aid provided that "the procurement of petroleum and petroleum products shall, to the maximum extent practicable, be made from petroleum sources outside of the United States and its Territories and possessions." Other provisions encouraged the acquisition of goods outside of the United States and directed the administration's attention to the effect of interim-aid purchases on domestic supplies and prices.[4]

These examples make it clear that domestic political interests were at stake in these months of discussion. With the 1948 election approaching, any act could take on partisan coloration, particularly since the legislative and executive branches were in the hands of different parties. Despite the opposition of many Democrats, President Truman was moving toward his candidacy for election in his own right; the chairman of the Senate Foreign Relations Committee, Arthur Vandenberg of Michigan, was mentioned as the possible Republican nominee. When Senator Carl Hatch (Democrat, New Mexico) wrote Truman on October 16, 1947, to advocate a special session of Congress in December to deal with interim aid, he based his argument not on the pressing needs of Europe but on his suspicion that "the brethren of the opposition are laying a trap." Without new monies approved in a special session, the president could either try to shift funds already appropriated for other purposes—in which case he would be denounced for usurpation of power—or await the regular session in January while eco-

---

4. Senate hearings, *European Recovery Program*, Pt. 1, pp. 262–66; House Committee on Foreign Affairs, *United States Foreign Policy for a Post-War Recovery Program* (1948), 343 (hereinafter cited as House hearings, *Post-War Recovery Program*); *Statutes at Large* 61 (1947), Sec. 2, p. 934. See also Senate Committee on Foreign Relations, *Hearings before the Senate Committee on Foreign Relations on interim aid to Europe* (1947), 138 (hereinafter cited as Senate hearings, *Interim Aid to Europe*); Marshall interview, October 30, 1952, p. 2, HSTL; General George C. Marshall, interview by Harry Price, February 18, 1953, p. 2, transcript in Oral History Interviews, Marshall Plan, folder for January–June, 1953, HSTL.

nomic deterioration continued in Europe—in which case he would be attacked for dereliction of duty. In either case, Hatch warned, the opposition hoped "to make much political capital" in the months ahead. When the president did call a special session, he in turn coupled the bipartisan foreign-policy issue of interim aid with measures having to do with the highly charged partisan issue of inflation. He requested a list of powers almost designed to be rejected, and those parts that Congress did approve it delayed until December 30, after the administration had tipped its hand on the Marshall Plan by sending up its draft legislation.[5]

In these ways, then, the political process leading to a historic initiative in American foreign policy was one of bargains and struggles among "special interests" economic, sectional, and partisan. To say this much is not to tell the whole story, however, for it is possible to find broader considerations at work in the development of the ERP as well. Such concerns transcending specific interest groups—one might call them attempts to discern the public interest—ran through the entire year leading up to the enactment of long-term aid to European recovery. Of such efforts, two of the most striking were the reports of the State Department Policy Planning staff and the Harriman Committee.

When Secretary of State Marshall returned from a meeting of the Council of Foreign Ministers in Moscow in April of 1947, he was convinced that action of some kind had to be taken to prevent Europe as a whole and Germany in particular from continuing to sink into an economic morass from which current efforts were incapable of extricating them. Further deterioration would only play into Stalin's hands. At the same time, divisions among the European countries themselves were a matter of concern. French officials were pressing for definitive, long-term agreements on German reparations that would, for example, earmark a sizeable portion of Germany's coal production for uncompensated shipment to French factories. American officials in Germany, on the other hand, led by General Lucius D. Clay, the deputy military governor, were becoming increasingly vocal in their contention that German recovery was essential to European recovery, and the retention in Germany of a greater part of that country's coal production was essential to German recovery. Immediately upon his arrival in Washington

5. Clifford Papers, ECA series, "Economic Cooperation Administration–Special Session of Congress" folder, in HSTL; *Public Papers of the Presidents of the United States: Harry S Truman, 1947* (Washington, D.C., 1963), 498.

on April 28, Marshall, faced with these threats and contradictory demands, directed the State Department's new Policy Planning Staff under George F. Kennan, as its first order of business, to draw up suggestions for a plan to deal with the facts that were already known. In effect, the PPS (whose very establishment was evidence of a desire for long-range thinking on the country's basic interest and policies) was to fit these crosscurrents and pressures into an overall conception of where the United States' national interest lay and to propose measures that would guide day-to-day actions without being consumed by them. No assignment could have been more congenial to Kennan's thinking. In an initial report on May 21 and a later one of July 23, he and his colleagues on the PPS laid out what was at stake for the United States in Europe. The earlier memorandum contained material that went almost unchanged into Marshall's address at Harvard on June 5.[6]

Meanwhile, outside the executive branch, demands were growing for a public justification of the sums that were beginning to appear in the press. This look at the national interest focused on the balance between the aims of European aid and the capabilities of the United States. How much could Washington afford to do—that is, how important to the overall good of American society were the interests at stake in Europe? How much did they count as compared with other desirable objectives that would have to be given up or deferred for lack of resources? Vandenberg began calling for examination of the issue in the summer of 1947; a June 19 PPS report agreed that such a study was desirable. Three days later, Truman announced the formation of three efforts to ascertain the capacity of the United States to undertake an as-yet-undefined Marshall Plan. The Council of Economic Advisers was to prepare a study of the impact of foreign aid on the domestic economy; a second committee, chaired by the secretary of the interior and drawing on the staff resources of a number of departments and independent agencies, was to report on the strain that a large new program of foreign assistance would place on the country's natural resources. The president also launched an extra-governmental investigation in establishing a bipartisan advisory council. This nineteen-member committee was composed entirely of private citizens, except for Harriman, its chairman, but the "Presi-

6. Charles Bohlen, *Witness to History, 1929–1969* (New York, 1973), 263. John Gimbel contends that the problem of reviving Germany without alienating France was more important than Russian intransigence in prodding the United States to sponsor the Marshall Plan. See his *Origins of the Marshall Plan* (Stanford, Calif., 1976).

dent's Committee on Foreign Aid" soon became known as the "Harriman Committee." Truman asked the group to study "the relationship between any further aid which may be extended to foreign countries and the interests of our domestic economy" and "to advise me, in the light of these facts, on the limits within which the United States may safely and wisely plan to extend such assistance."[7]

Both the July 23 study by the PPS and the report of the Harriman Committee on November 6 defined the fundamental issue as "the source of United States interest." Kennan's report elucidated two ways in which aid to Europe would affect the common good; the Harriman Committee identified three, beginning with the "humanitarian" element. By this term the committee meant something close to altruism, though the sense of obligation was still connected with the kind of society Americans had constructed for themselves—"to withhold our aid would be to violate every moral precept associated with our free government and free institutions." The United States could not deny assistance and still remain true to the principles it advocated; in that sense, aid was dictated by the public interest as a duty Americans owed to themselves more than to anyone else. But humanitarianism alone would not guide American actions. Finite resources required a selectivity among recipients and a determination that whatever plan was adopted would obviate the need for any further assistance.

Such concerns led to the second element of the public interest at stake for the United States: "our economic self-interest," which the Harriman Committee said was "closely related to the fate of Europe." Likewise, the PPS report granted that Americans "have a very real economic interest in Europe," stemming from "Europe's role in the past as a market and as a major source of supply for a variety of products and services." Yet an analysis based only on economic needs, or on economic and humanitarian con-

7. Arthur H. Vandenberg, Jr., ed., *The Private Papers of Senator Vandenberg* (Boston, 1952), 381; George F. Kennan, interview by Harry Price, February 19, 1953, p. 1, transcript in Oral History Interviews, Marshall Plan, folder for January–June, 1953, HSTL; Xerox 2051, photocopy of U.S. State Department Policy Planning Staff, "Studies Relating to the Impact of Aid to Foreign Countries on U.S. Domestic Economy and Natural Resources," June 19, 1947, Reports and recommendations to the Secretary of State and the Under Secretary of State, Vol. I, 1947, PPS/3, in George C. Marshall Research Library, Lexington, Va. (hereinafter cited as GCMRL); *Public Papers: Truman, 1947*, 301; Council of Economic Advisers, *The Impact of Foreign Aid upon the Domestic Economy: A Report to the President* (1947); J. A. Krug, *National Resources and Foreign Aid: Report of J. A. Krug, Secretary of the Interior* (1947).

cerns, was also inadequate. What was at stake, in the view of both groups, was the shape of the international system for years to come.

"The traditional concept of U.S. security," according to Kennan and his colleagues, was predicated both on a distribution of power in Europe that prevented any one state from dominating the Old World and using it as a springboard to threaten the United States, and on the continuation in the North Atlantic world of regimes sharing Americans' adherence to liberal democracy—"a considerable number of free states subservient to no great power, and recognizing their heritage of civil liberties and personal responsibility and determined to maintain this heritage." Further economic decline in Europe threatened social dislocations that would undermine both these foundation stones. "The implications of such a loss would far surpass the common apprehensions over the possibility of 'communist control,'" the memorandum warned. "United States interests in the broadest sense could not fail to be profoundly affected by such a trend of events." Itself adopting a broad definition of the common good of American society, the report concluded that while many uncertainties remained, "it is none too soon to begin the charting of a course of U.S. policy with relation to European recovery which would do justice both to the immediate national interests of this country and to the abiding concerns which the people of the United States feel for the continued vitality and prosperity of the European community."[8]

The Harriman Committee echoed this definition of the third interest, "which overshadows the others," calling for "an investment in the continued survival of a world economically stabilized and peacefully conducted, in which governments based on fundamental democratic principles can prosper, in which right, not might, prevails, and in which religious freedom, economic opportunity, and individual liberties are maintained and respected." Continued economic deprivation in Europe could drive its people to embrace communism or some form of authoritarianism in their revulsion against the failure of democracy. American aid would enable the Europeans to defend themselves in this "open ideological war. . . . But until that is done there can be no real balance in world affairs, and no real peace." The section concluded: "Thus broadly the United States' political interest may be de-

8. "Certain Aspects of the European Recovery Problem from the United States Standpoint," July 23, 1947, pp. 3–4, in Clifford Papers, ERP–Foreign Aid series, Folder 2, "European Recovery Program," HSTL. Joseph M. Jones discusses and quotes from the first PPS memorandum in his book *The Fifteen Weeks* (New York, 1955), 223–24, 239–41, 246–52.

fined. An objective analysis of the situation points conclusively to the need for courageous constructive action to aid Western Europe, both for its sake and for our own enlightened self-interest."[9]

While the Harriman Committee put more stress on communism than did the PPS, in both reports one finds an effort to recommend policy by identifying outside dangers that might threaten Americans' domestic search for their own collective definition of the good society. Collapse of the country's traditional economic partners could harm the national interest; so could the establishment of an international environment hostile to the country's fundamental principles. The national interest went beyond material needs, but it remained bound up with the United States' ability to continue to live under its chosen regime and was concerned with other states only as they affected the United States' prospects for doing so. Events in Europe posed risks both for American prosperity and for American principles as they affected American political life. Government actions, even highly expensive ones, were needed to minimize these risks, though only under clear conditions requiring serious efforts by the Europeans.

Finally, one might look at the very fact of a broad public debate as evidence that the common good was a touchstone in the national decision to offer aid to European recovery. While they differed in tone and emphasis, the reports of the Policy Planning Staff and the Harriman Committee served to engender discussion—the latter directly, the former indirectly as its arguments made their way into the public statements of administration spokesmen. In this debate, supporters of the European Recovery Program (as well as its opponents) had to make a reasoned case for their stand, and they tended to reason from, even if they did not in so many words refer to, an implicit idea of what the national interest required. Other arguments, based on personal advantage or interest group advancement, would not have been deemed legitimate in the sort of deliberative process that Marshall described when he denied that aid was a cover for domination: "Certainly, if this involved a conspiracy for economic imperialism, it would have to have a basis of more Machiavellian approach than is exhibited here with public hearings and public discussion on every side with regard to every issue."[10]

9. President's Committee on Foreign Aid, *European Recovery and American Aid: A Report* (1947).

10. House hearings, *Post-War Recovery Program*, 41.

True, arguments in this discussion were chosen with an eye to their political impact as well as their logical persuasiveness. Joseph Jones of the State Department's Office of Public Affairs, believing that what was needed for the European audience was "a highly attractive emotional and psychological appeal," drafted Marshall's Harvard speech with an emphasis on European unity so as to "convince Europe that our help was truly altruistic." At a department staff meeting the day of the speech, Undersecretary for Economic Affairs William Clayton urged that stressing "the importance of a European Economic Federation" would, among other benefits, "help sell an extensive aid program to Congress and the people." In the Senate hearings on the plan, Senator Alexander Wiley (Republican, Wisconsin) advocated obtaining military bases from the recipients of aid as a step that would allow proponents of assistance to "present all our sales arguments." True, those who were working for passage of the ERP sometimes used language that seemed to give credence to charges that fear of a collapse of capitalism was the sole reason to provide aid: Undersecretary of State Robert Lovett told a press briefing on November 26 that if Europe did not receive help, "the cost to you to try to readjust yourselves and to isolate yourselves against the impact of this is just going to make your hair curl"; Harriman contended at the Senate hearings that European recovery would bring "the restoration of Europe as a paying market for United States goods" and "bigger and sounder markets in Europe and elsewhere."[11]

Yet Lovett also reminded reporters of considerations of national security, and a Bureau of the Budget staff memorandum asserted that because the program was "predominantly political [and] . . . not commercial in character," its "success will not be measured in terms of a 'balance sheet' showing profits and losses but by the extent to which the United States achieves certain high policy objectives." The very length of time over which the plan was considered gave participants in the debate an opportunity to unmask deceptive arguments and permitted them to express in their actions, if not always in their words, their conception of the common good of the American regime, and of the policies that would serve this end. Along with indi-

11. Memorandum for the Files [dated July 2, 1947] Re: The Secretary's Harvard Speech of June 5, 1947, in Joseph M. Jones Papers, "Marshall Plan Speech" folder, HSTL; Xerox 2050/711.00, photocopy of General Records of the Department of State, Minutes, Staff Meeting, Thursday, June 5, 1947, p. 2, in Drawer 920, GCMRL; Senate hearings, *European Recovery Program*, 249, 484.

viduals' power struggles, bureaucratic logrolling, and interest-group maneuvering, there was insight and validity in Marshall's statement at the outset of his Senate testimony on the ERP: "Decisions of this magnitude and significance are dictated by the highest considerations of national interest." [12]

THE MARSHALL PLAN AND NATIONAL CLAIMS ABROAD

The national interest is largely inward-looking: in Kennan's words, "a function of our duty to ourselves in our domestic problems." [13] Once policy goals have been set—and quite independently of whether they were set with the society's common good in mind—there remains the task of justifying them in the international setting and persuading other international actors to accept their attainment by the state making the claim. In the events of 1947 and 1948, the preservation of a Western Europe of independent liberal democracies could itself be taken as a claim made by the United States on the international states-system, and statements such as the report of the Harriman Committee or the president's message to Congress accompanying draft legislation for the ERP could be viewed as arguments supporting an asserted interest. Beyond this round of claims and reasons, because Washington was bearing some considerable cost in financing its share of the Marshall Plan, policy makers felt justified in raising further interests and felt required to support them with convincing rationales. These claims were made against the prospective recipients of American assistance as a quid pro quo.

Because European recovery assistance would be large, because the circumstances of the aided countries varied widely, because the points of view of those who had to formulate and approve an aid package were equally varied, and because the international political conditions of the time were unsettled and unpredictable, the range of possible interests was broad. These potential claims had to survive a domestic process of review and se-

12. Press Conferences of the Secretaries of State, Ser. II (microfilm), Reel 11, November 26, 1947, p. 9, GCMRL; Staff Memorandum, "Use of a Government Corporation for Administration of European Recovery Program," November 3, 1947, p. 4, in James E. Webb Papers, "European Recovery Program—Items 1 through 3" folder, HSTL; Senate hearings, *European Recovery Program*, 1.

13. George F. Kennan, "The National Interest of the United States," *Illinois Law Review*, XLV (January–February, 1951), 730.

lection before they would be written into law and formally directed at other states. Nonetheless, foreign ministries in Western Europe could follow the American debate, and they were involved, at American insistence, in the construction of a complicated network of interlocking claims and obligations.

Many pressed for the United States to demand recompense in the form of raw materials. World War II had depleted American natural resources, and Marshall Plan aid would reduce them further. Why did a nation preparing to be a donor on this scale not have a legitimate interest in protecting its own future standard of living, an interest that would justify it in requiring the recipients of its assistance to make partial repayment in the form of raw materials, once they had completed their four-year march to recovery? Such payment in kind could come from the territory of the European metropoles; it could come, as Congresswoman Frances Bolton (Republican, Ohio) preferred, from the overseas possessions of European countries; or it could be purchased by the Europeans in third countries once their reserves of foreign currency allowed them to do so, and then shipped to the United States. As we have seen, Senator Lodge and Representative Lodge were especially worried about American petroleum reserves, and the third course was the one that both Lodges wished to take, not only with petroleum but also with other "strategic raw materials" after the immediate economic crisis had passed. Senator Lodge, for example, suggested at the Senate hearings that while it was contemplated that American assistance would be wound up within four years, the Europeans could in return agree to undertakings that would extend for ten, fifteen, or twenty years. Administration witnesses resisted this sort of requirement, arguing that to demand of the Europeans that they furnish the United States with raw materials for which they would not be paid in dollars would recreate the shortage of foreign exchange and the inability to pay for imports that had led to the need for aid in the first place. Secretary of the Interior Julius Krug warned against a "strait-jacket" that would "defeat the very purpose we are attempting to achieve, namely, to get their economy going again so that they can take care of themselves," and the ambassador to Great Britain, Lewis W. Douglas, a former senator brought back to Washington to present the administration's views on Capitol Hill, warned, "To the extent to which we exact a condition which increases the risks implicit in the venture, . . . we may be damaging our own long-term national interests." Both men did accept, however, that the administrator of ERP could look at specific countries and specific raw materials, and whenever he thought it prudent to provide assistance in the form of a loan repayable in such products, he should do so.[14]

Others hoped that the United States would assert an interest in obtaining overseas military bases in exchange for Marshall Plan assistance. Senator Wiley in particular was insistent that "the question of bases on the great strategic lands of the world . . . is something that fits into this picture." He noted that while "very cogent arguments" had been presented in favor of aid to Western Europe, "very little has been said . . . —outside of the general thesis that it is important economically to reconstruct Europe—along the line of what we are getting here and now for America." Calling on his colleagues to become "a little bit conscious of some of our own needs," he suggested saying to the recipient countries, "We are going to give billions; we are going to assist; we are going to be good samaritans; we are going to be good allies; we are going to give our substance, and we are going to tighten our belts, and now, is there not something, a little, forthcoming from you?" Although Secretary of Defense James Forrestal told Wiley that he "would not quarrel with your thesis," he termed the issue of bases a "collateral problem" and the restoration of economic balance to Europe "paramount." Marshall was more emphatic in rejecting an asserted claim on bases: "I think it is very important that . . . we do not introduce factors of that . . . nature because that would merely go to support the violent propaganda efforts against the whole procedure. We are not buying an advantage here for ourselves. We are trying to improve a very serious world situation which, in the end, it is of great importance to us that it be improved." Wiley favored asking for bases in return; Marshall opposed it; but both spoke the language of interests in debating which claims should be put to the Europeans and whether they could be justified in European eyes.[15]

If Marshall Plan aid could be reimbursed with raw materials or bases, it could also be repaid with dollars. Whether to provide assistance through loans or through grants was a continuing issue during Congress' deliberations, for it went to the core of the Europeans' obligations under the phrase accepted by all parties in the American debate: the efforts of the recipients of aid were to be marked by "self-help and mutual aid." Self-help included

14. House hearings, *Post-War Recovery Program*, 250–51, 343, 349–50; Senate hearings, *European Recovery Program*, 354, 368–69.

15. Senate hearings, *European Recovery Program*, 41, 481–84; Senate hearings, *Interim Aid to Europe*, 233.

repaying the Americans for their assistance wherever possible, but how often was it possible to assert this as an interest, consistent with the success of the program? For Senator Lodge, keeping grants to a minimum was entirely compatible with the objectives of aid because it would improve the transatlantic psychological climate by making "the whole thing . . . more self-respecting." Senator Bourke Hickenlooper (Republican, Iowa) maintained that "a part of the maintenance of [the Europeans'] self-respect is the meeting of obligations as opposed to the obtaining of a dole of some kind, or a hand-out," and Wiley observed, "The attitude in Europe, at least I have met it too frequently, is that all they have to do is come and get it." Hickenlooper expressed dissatisfaction with the administration's rough estimate that 20 to 40 percent of ERP aid would be in the form of loans and the remainder in grants. He argued for a requirement that grants should be used only for consumption goods, while any Marshall Plan funds that went to capital investment, public or private, should be provided as loans. As they had on other matters, administration witnesses criticized legislative restrictions on the actions of the program administrator and warned that loading the Europeans with dollar repayment obligations could defeat the purpose for which they were requesting help. Douglas did agree, however, that "where there is the ability to repay it is the intention to require repayment." [16]

Still other interests the United States might assert had to do with its access to information on the economies of recipient states and its influence over their policies. American officials had bitter memories of UNRRA funds that had gone to governments of which they disapproved, to support policies they believed would lead to economic ruin. They would not sponsor the infusion of further resources without a clear idea of current economic conditions in each European country, an accounting system that would allow them to trace the expenditure of all assistance, and a reliable set of indicators that would measure economic progress (or the lack of it) year by year and demonstrate the efficacy (or the lack of it) of measures funded in part by American taxpayers. On the other hand, too interfering a role for the United States not only would give aid and comfort, in the public debate, to those who castigated the plan as economic imperialism, but also would, in fact, strain the principle that Kennan and others asserted was the goal of

16. Senate hearings, *European Recovery Program*, 63–66, 437–43; Senate hearings, *Interim Aid to Europe*, 231–33.

assistance: the preservation of a system of independent states in Europe. Any plan would have to serve the two masters of accountability and sovereignty.

This was precisely the issue on which the first attempt at a common European response to the American offer foundered. Within a week of being informed of Marshall's Harvard speech, Ernest Bevin, the British foreign secretary, had publicly hailed the idea and was in private communication with France's premier, Georges Bidault. Within two weeks, Bevin was in Paris, accompanied by experts, holding talks with French Foreign Minister Robert Schumann. Two days later, the two men invited Soviet Foreign Minister Vyacheslav Molotov to join the discussions at the beginning of July, 1947, and he duly arrived, accompanied by a large party of experts. Tripartite cooperation went no further than this, however, because of basic differences, between Moscow on the one side and London and Paris on the other, over the relationship between the legitimate requirements of the donor and the continued sovereignty of the recipients in any program of assistance. The meeting broke down completely and was adjourned July 2.

Each side issued a public statement after the unsuccessful close of the discussions. Molotov stressed that the supranational European economic organization urged by his two Western counterparts, and especially its "Steering Committee" composed of the Big Three, would arrogate to itself decisions about the state interests of each of the participating countries too vital to be made by anyone but the affected country itself. Alternatively, if such decisions were to remain the province of national governments, and the search for shared economic interest continued on an ad hoc basis, Moscow would have no objection: "The Soviet Union favors the fullest development of economic collaboration between European and other countries on a healthy basis of equality and mutual respect for national interests." The greatest danger to the national interest of all European countries lay in their subjection to the dictation of a meddling supranational body dominated by a non-European power, "since it might lead to a denial of their economic independence." Because the proposals of France and Britain courted this danger, they had "nothing in common with the real interests of the peoples of Europe." Bevin called Molotov's statement "a complete travesty of the facts and a complete misrepresentation of everything the British Government had submitted," adding, "It is a fundamental principle by which we work not to interfere in the internal affairs of other countries and we hope the national sovereignty of European powers will be recognized and respected equally by everyone while this attempt is being made to achieve economic cooperation." Bidault asserted that Molotov's remarks contained an implied threat that "puts my country on guard." He echoed Bevin's theme that economic cooperation was the best means of preserving the recipient states' national interest—that is, their independence—by restoring them to economic health, and he laid stress on the innocuous nature of the Americans' desire for information: "It is simply a question of knowing the production and objectives of these various countries and of harmonizing them in complete liberty."[17]

As it happened, the Americans were themselves most uncertain of the scope of the demands they wished to put to the Europeans in return for aid. They were clearly pleased by Molotov's departure—a "hell of a big gamble," in the words of Charles Bohlen, counselor of the State Department, "based on our analysis that the Soviet Union could not tolerate the type of economic inspection and cooperation that would be required." Still, there would be supervision requirements, and timetables; the Europeans could "not merely submit shopping lists." The July 23 report of the interdepartmental Committee on European Recovery seemed genuinely torn. To pull the reins too tight "would tend to lend substance to charges that this Government was seeking a degree of dictation over the policies and acts of other governments"; to let them fall too slack would "constitute an open invitation to the abuse of United States readiness to assist and an act of irresponsibility toward the real needs of the European peoples concerned." On the whole, the committee leaned toward permissiveness. Similarly, the PPS report of May 21 portrayed the American role as a supporting one: "The initiative must come from Europe; the program must be evolved in Europe; and the Europeans must bear the basic responsibility for it."[18]

Others were far more willing to involve the United States both in the formulation of the plan and in its operation. In a memorandum of May 21 that helped to place the issue of aid to Europe at the top of the agenda in Washington, Clayton had pleaded, "*The United States must run this show.*" While he was never able to persuade Marshall to go this far, Clayton did

17. New York *Times*, July 3, 1947, Sec. 1, p. 4.

18. Charles Bohlen, interview by Harry Price, February 16, 1953, p. 2, transcript in Oral History Interviews, Marshall Plan, folder for January–June, 1953, HSTL; *The United States and European Recovery*, 32–34, 19, in Harry S. Truman papers, Files of Charles W. Jackson, "European Recovery Program—Printed Materials" folder, HSTL.

secure a reversal of an earlier American hands-off policy in the late summer, when the Europeans' own planning efforts seemed to be diverging widely from American wishes, and he then worked strenuously to change European positions on the major issues involved. Members of Congress largely sided with Clayton once their hearings began in the late fall. "I am not worried about their sovereignty much," proclaimed Senator Tom Connally (Democrat, Texas), the ranking minority member of the Foreign Relations Committee. "It is obvious they cannot eat sovereignty. We have to give them something besides sovereignty to get along with this program." Senator Lodge pressed for independent American inspectors to follow the uses to which American funds would be put, and raised the suggestion that an American be placed on the board of directors of any European corporation that received ERP aid; Senator Hickenlooper wished recipient governments to undertake that they would not tolerate a general strike. In the House Foreign Affairs Committee, Congressman Lodge wanted the bilateral agreements, to be signed by the United States and each recipient country, to contain pledges that the recipient would revalue its currency if that was deemed necessary; Congressman Karl Mundt (Republican, South Dakota) wanted a commitment from the recipients to provide the United States free air time on state-owned radio stations; Congressman Mike Mansfield (Democrat, Montana) elicited from Marshall a guarded prediction that if any of the projected participants in the plan adopted a Communist government, "they could not really go through with their pledges on such a basis as that." Arnold J. Wilson, president of the Illinois Manufacturers Association, testified before the Senate committee that the association was "opposed to the advancement of funds to other governments . . . to finance experimental schemes of socialization, nationalization, and monopolistic controls."[19]

Members of the administration were less enamored of strings legislatively attached to assistance. Undersecretary of State Lovett endorsed the most searching demands for information from the recipients of aid but was reluctant, in both his public and his private statements, to make so many suggestions to the Europeans in drafting the program that they would regard the United States as committed to its every provision when it was completed. In his congressional testimony, Douglas agreed that the demand for

19. Frederick J. Dobney, ed., *Selected Papers of Will Clayton* (Baltimore, 1971), 203; Senate hearings, *European Recovery Program*, 62–63, 228–33, 1023; House hearings, *Post-War Recovery Program*, 76, 260–62, 336–37.

information was a legitimate American interest, because "we want to be assured that the United States funds that are used will be put to their most effective use, and that they will be used in accordance with the conditions and for the purposes for which they are advanced." Beyond this point, he hesitated to go far in mandating policies by recipient countries. He told senators that placing an American government representative on the board of every European corporation that received aid "would hardly be consistent with the general conception of the way in which governments operate" and would be resented "as an unwarranted intervention by the United States Government in the private operations of a company." Douglas was similarly dubious about American intervention in the administration of foreign tax codes. Even the type of economy adopted in a recipient state was not necessarily an American interest, he told the Foreign Affairs Committee:

> The recovery of western Europe and the restoration of . . . stability is the purpose which we have in mind. If these countries . . . can achieve that purpose and fulfill their pledges under the mild type of socialism which exists in some of them, that is their business. It would be . . . too much of an invasion of the right of free people to determine the sort of economic system under which they wanted to live, provided always it is dedicated to the proposition that men should be free—it would be too much of an invasion on our part to undertake to dictate or influence them in the matter.[20]

Greater harmony reigned between Congress and the executive when it came to one of the central issues of policy: European cooperation. There was widespread agreement among the Americans that European rivalries had led to the war, that economic nationalism was severely hampering postwar recovery in Europe, and that the United States had a justifiable interest in conditioning aid on collaborative actions by the recipients. In his brief speech at Harvard on June 5, Marshall touched on the matter lightly, saying, "There must be some agreement among the countries of Europe as to the requirements of the situation and the part those countries themselves will

20. Press Conferences of the Secretaries of State, Ser. II (microfilm), Reel 11, August 27, 1947, pp. 8–9, GCMRL; U.S. Department of State, *Foreign Relations of the United States,* 1947, III, 350–51 (hereinafter cited as *FRUS*); Senate hearings, *European Recovery Program,* 229, 233; House hearings, *Post-War Recovery Program,* 203–204.

take," and noting, "The program should be a joint one, agreed to by a number, if not all, European nations." At a State Department staff meeting the same day, as we have seen, Clayton was arguing that a program organized on multilateral lines would be more popular with congressional and public opinion than would a plethora of aid packages directed to individual countries; a collective approach would also "help liquify inter-European trade [and] help set a better pattern for reconstruction developments." It was agreed that he should return to Europe to ask leaders there for "a rudiment of European initiative in cooperative efforts toward reconstruction" and to "suggest discreet, joint consultations among the European nations on various aspects of the problem."[21]

What the Americans got went well beyond "a rudiment of . . . initiative." After Molotov's departure from the Paris conference on July 2, Bevin and Bidault quickly agreed to invite all the states of Europe, East as well as West (except the Soviet Union and Spain), to meet for consultations. Only those outside what was just then coming to be called the Soviet bloc accepted, however, though Czechoslovakia and possibly Poland were thought to have been dissuaded from taking part only under heavy Soviet pressure. The participants therefore included Austria, Belgium, Denmark, France, Greece, Iceland, Ireland, Italy, Luxembourg, the Netherlands, Norway, Portugal, Sweden, Switzerland, Turkey, the United Kingdom, and representatives of the three Western occupying powers in Germany. Their conference, which convened on July 12 with the objective of preparing a report on Europe's needs by September 1, worked under the chairmanship of Bevin, who, along with the rest of the British delegation, "took the lead, provided the mechanics, and drove everybody mad."[22] Within four days, this temporary organization was succeeded by the long-term Committee of European Economic Cooperation. Also under British chairmanship, this body established an executive committee (composed of Italy, the Netherlands, and Norway, in addition to France and the United Kingdom) and a series of technical committees. By mid-July, then, the Europeans seemed well on the way to fulfilling their part of Marshall's implied bargain—producing a cooperative plan for utilizing the resources America would provide.

21. Xerox 2050/711.0016-547, photocopy of Minutes, Staff Meeting, June 5, 1947, in Record Group 59, Box 2353, GCMRL.

22. The comment of one member of the British delegation, quoted in Harry B. Price, *The Marshall Plan and Its Meaning* (Ithaca, N.Y., 1955), 36.

Yet, as the CEEC continued its labors from July into August, concern began to grow among the Americans that its report might crystallize in an unfortunate manner. Although Marshall's speech had included the offer of "friendly aid in the drafting of a European program," this phrase had been interpreted narrowly in the interest of encouraging European initiative. Such aid had been confined to providing data on American production capabilities and information on the needs of and the American plans for Bizonia, the Anglo-American zone in Germany; no American representatives had been allowed to attend the sessions of the conference. Indeed, Marshall later recalled issuing "an almost arbitrary, military-type command" to Clayton, Douglas, and others, forbidding them to advise the Europeans on the formulation of a plan.[23] But as the Americans clarified their objectives in their own minds, and the outlines of the European approach became more distinct, the two seemed increasingly to diverge. It appeared to the Americans that they would soon be presented with a demand that incorporated all the worst features they had hoped European initiative would avoid: it would be, not a European-wide plan of coordinated rebuilding, but simply the sum of the various inflated national recovery programs; it would contain only the most innocuous references to the austere financial and monetary policies Washington felt were necessary to halt inflation and stabilize exchange rates; it would do nothing to reduce tariffs and other barriers to trade; and it would give no assurance that at the end of the four-year program Europe would require no further assistance. In short, it would satisfy none of the interests the Americans believed they could legitimately press as the price for their aid.

Clayton, who had never been wholeheartedly in favor of the "hands-off" policy, and had conducted a sort of bureaucratic guerrilla warfare against it from Europe, seized his opportunity. From August 4 to August 6 he met in Paris with the American ambassador there, Jefferson Caffery; Douglas; Robert D. Murphy, U.S. political adviser for Germany; and Paul H. Nitze, deputy director of the Office of International Trade Policy, and convinced them to join him in appealing for authority to lodge American objections with the CEEC delegates. But any action would have to be taken quickly; the September deadline for the report was only three weeks away. From Washington, Lovett cautioned the group on August 11 that too exten-

---

23. Marshall interview, October 30, 1952, p. 2, HSTL.

sive an involvement by American officials in the Paris negotiations could make the resulting document more of an American plan than the administration wanted. Nevertheless, he agreed that an immediate decision on the nature of the United States' "friendly aid" was imperative. After consultations, he sent a message to Marshall, who was at that time attending a conference in Brazil. The August 24 telegram concluded with the advice, "I am convinced that the time has now arrived for us to give some indications that the present plan is not acceptable and to do so promptly." Marshall replied: "I concur completely in your views and action proposed. . . . I consider it essential that our people show great firmness and be most emphatic in stating our requirements."[24]

Showing firmness was of course easier said than done, and Clayton later admitted that "the whole situation got very tense." The objects of American firmness, the Europeans, were in general reluctant to accept the supranational features that would make the plan attractive in American eyes. In one of the daily meetings that Clayton, Douglas, and Caffery were holding with delegates to the conference, the representative of one state protested against Clayton's insistence that any regional organization set up to administer Marshall Plan aid should remain in existence to further European cooperation even after aid had ceased, saying that "European countries were not in the habit of looking over the back fence of their neighbors to see what they were doing." Clayton shot back that "perhaps we were all pursuing a will-o'-the-wisp and might as well forget about it." Despite this implied threat, approaches to the delegates in Paris proved unsatisfactory, at least in part because their instructions from their home governments did not give them the freedom of action to follow the Americans' suggestions. Therefore Lovett sent out a circular on September 7 to American diplomatic representatives in the participating countries, directing them to inform the host governments immediately of the American objections to the draft. While disclaiming any intention of "dictating," they were to present the Americans' view on what was required and to ask the governments to which they were accredited to instruct their representatives in Paris accordingly.[25]

24. *FRUS*, 1947, III, 349–51, 374, 375.

25. William L. Clayton, "GATT, the Marshall Plan and OECD," *Political Science Quarterly*, LXXXIII (December, 1963), 502; *FRUS*, 1947, III, 412–15. In addition, American representatives were now allowed to attend the conference committee meetings on an informal basis.

These efforts were only partially successful. Although the Europeans had already postponed the release of their report once—from September 1 to September 15—and feared that another delay would be taken as a mark of indecision on their part, they were at length persuaded to accept another week's postponement, until September 22. But they refused to make substantial alterations in the text; the estimates could not be pared without putting at risk the participation of some of the members. At most, they could only include language rendering it easier for the administration to make its own reductions while preparing legislation to submit to Congress; these face-saving clauses were inserted into the preamble. Moreover, in spite of Clayton's prodding, the report specifically abjured a permanent organization with broad powers to shape the direction of European recovery. While the CEEC, succeeded by the OEEC (the Organization for European Economic Cooperation), would be authorized to "ensure, to the fullest extent possible by joint action, the realisation of the economic conditions necessary to enable the general objectives to which each country has pledged itself to be effectively achieved," and to "make periodical reports to the various European Governments on the extent to which the programme is being realised," the individual states would gather for themselves the facts on which the reports and joint action would be based. The idea of an OEEC with an indefinite life-span was flatly rejected: "The organisation will be of a temporary character and will cease to exist when the special aid necessary for the recovery of Europe comes to an end." The aid request was more—or, more precisely, less—than the simple sum of the stated desires of each state; the members of one delegation at the conference, who "put in obviously inflated figures, were brought up short," and each country knew the workings of the others' economies well enough to prevent blatant padding. Still, cooperative measures were to be ad hoc, not permanently institutionalized, and each participant retained for itself the power to decide what its national interest required.[26]

This was a considerable disappointment to Washington. American officials had hoped for a thoroughly multilateral aid program in which a supranational organization received American funds and with them developed and mandated national acceptance of a regional recovery program. The op-

26. U.S. Department of State, *Committee on European Economic Co-operation: Volume I, General Report* (1947), 1, 40; Price, *The Marshall Plan and Its Meaning*, 36.

posite alternative to this approach was the Soviet suggestion voiced by Molotov in Paris in June under which each state, using its own estimates, would
make its own request to Washington, and then, once it had received a bilateral commitment of funds, would carry out its own recovery program. The
Europeans proposed to treat their interests as more interrelated than Molotov had demanded, but less so than Clayton had desired. They would act
on the broadened interest all shared in recovery, but at their own speed and
under no irrevocable conditions. In particular, they did not accept that the
Americans had made a good enough case to justify a national interest in
pressing the Europeans to establish a powerful supranational organization
capable of reviewing the actions taken by national governments and private
corporations and allocating American aid in accordance with its own plan
for coordinated recovery—demands that led one harried British diplomat to
remark somewhat tartly in the last stage of the CEEC deliberations, when
the American pressure to form such an agency was at its height, that some
people in free-enterprise America seemed to favor a directed economy.[27]
(Congressional statements during the interim aid debate, simultaneously de-
nouncing socialism in Europe and calling for a European supranational
body with greater power to guide economic recovery, evinced a similar
confusion.)

Members of Congress took the American interest in European pledges
of "mutual aid" very seriously. One important element of mutual aid was
the ending of economic nationalism through the reduction or elimination of
tariffs on all intra-European trade and the relaxation of currency restrictions
that impeded free international commerce. "There is quite a sentiment, as
you know, for the extension of this customs-union arrangement between
Belgium, Holland, and Luxembourg," Senator Barkley told Lovett at the
hearings on interim aid; and when the undersecretary said that the summer's
conference had been evidence of a willingness on the part of the Europeans
to undertake collaborative efforts, a skeptical Senator Connally suggested
using the four months of interim aid as "sort of a period of probation . . .
to determine . . . whether they mean it or not. . . . Saying they are going to
cooperate does not mean they are going to cooperate."[28]

Beyond seeing aid as a means to freer trade, members wanted to use it

27. William C. Mallalieu, "The Origin of the Marshall Plan: A Study in Policy Formation
and National Leadership," *Political Science Quarterly*, LXXVIII (December, 1958), 500.
28. Senate hearings, *Interim Aid to Europe*, 86, 88.

as leverage in securing European economic integration in general, which they valued not only for its benefits to Europeans but also for its usefulness to American interests in peace and prosperity. Senator Lodge argued to Lovett that "if we just go on perpetuating the regimes that existed in 1938, and never get Europe out of that rut, and just rebuild the same old firetraps and the same old tenements that twice have caused these world-wide explosions [*sic*], we are not accomplishing an awful lot," and urged that the plan could be used to encourage efforts in the Americans' preferred direction. In the House hearings, similar proposals were made. Congressman Mundt wanted the recipients of aid to commit themselves to send (it was unclear whether by sale or by gift) one another any surplus commodities they had. Congresswoman Bolton wanted a European executive committee established as the conduit for aid to all sixteen countries. Congressman Lodge wanted to require military cooperation and liaison among the sixteen in return for aid.[29]

But by the time of the hearings on interim aid, the administration had already made a tactical retreat. Even though it had been the integrative element in the Marshall Plan that Truman later said had most strongly captured his own imagination from the first, the Europeans had clearly dug in their heels against this asserted American interest. In his press briefing at the State Department on October 8, Lovett talked of moral suasion rather than supranational enforcement: "You must at some stage in international affairs rely on the combined moral strength of a group of nations," he said. "All of them [should] get together and have some multilateral sense of responsibility for the carrying out of engagements." When the administration submitted its draft ERP legislation to Congress on December 19, its earlier insistence on a vigorous European umbrella organization with the power to review the performance of the member states and with a strong voice in the allocation of assistance was nowhere to be found. The Europeans' refusal to go beyond a commitment in the CEEC report to form a multilateral consultative central agency had convinced policy makers in the executive branch that further immediate pressure on this point was useless. Included in the draft legislation was the requirement that the bilateral agreements between the United States and recipient countries, which were to be a condition for taking part in the European Recovery Program, were to contain

29. *Ibid.*, 98–99; House hearings, *Post-War Recovery Program*, 247, 250, 262–64.

provisions pledging the recipients to "cooperate with other participating countries in facilitating and stimulating an increasing interchange of goods and services among the participating countries and with other countries and to reduce barriers to trade among themselves and with other countries." Furthermore, Truman made this hopeful statement in his message: "When the representatives of sixteen sovereign nations, with diverse peoples, histories and institutions, jointly determine to achieve closer economic ties among themselves and to break away from the self-defeating actions of narrow nationalism, the obstacles in the way of recovery appear less formidable." Nevertheless, as the State Department's explanation of the proposed legislation indicated, American hopes for changing the Europeans' minds on the scope and function of their new multilateral body had become very modest indeed: "Although the United States should cooperate fully in the continuing work of the organization, the form of the organization and its powers must primarily be determined by the participating countries themselves." Getting some sort of recovery program started was plainly a more important interest to the administration than was using aid to promote European unity through a supranational cooperative organization, which might impose restrictions on private channels of trade and which the Europeans themselves did not want.[30]

INTERESTS ULTIMATELY CLAIMED BY WASHINGTON

If one turns from potential claims to interests that were in fact asserted in the final version of the legislation authorizing the Marshall Plan, one finds a much briefer list of demands made by the United States on the international states-system and more precisely on the states of Western Europe. Clearly, not every interest suggested by some participant in the debate leading to enactment of the Marshall Plan could have survived the process of committee hearings and deliberation, floor debate, consideration by confer-

30. Press Conferences of the Secretaries of State, Ser. II (microfilm), Reel 11, October 8, 1947, p. 5, GCMRL; Harry S. Truman, *Years of Trial and Hope* (New York, 1956), 137, Vol. II of Truman, *Memoirs*, 2 vols.; Senate Committee on Foreign Relations, *Outline of European Recovery Program: Draft Legislation and Background Information, Submitted by the Department of State for the use of the Senate Foreign Relations Committee* (1948), 9, 60; *Public Papers: Truman, 1947*, 519, 522.

ence committee, and final passage and signature, all with ongoing consultation with administration representatives who were in turn communicating with officials of other governments and the CEEC. Some of these potential interests were not advocated very strenuously even by their supposed sponsors; others were mutually inconsistent. Just as clearly, the legislative text did not necessarily represent a complete account of all the requests for which the United States would make a case abroad; congressional debate gave indications of concerns on Capitol Hill even when they did not appear in any specific provision of the law, and members of the administration had their own ideas of legitimate American requirements. Still, the statutory embodiment of the plan was as good a picture as any of the interests that the United States was prepared to avow and argue for in this case.

The act made provision for the protection of American subnational interests such as the shipping industry (by mandating, with certain escape clauses, that at least half of the commodities procured in the United States for the purposes of the Marshall Plan would be carried on American vessels) and farming (by directing that surplus agricultural commodities could be procured only in the United States, unless a commodity was produced in one country participating in the plan and destined for another, or the surplus in the United States was not sufficient to meet the needs of Europe). At the same time, those administering the ERP were to "minimize the drain upon the resources of the United States and the impact of . . . procurement upon the domestic economy, and . . . avoid impairing the fulfillment of vital needs" of Americans. Domestic grain supplies were to be protected, and petroleum and petroleum products were to be taken, "to the maximum extent practicable, . . . from . . . sources outside the United States."[31]

In return for its assistance—authorized at $4.3 billion for the first year—the United States was to be paid in some form, to the extent this was practicable and with a good deal of flexibility granted to the administrators. Assistance could be in the form of grants, or sales for cash or on credit, or in exchange for raw materials required by the United States. In decisions on which of these forms of aid was to be used, officials were to employ both the standard the administration had preferred—the capacity to repay without jeopardizing the attainment of economic recovery—and the standard

---

31. *Statutes at Large* 62 (1948). All passages from the European Recovery Act quoted through the end of this chapter are taken from this source.

preferred by some members of Congress—the character and purpose of the assistance. The troubled question of American natural resources received further attention. The administrator of the ERP was—again, whenever it was "practicable"—to promote increased production in the participating countries of materials in which the United States was deficient. "Recognizing the principle of equity in respect to the drain upon the natural resources of the United States and of the recipient countries," each participant was to agree to negotiate schedules for increased production and delivery of a "fair share" of such materials. Each was to facilitate the transfer to the United States, "by sale, exchange, barter, or otherwise for stock-piling or other purposes," of these materials, though only "after due regard for reasonable requirements for [its] domestic use and commercial export."

Beyond direct material returns, the ERP legislation sought to advance American interests in European policies. The use of "mutual aid" to lever the Europeans into economic and political cooperation, and ultimately integration, remained an objective, but the lever was a good deal shorter and less powerful than many in both the legislative and executive branches had once hoped. The OEEC would exist for the lifetime of the aid program at least, and it would constitute a standing forum that would force the Europeans to defend *their* asserted interests, or claims for assistance, before one another, thereby helping to hold down American expenditures. Aid was "contingent upon continuous effort of the participating countries to accomplish a joint recovery program through multilateral undertakings and the establishment of a continuing organization for this purpose" and upon an agreement by each recipient to cooperate with other participating countries "in facilitating and stimulating an increasing interchange of goods and services among the participating countries and with other countries and cooperating to reduce barriers to trade." There would be a "United States Special Representative in Europe," with the rank of an ambassador requiring Senate confirmation, who was to represent the United States before the OEEC, over and above the chief of a special mission for economic cooperation to be established in the American embassy in each participating country. This extra layer of American diplomatic representation might encourage the recipients to take more decisions at the European rather than the national level. In particular, the American agency that was to administer the aid program—to be called, revealingly, the Economic Cooperation Administration—was to encourage the OEEC to make itself the chief watchdog, "to ensure that each participating country makes efficient use of the resources of such country, including any commodities, facilities, or services furnished [by the United States], by observing and reviewing such use through an effective follow-up system approved by the joint organization." (Washington would do its own monitoring as well: participants' bilateral agreements, under which they gained access to Marshall Plan funds, were to pledge them to transmit to the United States quarterly reports on operations and to furnish any other information promptly upon request.)

Nor was this the end of the legislation's list of American interests to be asserted in return for assistance. Despite the fears of some Europeans, it was now American policy that mutual aid should include the western zones of Germany, and the act dealt with German equipment and manpower. For the first, it foresaw that the removal of capital equipment from Germany, already scheduled as war reparations, might have to be canceled and the equipment retained in German hands, "if such retention will most effectively serve the purposes of the European recovery program." For the second, it noted that the repatriation of all (in effect, German) prisoners of war by January 1, 1949, had also already been agreed upon, implying that this accord, by contrast, was not to be altered. Strategic trade with the East financed by the United States was ruled out. (The circumlocution employed applied to "any country wholly or partly in Europe which is not a participating country" and to all commodities that "would be refused export licenses to those countries by the United States in the interest of national security.") Other donors, particularly in the Western Hemisphere, were welcome, and the president was to keep the United Nations informed of the operation of the plan and request its cooperation if need be, but none of this was to be allowed to dilute American control through "delegat[ing] to or otherwise confer[ring] upon any international or foreign organization or agency any . . . authority to decide the method of furnishing assistance under this title to any participating country or the amount thereof." Limitation of the role of the UN did not mean a free hand for national governments, and especially state-run trading entities; "to the maximum extent," the plan was to "utilize private channels of trade."

Such were the claims made by the United States in launching the European Recovery Program. One may note the limited scope of American claims, even in a case in which Washington might have been thought to occupy a strong position for driving a hard bargain with the impecunious and desperate countries asking for its help. By and large, they were limited to interests that could be fairly drawn from Americans' duties to themselves and the rule of warding off outside interferences—in the form of a Western Europe controlled by a hostile power and hostile ideologies—to Americans' ongoing endeavor to carry out those self-regarding duties among themselves. Hadley Arkes has described the official American attitude as "pluralist" in its sympathy for the independence of both foreign states and private entities within the United States and in its reluctance to replace such decentralization with more hierarchical relationships in which the American government gave marching orders to others. To take the example of East-West trade, Washington did not insist on a complete cessation of commerce with the Soviet bloc. It did not even demand the cutoff of trade in "strategic" goods by the Europeans, though it was banning such trade itself. It merely stipulated that no *American* commodities could be transshipped to the East, or used in the production of goods sold there, if the product ultimately exported would be illegal if shipped from the United States itself. Likewise, on the question of European integration, even though Washington strongly wished for cooperation and mutual aid to lead to something more far-reaching and long-lasting, it largely acquiesced when the Europeans refused to acknowledge this end as a justifiable American interest, even in exchange for a sizeable program of economic assistance. Reflection on the relative modesty of what the United States gained on these issues should prompt renewed attention to the stringent justifications often required by other states for interests claimed abroad—that is, to the prerequisites of success in the society of states, prerequisites that distinguish interests from idle wishes or unlimited desires.

VII The Korean War

DECIDING WHETHER, IN what manner, and with what objectives to
intervene upon the outbreak of war on the Korean Peninsula involved the
United States in a process of clarifying its interests that was quite unlike the
steps leading to the Marshall Plan. Instead of prolonged deliberation over
months, there was a rapid series of decisions, taken within a period of little
more than three weeks. Instead of exhaustive studies that compiled mas-
sive quantities of information, decision makers proceeded on the basis
of sketchy, hurried reports straight from the battlefront, combined with
hunches in Washington. Instead of an open debate involving Congress, interest groups, and shoals of executive-branch agencies, there were necessarily confidential meetings of the president with a small band of senior military and diplomatic advisers, later broadened to include their economic
counterparts and congressional leaders. Where in 1947 and 1948 there was
an extended transatlantic give and take over the parties' interests and policies, in 1950 other countries tended to wait to see what the United States
would do, and their most significant influence on the course Washington
would take came in the UN Security Council debates held very early in the
crisis. In the one case, the United States chose to proceed outside the framework of the United Nations and its associated agencies; in the other, American actions were tied to the UN from the outset.

In spite of all the differences, however, the decision to go to war in
Korea was in one way like the decision to offer the Marshall Plan: it was
one of the decisive steps in the creation of the postwar world. As the one
crystallized the United States' interest in the economic health (and ultimately
the security) of Western Europe, so the other solidified its interest in the
security (and therefore the economic well-being) of North Asia. Both episodes defined the Cold War by demarcating its front lines, and the second
accelerated its militarization. In both cases unwelcome events forced Ameri-

can policy-makers to think again about just what claims they intended to assert in distant regions and how far they intended to defend those interests with commitments of substantial resources. And in both instances the roster of interests asserted turned out to differ from that which leaders might have put forward in the abstract, before they were confronted by the case at hand. Indeed, one of the more remarkable features of the Korean case was the speed with which the outbreak of fighting caused the American government to change the claims it was prepared to argue for before the world.

THE UNITED STATES' PREWAR CONCEPTION
OF ITS NATIONAL INTERESTS

Leland Goodrich has summarized American policy toward Korea in the decade following World War II by pointing to two broad aims: "first, to achieve the establishment of a unified, independent and democratic Korea, . . . and secondly, pending or failing the achievement of that goal, to contain Communist expansion and prevent the Communists from taking over the whole of Korea."[1] These interests were asserted in American policy in a less-than-wholly consistent manner, and Washington was making other claims as well. During the prewar period the United States tended to shift from one interest to another, though none of the changes was as dramatic as those that occurred beginning in June, 1950.

It is certainly true that the United States had declared an interest in a unified, independent Korea. The Cairo Declaration—agreed to by the United States, Great Britain, and China in 1943 and endorsed by the Soviet Union upon its entrance into the war against Japan in 1945—called for such a step "in due course." In negotiations with the Soviets, American decision-makers pursued this goal for two years after the end of the war.

The failure of these negotiations was both a product and a source of the hostility between Washington and Moscow that deepened between 1945 and 1950 and accounted for the appearance of the second American goal: preventing the Communists from taking over the whole of the peninsula. That this goal existed even before the war ended was evidenced by the hurried American decision in August and September of 1945 to accept the sur-

---

1. Leland Goodrich, *Korea: A Study of U.S. Policy in the United Nations* (New York, 1956), 5.

render of Japanese troops south of the 38th parallel, rather than allowing Soviet forces to accept the enemy's surrender throughout Korea.

Both before and after the withdrawal of Russian troops and the establishment of a North Korean government in late 1948, American policymakers were certain that any Communist regime on the peninsula was completely under Soviet control. The National Security Council study (NSC 8/2) guiding basic American policy in Korea in 1950 spoke of a "puppet government which can be used as a vehicle for the eventual extension of Soviet control throughout the peninsula," and concurred in the opinion of the American mission in Seoul that the "Soviets have fashioned their north Korean creature in typical Communist monolithic disciplined mould and in the circumstances there is virtually no scope for deviations from soviet desiderata, however minute these may be." [2] Equating unification of Korea on the North's terms with Soviet control of the entire peninsula meant that the unfolding Cold War rivalry would powerfully affect perceptions of the stakes involved. The consequences to American interests of allowing Korean territory south of the 38th parallel to fall into Communist hands had been spelled out in a report on the situation in Korea submitted by Lieutenant General A. C. Wedemeyer in September of 1947. It spoke of "an immense loss in [American] moral prestige among the peoples of Asia, . . . serious repercussions in Japan . . . [and] opportunities for further Soviet expansion." [3] Such fears were surely on the mind of the United States ambassador to South Korea, John J. Muccio, when, at an interdepartmental meeting held on April 27, 1950, while he was in Washington for consultations, he said that Korea was a "symbol of U.S. interest in Asia." [4]

Negotiations aimed at resolving the Korean impasse floundered for two years, between September, 1945, and September, 1947, and negotiators could discover no basis for agreement. Unwilling to face a deadlock indefi-

---

2. U.S. Department of State, *Foreign Relations of the United States,* 1949, VII, Pt. 2, p. 974 (hereinafter cited as *FRUS,* 1949). The paper quoted here, NSC 8/2, was issued March 22, 1949; it was a revision of NSC 8, dated April 2, 1948.

3. Quoted in Senate Committee on Armed Services and Committee on Foreign Relations, *Military Situation in the Far East* (1951), Pt. 3, p. 1988 (hereinafter cited as *Military Situation* hearings). See also Senate Committee on Armed Services, Report to the President submitted by Lt. Gen. A C. Wedemeyer, September, 1947, *Korea* (1951) (hereinafter cited as *Wedemeyer Report.*)

4. *FRUS,* 1949, VII, Pt. 2, p. 975; U.S. Department of State, *Foreign Relations of the United States,* 1950, VII, 49 (hereinafter cited as *FRUS,* 1950).

nitely, the United States took steps to turn over many of the responsibilities of government to the South Koreans, even without the cooperation of the Soviet Union. Yet this alternative was not cost-free. Clearly, such a policy of devolving power upon Korean authorities in Seoul and supplying those authorities with economic and military assistance made it less likely that the other American interest—that of unification—could be achieved. The more the South took on the attributes of an established government, the more complete would be the transformation of the parallel from a line delimiting temporary zones of military responsibility into a permanent international boundary; and the likelihood of an acceptable arrangement establishing one Korean government would thereby be reduced.

The unresolved tension between these two interests produced a policy characterized by unsatisfactory compromises. Some of these decisions tilted toward one objective and slighted the other while pretending to be even-handed. Consider the State Department's rationale in early 1950 for supplying military advisers to Seoul in order to train South Korean pilots: "the Department would not consider the furnishing of advisory personnel as a commitment in support of an autonomous Korean air force. That is, the Department does not consider that it is supporting the creation of an autonomous Korean Air Force by suggesting to the Department of Defense that air advisers be assigned to Korea."[5] It is difficult to understand how the training of South Korean pilots would *not* be at least a step toward an autonomous South Korean air force. But to admit this would have been to admit that a choice between the two interests had been made explicit, and this the State Department was not willing to do. (At any rate, whether because it did not accept the State Department's reasoning or because it preferred to allocate its funds elsewhere, the Defense Department did not accede to the request.)

In other cases, American policy-makers searched for courses of action that held out some hope of achieving both ends, perhaps one after the other. This might be said of Secretary of State Dean Acheson's treatment of Korea in his testimony before the Senate Foreign Relations Committee on March 7, 1950. In the course of his review of the administration's request for funds for the Economic Cooperation Administration, he outlined a plan

5. January 31, 1950, memorandum from John M. Allison, director of the Office of Northeast Asian Affairs, to Najeeb Halaby, director of the Office of Foreign Military Affairs in the Office of the Secretary of Defense, in *FRUS*, 1950, VII, 24.

for making South Korea both strong enough to maintain its independence and attractive enough to "serve as a nucleus" to entice Koreans from the North into joining a unified government.[6] This attempt to make South Korea a "showcase" (to use Goodrich's term) was an appealing option because, in giving promise of attaining both objectives, it did not force officials to choose between them.

Uncertainty seemed to characterize even the manner of identifying the entity with which American policy was concerned. At times, State Department cables and internal communications spoke of "South Korea," presumably referring to a sovereign state to which the United States and more than thirty other countries had granted diplomatic recognition. At other points, the phrase "south Korea" was employed. Through the substitution of a lower-case for a capital letter, what had seemed to be the name of an independent country took on more the character of a mere geographical description—the unnaturally truncated southern half of the Korean Peninsula, or the southern part of the Korean nation. If usage of the two forms was inconsistent, so were American actions.

There was one final means of preserving both of the major strands in the tangled web that was the United States' policy. Washington, if it chose, might attempt to implement its wishes for democratic elections throughout Korea regardless of Moscow's objections. Both facets of the American interest would be served: elections would provide the basis for a single government with authority over all Korea, and American decision-makers were certain that a fair ballot would deliver that government into non-Communist hands. The difficulty with such an Elysian prospect, of course, lay in the certainty that Moscow would object; and in a region so close to the borders of Russia itself, it seemed more than likely that such objections would be backed by force. Implementation of this plan, in other words, might require an American willingness to fight at least a limited war.

Such willingness was entirely absent prior to the summer of 1950. The question being debated within the American government was not whether to send an invasion force into North Korea, but how soon to withdraw those troops already stationed in South Korea. In fact, for many the objective of avoiding a commitment of forces to Korea became the paramount interest for Washington, even if this meant putting at risk both unification

6. Quoted in U.S. Department of State, *Bulletin*, XXII (March 20, 1950), 454.

and the denial of at least part of the peninsula to the Russians. This line of thinking was especially prevalent within the precincts of the Department of Defense. Interests tied up with Korea—including "prestige" and the use of American troops as a bargaining chip—had always been of a more political than military nature, and it was the State Department that pressed them most vigorously. Military spokesmen were considerably less inclined to see vital American interests in the area. The Joint Chiefs of Staff made this hesitancy quite clear in the comments they submitted in a memorandum of June 27, 1949, from the Department of the Army to the Department of State: "From the strategic viewpoint, . . . Korea is of little strategic value to the United States and . . . any commitment to United States use of military force in Korea would be ill advised and impracticable in view of the potentialities of the over-all world situation and of our heavy international obligations as compared with our current military strength." This reasoning continued to guide the thinking of the Defense Department through the following year.[7]

As the JCS memorandum explained, military analysts saw two basic reasons for refusing to commit American troops to South Korea. First, in view of the pressing need to assign Washington's limited forces to other trouble spots around the world, the commitment to an area of such slight military value as Korea of any contingent large enough to be effective could not be justified. True, the occupation of all Korea by a hostile force was not desirable, particularly because of the peninsula's proximity to Japan; but as General Omar Bradley later said, "You always have to stop your front line somewhere." Second, in the event of a general war in Asia, American ground forces in Korea would prove to be a liability, not an asset. According to the military's studies, if an invasion of the Asian mainland were called for, it would be launched against China or Siberia by sea, rather than from a foothold in Korea. If there were enemy forces on the peninsula, they could presumably be neutralized by air strikes. Moreover, it was feared that in circumstances of general war South Korea would be indefensible; the most likely end for any American garrison stationed there would be a disorganized and hurried withdrawal, if not a complete rout. The memorandum termed a unilateral American intervention if war should break out in Korea "a retrogressive step" filled with "complications" that would be "unsound

7. *FRUS*, 1949, VII, Pt. 2, p. 1056; *FRUS*, 1950, VII, 79.

from a military point of view." The last American soldiers left South Korea in mid-1949, though Washington continued to supply Seoul with military assistance other than advanced or heavy weapons.[8]

This constituted the "bilateral" track of American policy toward Korea. But there was a second, "multilateral" track, simultaneously pursued; and though it employed different means, it was directed toward the same end: relieving the United States of an unwelcome responsibility for South Korea without renouncing American hopes for the future of the peninsula. This second track aimed at making Korea a United Nations problem. Goodrich has questioned the wisdom of this course of action, asking whether it did not overload the capabilities of the relatively new international organization, but to decision makers in Washington the policy had much to recommend it.[9] The more responsibility the UN took from American shoulders, the more Korea would come to be seen as a UN rather than an American protégé, the less American prestige would be tied up with events on the Korean Peninsula, and the greater would be the likelihood that Washington could avoid military reinvolvement there. Second, if the Russians could be persuaded that in Korea the UN was a neutral arbitrator, they might accept proposals from it that they would have rejected coming from the United States. There was at least a chance that this might move negotiations off dead center and eventually lead to an agreement on unification that would not place the new government in Communist hands. Third, if unification should prove impossible, the UN stamp of approval on the government in the South might be of some help in deterring attacks on that government.

Although as time went on the first and third of these objectives came more and more to dominate the second, this did not alter the basic American policy of seeking to deepen the involvement of the UN in Korean affairs. The United States placed the question of Korea's future before the General

8. *Military Situation* hearings, Pt. 2, p. 1111; *FRUS*, 1949, VII, Pt. 2, p. 1055. See also Ernest R. May, *"Lessons" of the Past: The Use and Misuse of History in American Foreign Policy* (New York, 1973), 58–61. The costs of a Korean commitment also lay behind what Acheson later identified as the "great Congressional hostility to American activities in Korea." The country seemed to many members of Congress "a long way off, something not intimately connected with American interests, a further drain of Money" (Dean Acheson, Princeton seminar, February 13–14, 1954, p. 9, in Dean Acheson Papers, Princeton Seminars series, Harry S. Truman Library, Independence, Mo. [hereinafter cited as HSTL]). *FRUS*, 1950, VII, 84–85, 104, 110–11; *FRUS*, 1949, VII, Pt. 2, p. 1103; *Military Situation* hearings, Pt. 3, pp. 1990–91.

9. Goodrich, *Korea: A Study of U.S. Policy*, 93–99.

Assembly in September, 1947, and the resolution adopted by that body on November 14 stated that the Korean people themselves should create a provisional government through free and secret elections, which Washington believed would produce a unified, non-Communist government. The resolution also declared that, subsequently, foreign troops should be withdrawn from Korea. This section ratified what American military planners wanted to do in any event and put pressure on Moscow to withdraw its forces from the North as well. And it created a United Nations Temporary Commission on Korea (UNTCOK) to observe the elections and to consult with the newly elected representatives and their government, effectively putting that government under an implicit form of UN sponsorship.[10] When authorities in the North refused to take part in the elections or to recognize the existence of UNTCOK, the Americans persuaded the commission to observe and endorse elections held in the South alone. The elections were held on May 10, 1948; UNTCOK adopted a resolution on June 25 stating that the elections were valid; and the United States gave formal diplomatic recognition to the resulting government of the Republic of Korea on January 1, 1949.

This policy of strengthening ties between the UN and Korea continued through the prewar period. In December of 1948, the United States supported the replacement of UNTCOK with the permanent United Nations Commission on Korea (UNCOK). It cooperated with UNCOK's requests, invited it to verify the withdrawal of American forces in June, 1949, and in December of that year supported the resolution adopted by the General Assembly broadening its functions to include the investigation of developments that might lead to military conflict in Korea. Washington's endorsement of a South Korean application for United Nations membership in April, 1949, was thwarted by a Soviet veto, but during 1949 and 1950 Seoul did become associated with several UN-related agencies. By mid-1950 the links had become so numerous that on his brief trip to South Korea just prior to the invasion, John Foster Dulles, at that time a consultant to the State Department charged with the preparation of the Japanese peace treaty, could say to his hosts that Washington looked on them as, "spiritually, a part of the United Nations."[11]

In general, therefore, American policy before the outbreak of the war

10. See U.S. Department of State, *The Conflict in Korea: Events Prior to the Attack on June 25, 1950*, Far Eastern Series 45, Pubn. No. 42266 (1951), 15.

11. U.S. Department of State, *Bulletin*, XXIII (July 3, 1950), 13.

followed the guidelines contained in NSC 8/2 in seeking "to promote sympathetic interest and participation in the Korean problem" by the UN. But this goal appeared to be less important than that of keeping American troops out of Korea; indeed, it had been adopted at least partly as a means of allowing American forces to leave. If the two interests were ever to come into conflict, it seemed that the desire for disengagement would prevail. The Department of the Army's June 27, 1949, memorandum, "Implications of a Possible Full Scale Invasion from North Korea Subsequent to Withdrawal of United States Troops from South Korea," made this clear. While it endorsed the use of force to evacuate American personnel in such an event, and stated that presentation of the problem to the Security Council for emergency consideration as a threat to the general peace would be a "logical and necessary" step, it concluded: "To initiate police action with U.N. sanction by the introduction of a military task force into Korea composed of U.S. units, and units of other member nations of the United Nations with the objective of restoring law and order and restoration of the 38th parallel boundary inviolability . . . involves a militarily disproportionate expenditure of U.S. manpower, resources, and effort at a time when international relations in Europe are in precarious balance . . . [and] is unsound militarily." [12]

In sum, then, American policy toward Korea after World War II had begun with an interest in a nonhostile regime in Korea; this interest was to be advanced through the objectives of unifying the peninsula or denying at least part of it to Communist control. These had in time been overshadowed by the aim of withdrawing from Korea; this new aim was a product of the belief that any new war would be worldwide and that under such circumstances American forces in Korea would represent an unjustifiable diversion from more important areas. In order to aid their withdrawal, American decision-makers attempted to turn the problem of Korea over to the United Nations while they readied the Seoul government to defend itself in a guerrilla war. (Muccio summed up American policy: "Putting it bluntly, the plan was to turn the problem over to the U.N. and to get out the way in case of trouble.") Acheson's National Press Club speech of January 12, 1950, in which his main argument on American Far Eastern policy was later overshadowed by controversy over his location of Korea and Taiwan outside the American "defense perimeter," indicated these newer aims; so did similar

12. *FRUS*, 1949, VII, Pt. 2, pp. 978, 1054.

statements by General MacArthur in a New York *Times* interview in 1949 and by Senator Tom Connally, the chairman of the Foreign Relations Committee, in a *U.S. News & World Report* interview of May 5, 1950. Those seeking evidence that the United States had no interests for which it was willing to fight in Korea could also point to a 193–191 vote in the House of Representatives on January 19, 1950, that defeated a bill authorizing $120 million for economic assistance to South Korea. After a determined lobbying effort by administration figures from the president on down, the House reconsidered and on February 9 passed a Senate bill authorizing the funds, but only after adding an amendment expressing the Congress' understanding that the measure "did not constitute any commitment beyond 30 June."[13]

THE BEGINNING OF THE WAR AND THE AMERICAN RESPONSE

By June 30, of course, the United States was at war in Korea, and its efforts to hold what it by then had decided was a vital interest went well beyond what its previous statements and actions would have led one to predict.[14] The outbreak of fighting so altered the psychological setting in which decisions were made that those precepts that formerly had been invoked as reasons to stay out of Korea now became forces compelling the United States to enter the conflict. Washington still wanted to make a convincing case for its asserted interests; ironically, many of the same arguments on which it had relied in pulling back from a commitment in Korea were now used to explain why it had interests worth fighting for in the area.

The influence of prewar assumptions

A case in point was the belief that an attack on the Republic of Korea would come only as part of a wider war of aggression directed by the Soviet Union.

13. John J. Muccio, Oral History Interviews, 14, in HSTL; Barton J. Bernstein and Allen J. Matusow, eds., *The Truman Administration: A Documentary History* (New York, 1966), 435–36; *Military Situation* hearings, Pt. 3, pp. 1740–41; New York *Times*, March 2, 1949, Sec. 1, p. 22; *U.S. News & World Report*, May 5, 1950, p. 30; *FRUS*, 1950, VII, 12, 28, 77, 85.

14. For the chronology of events during the first week of the war, see Glenn D. Paige, *The Korean Decision: June 24–30, 1950* (New York, 1968); Beverly Smith, "The White House Story: Why We Went to War in Korea," *Saturday Evening Post*, November 10, 1951, pp. 22ff.

When war came to the Korean Peninsula alone, American decision-makers did not discard this idea; nor did they waver in their belief that it was a primary American interest to resist the extension of Soviet power. But whereas previously the attacks at several points around the globe had been expected to come *simultaneously,* they were now anticipated to fall *sequentially.* Soviet expansionism would strike again if it was successful in South Korea. Therefore, the strategic value of the ROK took second place to its symbolic importance. A commitment that had been considered militarily unsound as a battleground under conditions of general hot war now became highly significant as a testing ground under conditions of militarized cold war. If the bitter experiences of the 1930s had taught American policy-makers but one lesson, it was the necessity of avoiding appeasement. In the light of this lesson, a country that had been secondary now became central; actions that had been diversionary now were decisive. Truman later recalled that as he pondered the situation during the three-hour flight from his home in Independence, Missouri, to Washington on the afternoon of June 25, he "felt certain that if South Korea was allowed to fall Communist leaders would be emboldened to override nations closer to our own shores." If decisive action in opposition to Soviet threats to American interests was required to ward off World War III, Truman was ready to take it; he told Secretary of Defense Louis Johnson, who met him at the airport in Washington, that he wanted to "hit them hard." [15]

The president found his advisers in a receptive mood for such directives. At the first conference on an American response held at Blair House after dinner on June 25, Secretary of the Air Force Thomas K. Finletter "stressed the analogy to the situation between the two world wars. He thought we should take calculated risks hoping that our action will keep the peace." Johnson agreed, pointing to the importance of attitudes abroad. In later congressional testimony, Bradley emphasized the fact that action was taken less to save Korea itself than to "stop an aggression and avoid an appeasement in the case." As Acheson later remembered his state of mind on that afternoon, it was one of resolution against "an open, undisguised challenge to our internationally accepted position as the protector of South Korea, an area of great importance to the security of American-occupied Japan." "To

---

15. Harry S. Truman, *Years of Trial and Hope* (New York, 1956), 332–33, Vol. II of Truman, *Memoirs,* 2 vols. See also May, *"Lessons" of the Past,* 70–86.

back away from this challenge," he now believed, "would be highly destructive of the power and prestige of the United States." This analysis gave South Korea much greater significance than prior American statements (including Acheson's) had accorded it, but an intelligence report issued on June 25 by the Estimates Group of the Office of Intelligence Research concluded that the Kremlin, too, "must . . . have . . . considered Korea as more important than we have assumed." The study went on to say: "It is not believed that the attack on South Korea was resorted to merely for the purpose of achieving or furthering local Korean aims. Considering the apparent U.S. commitments to South Korea, it is estimated that Moscow would not have taken the risks involved—even allowing for a heavy discounting of these risks—unless liquidation of the South Korean Government was called for by the Kremlin's global strategy, as distinct from North Eastern Asian strategy." The intelligence estimate, like Acheson's musings, assumed that the Russians must have known of, and were deliberately challenging, a commitment from which American policy-makers had just spent two years endeavoring to escape.[16]

Washington remained uncertain for some time whether Moscow's expected military thrusts would in fact be sequential rather than simultaneous; the fear of tying down American forces in the secondary Korean theater died hard. MacArthur subsequently criticized the concern expressed by administration figures about Russian moves in other regions, recalling that "it could not fail to be obvious even to the non-military mind that Soviet military dispositions in eastern Europe were defensive rather than offensive." But the general's superiors in Washington were genuinely fearful that a second Russian attack, on Europe or on other areas, was in the offing. At the series of sessions held at Blair House from June 25 to June 30, at which the decisions for intervention were taken, the president frequently asked his advisers for information that would indicate whether the Soviet Union was planning to strike elsewhere through another client state. At the NSC meeting on the June 28, he "said he didn't intend to back out unless there should develop a military situation which we had to meet elsewhere."[17] He may

16. *FRUS,* 1950, VII, 149, 140, 160; *Military Situation* hearings, Pt. 2, pp. 1070, 1110–11, Pt. 4, p. 2585; Dean G. Acheson, *The Korean War* (New York, 1971), 20; George M. Elsey, notes of June 26, 1950, p. 1, in George M. Elsey Papers, Korea series, folder for June 26, 1950, HSTL.

17. Douglas MacArthur, *Reminiscences* (New York, 1965), 383; Paige, *The Korean De-*

have delayed a final decision to introduce ground troops until June 30 in order to give himself as much time as possible to see whether Korea was only a feint, designed to pin American forces down while the Russians moved on some other area of greater strategic importance.

Even after June 30, officials wished to leave open the possibility of withdrawal in the event of general hostilities. "If the Soviets come in, I should think that we still have to fight it out in Korea unless and until the war becomes general," Acheson wrote on July 12. "At that point general military judgment might well be different." What this judgment would be was forecast in a memorandum of July 10 to Johnson in which the Joint Chiefs of Staff pronounced themselves "concerned . . . lest political considerations demand excessive commitments of United States military forces and resources in those areas of operations which would not be decisive. Therefore, if major USSR combat units should at any time during military operations of the Korean area of hostilities engage or clearly indicate their intention of engaging in hostilities against U.S. and/or friendly forces the U.S. should prepare to minimize its commitment in Korea." In response to such fears, Charles Bohlen was called to Washington to spend a month searching, in vain, for evidence that "the Korean invasion was the forerunner of similar Communist military moves elsewhere in the world."[18]

At the same time, the wish was strong to leave the way open for a Soviet withdrawal from the conflict. At the meeting on June 27 at which Truman and his senior advisers briefed congressional leaders on the background of the president's statement on Korea issued that day, it was suggested that public silence on Moscow's role in events might bring about such a backing away. The secretary of state argued, "If we publicly say that the Soviets are responsible for the actions of the communists in North Korea then, as a matter of prestige, the Soviet government will be forced to continue supporting the North Korean forces and we will find ourselves with a really

cision; Dean Acheson, notes of June 28, 1950, p. 4, in Acheson Papers, Memos of conversations, folder for May–June, 1950, HSTL; Congressional leaders' meeting, June 30, 1950, p. 6, in Elsey papers, Korea series, HSTL.

18. Dean Acheson to Paul [Nitze?], July 12, 1950, p. 1, in Acheson Papers, Memos of conversations, folder for July, 1950, HSTL; JCS memorandum for the Secretary of Defense, "U.S. Course of Action in the Event Soviet Forces Enter Korean Hostilities," July 10, 1950, p. 236, in Korean War documents file (Defense), Pertinent papers on Korean situation (Vol. II) HSTL; Charles Bohlen, *Witness to History, 1929–1969* (New York, 1973), 292.

tough scrap on our hands. If, however, we leave the door open the Soviet Union may well back down and call off the North Koreans." Acheson spoke with the fervor of a convert, for only the day before he had been persuaded by similar arguments from the American embassy in Moscow to refrain from making an immediate public accusation naming the Russians as the instigators of the conflict. Thus, the decision to portray the war as one of opposition to "communism," rather than to the power of the Soviet or Chinese state—often criticized for loading the conflict with ideological freight that made it difficult to arrive at a settlement—seems to have been attributable, at least in part, to a desire to respect Soviet sensibilities and avoid the exacerbation of tensions.[19]

By contrast, while continuing apprehensions over a wider war pulled policy makers toward caution, the continuing link between South Korea and the United Nations now impelled them toward action. Turning various responsibilities in South Korea over to the UN, in the hope that this would compensate for, and in some ways camouflage, the withdrawal of an American commitment, had seemed an effective substitute for what the Department of the Army in 1949 called "the unilateral course of action and responsibility in Korea from which [the United States] so recently has struggled to extricate itself." But with the outbreak of fighting, American decision-makers felt themselves trapped by their own prior success in this endeavor; as NSC 8/2 had warned: "The overthrow by Soviet-dominated forces of a government established in South Korea under the aegis of the UN would . . . constitute a severe blow to the prestige and influence of the latter; in this respect the interests of the U.S. must be regarded as parallel to, if not identical with, those of the UN." South Korea and the United Nations had become so closely identified that to allow the ROK to fall now with nothing more than a protest before the Security Council would be, as American officials saw it, a threat to the UN itself and to collective security, both of which were at the time considered cardinal American interests. UN involvement in Korean affairs, which had been used to ease an American departure, now appeared to demand an American return.[20]

From the beginning, action in Korea was, for American policy-makers, linked to the UN. When John D. Hickerson, the assistant secretary of state

19. Memorandum for Matthew Connelly from Charles S. Murphy, June 27, 1950, pp. 7, 8, in Elsey Papers, Korea series, folder for June 27, 1950, HSTL; *FRUS*, 1950, VII, 148, 169–70, 174–77, 197.

20. *FRUS*, 1949, VII, Pt. 2, pp. 975, 1055.

for United Nations affairs, telephoned Acheson at his Maryland home as the earliest fragmentary reports of the invasion were coming in, his first recommendation to the secretary was to request that United Nations Secretary-General Trygve Lie convene an emergency meeting of the Security Council the following morning to call for a cease-fire. Acheson approved, and confirmed the order immediately in a call to Truman in Missouri. At the Blair House meetings after Truman's return to Washington, the UN was never absent from the president's calculations. That he associated intervention in Korea with obligations to the United Nations was made clear at his meeting with congressional leaders on June 27, when he carefully distinguished between this action and the other steps taken simultaneously by the United States unilaterally to improve its military position elsewhere in the Far East.[21]

American representatives were meanwhile employing the same rationale before the UN itself. In presenting his government's request for a cease-fire resolution at the Security Council's emergency session on June 25, Ernest Gross, the deputy United States ambassador, asserted that the links the organization had developed with Seoul now made an international response to the attack imperative: "Such an attack openly defies the interest and authority of the United Nations. Such an attack, therefore, concerns the vital interest which all the Member nations have in the Organization." A July 3 memorandum by the State Department insisted that the survival of the United Nations had become synonymous with the survival of South Korea. Since "the continued existence of the United Nations as an effective international organization" was "a paramount United States interest," Washington had to intervene to protect both. Speaking on July 10 before the Institute of Public Affairs at the University of Virginia, Ambassador-at-large Philip C. Jessup reiterated that "we shall continue our policy of supporting the United Nations in its efforts to secure a permanent adjustment of the situation in Korea in the interest of the Korean people. We have no other or separate interest of our own."[22]

At the same time, the administration was not unaware of the propa-

21. Truman, *Years of Trial and Hope*, 333; *FRUS*, 1950, VII, 160, 183, 201–202; Tom Connally and Alfred Steinberg, *My Name Is Tom Connally* (New York, 1954), 346–47.

22. U.S. Department of State, *Bulletin*, XXIII (July 17, 1950), 84, 87, (July 30, 1950), 176–77; *Military Situation* hearings, Pt. 3, p. 1818; United Nations Security Council, *Official Records*, Fifth Year, No. 15, p. 4 (June 25, 1950). See also the statements to the Security Council of the American ambassador Warren Austin on June 27 (pp. 3–5) and June 30 (p. 11).

ganda advantages to be derived, both at home and abroad, from tying American action to the UN rather than taking it unilaterally. Kennan, fearing that multilateral action would push the United States beyond the limited response in Korea that he favored, was almost alone in his opposition to those he termed "wide-eyed enthusiasts for the UN." Nevertheless, it is far from certain that the UN was the deciding factor in the calculations of his colleagues. At the same congressional leadership briefing on June 30 at which Truman stated for the record that the United States was acting as part of the UN and that MacArthur was a UN officer, the president implied that the international organization was in some respects a façade for American action, though his own control over MacArthur's actions, for example, could not be stated publicly.[23]

Similarly, a note of thanks sent by Truman to Acheson on July 19 recalled: "Your initiative in immediately calling the Security Council of the U.N. on Saturday night [June 24] and notifying me was the key to what followed afterwards. Had you not acted promptly in that direction we would have had to go into Korea alone." Clearly, the president was prepared to intervene even without UN support. In and of itself, this does not mean that Truman did not feel that resistance to aggression in Korea would be an important service to the UN. He and his advisers could have reasoned that opposition by any state to the North Korean invasion would further the United Nations' goal of a peaceful, stable world, and that if, for whatever reason, the UN proved unable to act, the United States, through unilateral intervention, would be defending the world body in spite of itself. But the note does indicate that the president favored a forceful American response, regardless of whether the UN agreed with Washington's perception of the threat and requested action. Acheson's later discussion of the usefulness of the United Nations to American policy-makers tended to confirm this instrumental view. Asked whether UN involvement had eased the task of defending intervention before the American people and the allies, he replied, "I should think that was true. I think that the whole attitude of the country was much more attuned to the prevention of acts of this sort through the Charter and the principles . . . of the U.N. than it would have been without

23. Connally, *My Name Is Tom Connally*, 349; George F. Kennan, *Memoirs, 1925–1950* (Boston, 1967), 490–91; Congressional leaders' meeting, June 30, 1950, pp. 11–12, in Elsey Papers, Korea series, HSTL.

it. I'm not at all sure that we wouldn't have done the same thing, but you might have had more inertia to overcome in doing it."[24]

Other potential interests

Harried officials like Acheson had a multitude of questions to answer as the days rapidly passed in June and July. Among them, two of the most important had to do with other interests the United States might press on an unsettled society of states. One concerned the ends of the war: Was the war aim of the UN force to be the reestablishment of the previous border between the two Koreas, or its obliteration? The other concerned the means of the war: How much assistance should the United States expect from its allies and other UN member states in prosecuting this experiment in collective security?

On the first, there was no settled answer in Washington, because, in a final ironic twist, the armed intervention that American policy-makers had attempted for so long to avoid now reopened the original debate on the primary interest of the United States. Was it to achieve a unified, independent Korea? If so, the large American ground forces soon to arrive on the Korean Peninsula might make it possible to reach that goal, if they were ordered to occupy all of North Korea. Or was the main American interest to prevent a Communist occupation of the entire peninsula? This more limited goal could be achieved by a restoration of the *status quo ante bellum*, the division of the peninsula at the 38th parallel.

When later asked for the thinking of the administration officials on this issue during the Blair House meetings June 25 through June 30, Johnson replied, "There were no expressed conclusions at that time in my presence on any one of these points. In other words, no one . . . said we stopped at the thirty-eighth, we stopped at the Yalu, or what." But if the matter was not raised at these earliest discussions, it became a matter of controversy

24. Dean Acheson, *Present at the Creation: My Years in the State Department* (New York, 1969), 415; Dean Acheson, comments from February 13, 1954, p. 6, transcript in Acheson Papers, Princeton Seminars series, folder for February 13–14, 1954, HSTL. See also Edwin C. Hoyt, "The United States Reaction to the Korean Attack: A Study of the Principles of the United Nations Charter as a Factor in American Policy-Making," *American Journal of International Law*, LV (January, 1961), 45–76.

soon thereafter. Kennan and Bohlen favored no American advance beyond the narrow "waist" of Korea, which roughly coincided with the prewar frontier, and an address by Acheson on June 29 apparently accepted their view, though his words were not wholly free of ambiguity. The secretary declared, "This action pursuant to the Security Council resolutions is *solely for the purpose of restoring the Republic of Korea to its status prior to the invasion from the North* and of re-establishing the peace broken by that aggression." Austin quoted this speech before the Security Council the following day.[25]

On the other hand, a memorandum of July 3 by John Allison, director of the State Department's Office of Northeast Asian Affairs, endorsed by Assistant Secretary of State for Far Eastern Affairs Dean Rusk, warned that a suggested presidential statement pledging to advance no further than the 38th parallel would be "unrealistic," "unwise," and "fatal to what may be left of South Korean morale." Allison went on to state, "I personally feel that if we can, and I am not at all certain we can, we should continue right on up to the Manchurian and Siberian border, and having done so, call for a UN-supervised election for all of Korea." In a second memorandum on July 13, this one endorsed by Dulles, Allison complained that a public statement by an army spokesman in the Far East that American troops were involved in the war only for the purpose of driving North Korean forces back to the original boundary "should never have been made," and was "folly."[26]

Whether the president was convinced by, or even knew of, Allison's arguments is unclear, but when he was given the opportunity at a news conference on July 13 to make a statement disclaiming any interest in forcible reunification, he refused to do so, saying only that he would "make that decision when it becomes necessary to do it." In private, he placed more stress on being "damn careful" not to take aggressive actions in North Korea. When he approved MacArthur's orders on June 29, Truman insisted that geographical restrictions be placed on the conduct of air operations; he was quoted as stating "that he only wanted to restore order to the

25. *Military Situation* hearings, Pt. 4, p. 2586; U.S. Department of State, *Bulletin*, XXIII (July 10, 1950), 43 (emphasis added), (July 17, 1950), 87; Bohlen, *Witness to History*, 292–93; Kennan, *Memoirs*, 487–90, 496.

26. *FRUS*, 1950, VII, 272, 373.

38th Parallel; he did not want to do anything north of it except to 'keep the North Koreans from killing the people we are trying to save.'"[27]

As for naval action, the American blockade announced by Truman on June 30 was publicly defined as including "the entire Korean coast." In fact, however, because the United States did not have sufficient forces available to undertake this task completely, and because, as Johnson was reminded on July 6 by the liaison officer of the secretary of defense with the State Department, Major General James H. Burns, "we wish to stay well clear of Russian and Manchurian waters," the blockade extended only to the 41st parallel on the east coast of the Korean Peninsula and to 39 degrees, 30 minutes on the west coast, leaving the United States with a less effective but possibly less provocative "paper blockade" of the northernmost part of Korea's coastline nearest the Soviet and Chinese borders.[28] Moscow's sensitivities about an area close to its own territory, West European apprehensions that the United States would be diverted from the main arena of world politics (in Europe), and American uncertainty that a drive to the Yalu was within the country's capacities: all these combined to cast doubt on the notion that a Korea unified by force of arms under the UN flag was an American interest that could be sustained. Still, there were arguments on both sides, and, as the events of the fall would demonstrate, the question was by no means closed.

While the president and his advisers debated the extent to which an interest in a unified, non-Communist Korea could be pressed, attention outside the upper reaches of the executive branch was concentrated more on the immediate means of fighting the war, and particularly on the issue of other states' contribution to this multilateral effort at collective security. Was the demand for military and other assistance to the UN forces an interest the United States could reasonably and successfully press on members of the states-system? At Truman's meeting with congressional leaders on June 30, the matter was the primary subject of discussion, as legislators tried to impress on the president the desirability of quickly supplementing Ameri-

27. *Public Papers of the Presidents of the United States: Harry S. Truman, 1950* (Washington, D.C., 1965), 513, 523; NSC meeting, June 29, 1950, pp. 1–2, in Elsey Papers, Korea series, HSTL.

28. Korean-UN data, July 6, 1950, in President's Secretary File, Korean War, General U-W series, HSTL.

can troops with those of other countries. Senator Millard Tydings (Democrat, Maryland) was "certain that some show of *Allied* as distinct from American forces was necessary," both to sustain the American people "once the casualty lists began to appear" and to scotch any belief abroad that "this was a private American war." He repeated his plea twice during the meeting, with the refrain, "just a company, just a company or two." His Senate colleague Scott Lucas (Democrat, Illinois) endorsed the idea, as did Congressman John Vorys (Republican, New York), who noted the particular importance of Asian ground forces: "If we got a few Asiatics into the fighting, it wouldn't look so much like 'White man's imperialism.'" Meanwhile Senator Wiley pressed to know "if the State Department was working to get other countries into the fighting with us."[29]

To such concerns the president at least initially appeared sympathetic. He told the NSC on June 28 that Great Britain's reported offer of naval forces should be accepted as soon as it was received, and when Johnson reminded him that the American navy had not wanted foreign vessels and crews in the Second World War due to differences in signals, Truman responded, "That was a different situation. We do want them now." Likewise, he told Acheson and Johnson the following day that the answer to offers from Australia, New Zealand, Canada, and the Netherlands should be to "take everything. We may need them." (The president did, however, insist that all contributions of armed assistance be accepted for the United Nations, not the United States.)[30]

Others were less enthusiastic at the prospect of a UN command with large contingents not drawn from the United States and South Korea. In response to questions from the State Department and the secretary of the army, the Joint Chiefs of Staff sounded a note of caution, on grounds of military efficiency. While they conceded that "certain Latin American countries [and others] might easily be induced to come forward with assistance offers," they warned that acceptance should be conditioned on a number of considerations: "the efficiency of the units offered, their availability and suit-

29. Congressional leaders' meeting, no date, in Elsey Papers, Korea, series, HSTL; Dean Acheson, press conference of July 5, 1950, in Acheson Papers, Press Conferences, 1949–51, series, folder for January–December, 1950, *ibid.*

30. NSC meeting, June 28, 1950, p. 2, in Acheson Papers, Memos of conversations, folder for May–June, 1950, *ibid.*; George Elsey, notes from June 29, 1950, pp. 5–6, in Elsey Papers, Korea series, *ibid.*

ability for early employment, logistical and transportation considerations involved, and the likelihood of such units being employed profitably in Korea by the Commander in Chief, Far East in cooperation with the other forces under his command." A follow-up JCS memorandum doused the idea with more cold water. Assistance from the United Kingdom, Australia, New Zealand, Canada, and Pakistan could be "useful," but the Joint Chiefs recommended that "no aid be requested from the Philippines, Italy, Turkey, or Saudi Arabia since these countries may have urgent need for their own use of all of the forces which are available to them." Even Truman, for all his blunt talk of taking all help from third countries, thought there were some cases in which wider considerations made accepting, let alone soliciting, military forces diplomatically awkward or strategically unwise. At the session with congressional leaders he remarked that the idea of encouraging "Asiatics" to fight on the UN side was "a very difficult matter, because if we got some Asiatics—like Chiang's men on Formosa, for example—we would have to be awfully careful of the Chinese Communists."[31] Although it was generally believed within the American government that the United States had a good case and a justifiable interest in securing military and other aid from all states that supported the UN action, then, many feared that pressing too hard in particular cases would imperil other interests.

KOREA AND THE COMMON GOOD

To abstract discussions of the common good of the American people, policy makers did not devote much time in the frantic weeks after June 25. Nor had they conducted such seminars in the slightly more leisurely months before the invasion. If, then, one wishes to see whether any consideration of national interest underlay American policy, and what the national interest was thought to entail, one can approach the problem in two ways: by ex-

31. "Check List #1," June 30, 1950, in Acheson Papers, Memos of conversations, folder for May–June, 1950, *ibid.*; JCS Memorandum for the Secretary of Defense, "Subject: United States Courses of Action in Korea," July 14, 1950, p. 244, and JCS Memorandum for the Secretary of Defense, "Subject: Joint Chiefs of Staff Views on Proposed State Department Request for Assistance in Korea from Certain U.N. Nations," July 14, 1950, p. 246, both in Korean War documents file (Defense), Pertinent papers on Korean situation (Vol. II), *ibid.*; Congressional leaders' meeting, June 30, 1950, p. 6, in Elsey Papers, Korea series, *ibid.*

amining the record for evidence of alternative motives for action, and by recalling what officials did and the reasons they gave for doing it.

The interpretation that policy is the product of pressures by special interests, often of an economic sort, finds little support in the Korean episode. Domestic interests played a far smaller role in shaping American actions in Korea from 1945 to 1950 than they had in policy toward Western Europe prior to the Marshall Plan. In 1947 the Wedemeyer Report had somberly summarized the condition of the South Korean economy: "South Korea is a depleted and eroded country with no minerals worth mentioning, an agriculture dependent on nitrate input, and a backward people."[32]

Faced with these obstacles and with the dangers and uncertainties attendant upon ongoing border clashes and guerrilla warfare between North and South, American businessmen had made no great move to explore opportunities for economic contacts with South Korea and evinced no desire to do so in the future. Beyond their hope for stability in the area that might encourage greater investment at some point, American officials made Korean policy on the basis of considerations other than the effect on American economic interests.[33] Nor were there other domestic interest groups that had any degree of influence over Washington's actions. No large group of Korean immigrants or persons of Korean descent existed in the United States to press decision makers to be more concerned with the future of South Korea. Members of the "China lobby" did strongly attempt to influence America's Asian policies, but for them South Korea was of distinctly secondary importance, an object of concern only insofar as it affected the Nationalists' struggle in China. Indeed, it was members of Congress most sympathetic to Chiang Kai-shek, along with other members intent on economy, who defeated the House bill for aid to South Korea in January, 1950, relenting only after funds for China were added to the measure.

Of course one could argue that American actions, first in endeavoring to make South Korea a ward of the United Nations and then in intervening militarily when war came, were dictated by a broader policy of keeping as

32. Wedemeyer Report, 21.
33. See Kwak Tae-Hwan, "United States-Korean Relations: A Core Interest Analysis Prior to U.S. Intervention in the Korean War" (Ph.D. dissertation, Claremont Graduate School and University, 1969); Jung Yong Suk, "The Rise of American National Interest in Korea: 1845–1950" (Ph.D. dissertation, Claremont Graduate School and University, 1970); Fred Harvey Harrington, "Beard's Idea of National Interest and New Interpretations," *American Perspective*, IV (Fall, 1950), 342–44.

much of the world as possible open to a free international economy—or, to put it pejoratively, maintaining an "Open Door" around the world for the benefit of American corporations. In the grip of a sort of economic determinism, decision makers in Washington needed to preserve a principle— that no region should be closed to Western investment—at least as much as whatever real opportunities for investment existed in the case. Still, when the views of the business community did come up in the deliberations of late June and early July, the president's economic advisers usually cited them as a reason to do less rather than more, later rather than sooner, at a lower rather than a higher cost.[34] These concerns conveyed the impression, not that interest groups were demanding strong American action in Korea, or that the interests of capitalism required intervention, but just the opposite—that officials were setting their course based on other considerations while seeking ways to bring the business community along in support.

What these other considerations were, subsequently became a matter of dispute. Reviewing in his diary on July 28 the discussion of that morning concerning American policy on Korea and two other issues with which it had become intertwined—the defense of Taiwan and the seating of the Chinese Communist regime in the United Nations—Kennan asserted, "What we were dealing with here was a conflict of interest, founded in bitter strategic and political realities. It could not be considered a moral issue." Kennan's colleague, John Carter Vincent (one-time director of the State Department's office of Far Eastern affairs, in 1950 minister to Switzerland), later disagreed: "Our reaction to the aggression can be explained, it appears, only in moral or ethical terms. Truman and Acheson assumed a moral leadership and received the support of the American people because we felt that there was a moral commitment to defend South Korea. The material or observable evidence at the time certainly could not have warranted a prediction that such would be our reaction." The national interests asserted and acted upon by Washington prior to the invasion would seem to support Vincent's claim that particular material interests had not kept the United States in Korea. Yet Kennan was also correct in arguing that the Americans were not brought back to Korea solely by the influence of abstract moral principles or ideals. Rather, there were intermediate considerations—

---

34. "Some Implications of the Korean Situation," July 12, 1950, p. 1, in Elsey Papers, Korea series, "Message to Congress on Korean Situation" folder, HSTL; Notes on cabinet meetings of July 8, July 14, 1950, in Matthew J. Connelly Papers, Notes on cabinet meetings series, folder for January 6–December 29, 1950, *ibid.*

specific principles intimately bound up with the nature of the American regime that convinced policy makers in Washington that they could not abandon South Korea and still remain true to the United States' own common good. Kennan himself recognized this when he later said, "It was always my feeling that in the interval between the time when the Japanese surrendered to us unconditionally and the time when there was a peace treaty which returned the fundamental responsibility to the Japanese, we Americans were responsible for peace and security in that area." That sense of "responsibility" stemmed less from the specific interests at stake in the Korean Peninsula than from a feeling of duty that in turn sprang from a self-definition of the kind of people Americans were. Americans, Kennan hoped, were people who, once they had exercised power in a situation and therefore assumed some responsibility for it, would not shirk the resulting obligation or walk away from a problem in which, through their own actions, they had become entangled. This duty was particularly keen when norms in favor of self-determination and against aggressive war were flouted in an egregious way that most Americans professed to find (and generally *did* find) morally repugnant. "The real basis of the Korean decision had almost nothing to do with Korea," one participant in the deliberations argued. "It had to do with aggression."[35] A sense of outraged honor pervades the public statements of American officials at the time and their recollections afterward. Such talk can be nothing more than self-serving posturing. What is more striking is the almost automatic unanimity with which decision makers determined to intervene in force in a situation in which they had previously discerned few self-interested reasons to be involved and under conditions in which they faced few if any pressures from subnational groups to act as they did.

MAKING THE PUBLIC CASE

Punctuating the confidential discussions and decisions through late June and early July was a series of public remarks by the participants. During this time, the White House issued four presidential statements on Korea—on June 26, 27, and 30, and July 8—and Truman held three news confer-

35. Kennan, *Memoirs*, 494; New York *Times*, January 30, 1957, Sec. 1, p. 28; George F. Kennan, "Morality, Politics and Foreign Policy," in *The Virginia Papers on the Presidency*, ed. Kenneth W. Thompson, the White Burkett Miller Center Forums, 1979 (Washington, D.C., 1979), 22–23; Paige, *The Korean Decision*, 298.

ences—on June 29, and July 6 and 13. Acheson and his aides were providing press briefings at the State Department, and statements were made by other executive agencies and by members of Congress. The result of all these comments was to establish the outline of a consensus on the interests at stake, but the constituent elements were scattered and the connections among them were not always clear. A more fully thought-out and carefully worded definition therefore had to wait until July 19, when the president presented two statements that for the first time publicly reviewed at length the considerations underlying the administration's actions in the Far East. In a special message sent to Congress at noon of that day (not delivered in person) and in a live radio and television speech to the public at 10:30 P.M. (the first televised presidential address to the nation in history), Truman made his case for defining an interest in military efforts in cooperation with others aimed at safeguarding South Korea's independence.[36]

That case rested on an argument justifying American intervention. Was Korea linked to the United States' national interest so closely as to give Washington grounds for using armed force there? The president insisted that it was, telling Congress that the invasion "created a real and present danger to the security of every nation" and, making the point more specific, telling the public that "what is at stake here is nothing less than our own national security." This was of course a very strong statement, given the absence of any immediate threat to American territory and the inability of the North Koreans, unaided, ever to mount such a threat; and Truman acknowledged that "Korea is a small country, thousands of miles away." He contended, nevertheless, that "what is happening there is important to every American," for two reasons: opposition to aggression and support for the United Nations. "I think it is important that the nature of our military action in Korea be understood," he said in his message to Congress. "It should be made perfectly clear that the action was undertaken as a matter of basic moral principle. The United States was going to the aid of a nation established and supported by the United Nations and unjustifiably attacked by an aggressor force."

The North Korean attack was "naked, deliberate, unprovoked aggres-

36. See *Public Papers: Truman, 1950*, 491–92, 502–506, 513, 516–18, 520, 522–25, 527–42. Truman's quotations in subsequent paragraphs are from this source. The president also sent a message thanking Governor Thomas E. Dewey for his telegram of support in the crisis (see p. 496), and made brief scattered references to the conflict in other public remarks during this time.

sion, without a shadow of justification," the president told Congress, noting that field observers attached to UNCOK had completed a routine tour of the border only the day before the invasion and had found South Korean forces neither organized nor equipped for anything but defense. It was clear which side had crossed the border. Faced with this act and with the implications they felt it entailed, the United States and its allies had responded with vigor and dispatch, because "the fateful events of the 1930's, when aggression unopposed bred more aggression and eventually war, were fresh in our memory." The "free nations had learned the lesson of history," Truman proudly stated, and thus "this united and resolute action to put down lawless aggression is a milestone toward the establishment of a rule of law among nations."

Citing the example of appeasement in the interwar period could mean that stopping aggression in 1950 had more than moral or legal significance; it also had the quite self-interested intention of deterring future moves against areas more important to the United States by exacting a penalty in Korea. But Truman did not speak in the language of the strategic calculations that had been a part of his administration's discussions both before and since June 25. Indeed, the president's messages gave very little attention to the interests of two states most intimately involved in the war, Japan and South Korea itself. Japan, which had loomed large in the thoughts of decision makers wrestling with the Korean problem before the invasion, was not mentioned at all except in a brief reference, found in Truman's speech to the nation, to Korea's pre–World War II history. Even more surprisingly, the interests of South Korea received equally slight notice. The president recognized that what the United States was doing would serve the most basic survival interest of South Korea when he affirmed that Washington would "support the United Nations in its effort to restore peace and security to Korea." But this commitment, rather than being the fruit of an advocacy of South Korea's interests or any obligation to that country, was represented as "the carrying out of our obligations *to the United Nations* in Korea [emphasis added]." The ROK was not so much an independent actor whose interests coincided with those of the United States as the site on which an American commitment to a third party, the UN, was being tested.

The United Nations occupied a prominent place in both of Truman's statements. He began his radio and television address by pointing out that the well-being of the UN was tied to that of South Korea: "The attack upon

Korea was an outright breach of the peace and a violation of the Charter of the United Nations. By their actions in Korea, Communist leaders have demonstrated their contempt for the basic moral principles on which the United Nations is founded." The disregard for the UN and its ideals implied in the invasion was especially damaging in view of the active role taken by the international body in the establishment and development of South Korea. "The attack on the Republic of Korea, therefore, was a clear challenge to the basic principles of the United Nations Charter and to the specific actions taken by the United Nations in Korea." Truman recounted the Security Council's resolutions asking for help to Seoul. The United States, if it was to remain true to its own principles and those embodied in the charter, had no choice but to concur in "the prompt action of the United Nations to put down lawless aggression" and intervene: "If this challenge had not been met squarely, the effectiveness of the United Nations would have been all but ended, and the hope of mankind that the United Nations would develop into an institution of world order would have been shattered."

Thus, the president drew the connection between Korea and the American national interest in broad and somewhat abstract terms, availing himself of neither the language of material calculation (which might have been thought uninspiring) nor the discourse of self-respect, responsibility, and honor (though these considerations had also played some role in the decisions of the preceding weeks). In his references to the specific interests that the United States would assert in this case, and the claims of others that it would recognize, his words were at some points equally guarded, though for very concrete reasons.

That the interests of the Soviet Union still weighed heavily on the minds of administration officials was clear from the president's treatment of them. He strongly condemned Moscow for its refusal to call off the North Koreans, noting, "The attitude of the Soviet Government toward the aggression against the Republic of Korea is in direct contradiction to its often expressed intention to work with other nations to achieve peace in the world." Truman recounted that an American diplomatic approach to the Soviets, asking them to use their influence with Pyongyang, had been met with the Soviet government's reply that South Korea had started the war and the Security Council's actions were illegal. Truman contended: "These Soviet claims are flatly disproved by the facts."

Despite the vigor of this denunciation, a desire to leave the Soviet Union a face-saving way out of the crisis—which had restrained the Americans since its beginning—was also evident. Although Truman criticized Moscow for not helping to end the war, he did not blame it for starting the conflict. Instead, he laid that indictment against a vaguer and more general enemy, "communism." Just as Acheson had pleaded with congressmen not to assign guilt publicly and thus not to trench unnecessarily on Soviet prestige, so now Truman avoided wording that would tie the Soviet Union's standing to the success of North Korean arms. Nevertheless, if the American response was to serve its purpose of deterring future Soviet-inspired aggression, it had to be coupled with a threat of sanctions against Moscow itself and not only against its proxies. The president's warning of an enlarged crisis was veiled but firm as he said, "I am sure that those who have it in their power to unleash or withhold acts of armed aggression must realize that new recourse to aggression in the world today might well strain to the breaking point the fabric of world peace."

The president's messages had the difficult task of mirroring American actions in the attitude toward Soviet interests that they were intended to convey. Like the tough military response to the attack, Truman's warning that further breaches of the peace could provoke a wider war was meant to deter Moscow from sponsoring other assaults. Like the plea of the American Embassy in Moscow to the State Department, and the request by the Secretary of State to members of Congress, not to blame the Soviets publicly, Truman's refusal to charge explicitly that the war had begun at the Soviet Union's direction left the door open for a quiet withdrawal of support from the North Koreans that would not unduly harm Russian prestige. The passages of the two addresses dealing with Soviet interests, which Marshal Shulman, then a Soviet specialist in the State Department, had helped to draft, reflected the care that was required to send the proper signal to the Kremlin.

In a balancing act of equal delicacy, Truman acknowledged the interests of other states allied with or friendly toward the United States. Neither immediately menaced by the attack nor entirely certain that they would not be the target of a similar threat in the future, these states required assurance on two fronts: first, that Washington would stand by its commitments (even if, as in the case of South Korea, it had been attempting for at least two years to escape any commitment); and, second, that it would not become so preoccupied by its defense of South Korea that it neglected the needs of others.

Truman's messages addressed both of these concerns. He hoped to satisfy the first by his resolute tone, as he praised the fifty-two members of the United Nations (of a total of fifty-nine) that had expressed support for the Security Council resolution calling for assistance to the Republic of Korea. He further commended the action of those states that had agreed to provide tangible assistance to the UN forces, and he specifically mentioned the two countries that had provided aircraft and the five that had provided naval vessels, though he did not publicly ask for more.[37] The president pledged that the United States would stand fast in its support of South Korea throughout what would be "a hard and costly military operation" in which "we can expect no easy solution." American intervention, he asserted, had already had an invigorating effect on the non-Communist world—"where there had been dismay there is hope; where there had been anxiety there is firm determination."

But if Korea was a testing ground for American will, it could also be seen as a distraction from other tasks and the needs of other countries. Truman wished to assure all third parties that South Korea was not the United States' sole concern, noting the need "to consider [the war's] implications for peace throughout the world" and declaring that the attack "makes it plain beyond all doubt that the international communist movement is prepared to use armed invasion to conquer independent nations." In "recogniz[ing] the possibility that armed aggression may take place in other areas," the president reiterated and defended the package of broader measures announced during the first week of the crisis: increased aid to the Philippines and to the French forces in Indochina and the redeployment of the 7th Fleet between China and Taiwan. Truman also promised that not only would the outbreak of war in Korea not hinder American efforts to strengthen the security of other states, it would spur them on. The president referred to the collective efforts embodied in the Marshall Plan, the Rio Pact, and the North Atlantic Treaty, and to American assistance to individual countries such as Greece, Turkey, and Iran. As proof of the United States' commitment to continue aiding all these areas, he called on the

37. Probably in response to a request from those preparing Truman's two addresses, the State Department had supplied an eight-page compilation of the responses by all countries to events in Korea. See "Tabulation of Replies to UN Secretary-General with Respect to Security Council Action on Korea," July 13, 1950, in Elsey Papers, Korea series, "Message to Congress on Korean situation" folder, HSTL.

House of Representatives to enact without delay the authorization bill then pending for the Mutual Defense Assistance Program for 1951, and promised to lay before Congress requests for additional funds for this purpose, in which increased aid to the North Atlantic area would play a particularly important part. He laid down the expectation that American allies would also do more for their own security—"The other nations associated with us . . . , like ourselves, will need to divert additional economic resources to defense purposes"—and pledged to help them do so. "The free nations face a worldwide threat," he declared to the people in his speech that evening. "It must be met with a worldwide defense."

While he was warning Moscow that it had gone beyond he bounds of its reasonable interests, putting the allies on notice that greater efforts at defense would be required of them, and pledging the United States to oppose the one and assist the other, the president took care to abjure one potential American claim or interest. To try to blunt the charge that Washington's entrance into the war in Korea and, even more clearly, its actions in Taiwan, the Philippines, and Indochina evidenced an imperialist or neoimperialist intent in East Asia, Truman assured the nation, "For ourselves, we seek no territory or dominion over others." Similarly, in his message to Congress, he said, "In order that there may be no doubt in any quarter about our intentions regarding Formosa, I wish to state that the United States has no territorial ambitions whatever concerning that island, nor do we seek for ourselves any special position or privilege on Formosa."

Finally, just as the advantages or disadvantages to be derived by domestic interests from the government's action had not seemed to occupy decision makers in their private discussions during the past three and one-half weeks, so now Truman paid them little attention in his public messages. His only references to them in fact were assertions of the supremacy of the national interest over domestic interests, combined with pledges that all interests would share equally in the sacrifices that would be necessary. As part of these efforts, the president denounced both hoarding by consumers and profiteering by businessmen as economically ruinous actions that, while they might benefit those interests temporarily, would undermine the greater common interest in price and wage stability. Truman called hoarding "foolish," "very selfish," and "perfectly ridiculous" and claimed that the only shortages the country had to fear were those that hoarding might artificially create. He threatened "the more drastic measures of price control and rationing" if business, labor, farmers, and consumers did not voluntarily restrain wages and prices, and used strong language against gouging: "Every businessman who is trying to profiteer in time of national danger—and every person who is selfishly trying to get more than his neighbor—is doing just exactly the thing that any enemy of this country would want him to do." He pledged to favor no domestic interests when he submitted to Congress his proposals for tax increases to pay for war-related expenditures and concluded his address to the public with a tribute to national unity: "Our country stands before the world as an example of how free men, under God, can build a community of neighbors, working together for the good of all."

The two messages had been carefully prepared. (Truman's speechwriters went through seven drafts of the message to Congress and a comparable number with the public speech, in a process of laborious consultation with others in the White House and with the departments directly concerned.)[38] They represented the administration's effort to make the most convincing and inspiring argument for its actions, before both a domestic and a foreign audience. In them one finds claims that few in the American government would have thought of asserting as American interests a month before. If the Marshall Plan demonstrates the limitations on the interests that even great powers can put forward without arousing opposition, then intervention in the Korean conflict illustrates the speed with which a state's asserted interests can change, even when the underlying ideas giving rise to those interests do not themselves change. For the conceptual foundation of the United States' policy—opposition to Soviet expansion in the Far East, denigration of the strategic significance of Korea relative to other regions, a desire to associate South Korea with the United Nations, and a hope to deter a broader war with Moscow—remained unaltered. What shifted were circumstances, which convinced policy makers that through its own actions, the United States had developed greater responsibilities and commitments in Northeast Asia than they had thought. These duties (which the United States owed primarily to itself, if it was to retain its sense of honor and self-respect), combined with narrower strategic considerations and broader ethical ones, brought Washington to intervene. Yet while the twin goals of de-

38. "Memorandum For File. Subject: Preparation of President's Message to Congress on Korea, July 19, 1950," in Elsey Papers, Korea series, folder for June 25, 1950, *ibid.*; "Memorandum For File. Subject: Preparation of the President's Radio Address on Korea, Wednesday, July 19, 1950," in Elsey Papers, Korea series, "Radio Address on Korea," folder, *ibid.*

terrence and responsibility made a convincing case for the argument that the overall national interest, as that term has been understood here, required intervention, only the more abstract or altruistic of these motives made their way into Truman's speeches to be treated at any length. Under the new circumstances of the late summer of 1950, anticommunism and construction of world order were more potent symbols in public debate. Without the basic sense that the common good of the American regime required shouldering responsibilities the country had (perhaps unwittingly) assumed, and the assertion of specific interests that flowed from those responsibilities, however, there would have been no intervention for the messages to justify.

VIII   The Nixon Doctrine

THE WORLD VIEW that came into being in 1947 and 1948 in Western Europe and in 1950 in Korea informed American actions for a remarkably long time. Despite Tocqueville's fear that liberal democracies would be unable to sustain any foreign policy long enough for it to be effective, the United States hewed to the decisions made in those instances—that Washington had an important stake in the economic health, the political orientation, and therefore the character of societies in large stretches of the globe, and that it was prepared to intervene with its own forces if those values were militarily threatened—for some twenty years. Such impressive continuity came about partly because of the bipartisan containment consensus that solidified around the general precepts guiding this conception of national interest and shaped the thinking of the establishmentarians who applied it in the circumstances of their day. More than this, the edifice held firm because its floor plan seemed to correspond to the working environment in which policy makers found themselves: a world in which two great rivals confronted each other over power, ideas, and influence, and in which the United States could carry on the competition without excessive costs and risks.

Buttressed by these strengths, the containment fortress might have stood for years longer if it had not been ground down by the war in Vietnam. Far more costly than anyone in authority had ever expected, or had prepared public opinion to expect, American participation in the war came to be viewed as an enormous (and dangerous) cul-de-sac. It was an irritant in relations with the country's major allies, who felt it distracted the United States from more important tasks. In relations with American adversaries, it diverted Washington both from possible avenues of cooperation (as in the hostility toward Hanoi's supporter, China, which delayed any rapprochement with that country), and from confrontation with rivals over issues elsewhere. Physical resources, manpower, and, not least, the energies of policy makers drained into the seemingly bottomless pit of Indochina. At base, however, it was not the sheer cost of the venture that made it unsupportable; it was the apparent inability of the Johnson administration to make a convincing case for the necessity of the war to American citizens and for the acceptability of American participation in the war to a significant section of international society—to demonstrate that Washington was pursuing a real national interest and not a bluff, a crusade, or a dream—that made American actions increasingly unpopular.

Dissatisfaction with the justifications offered for, and the frustrating conduct of, the American war effort spilled over into an assumption that containment as a whole was flawed. Partly this equation was a result of the efforts by the administration to bolster popular support for its actions by buttressing them with what seemed to be an unshakable containment consensus. The rhetoric of containment served as the basis for American intervention, and official explanations argued that the domino theory was the logical extension of the reasoning behind the Marshall Plan and Korea. No matter that Kennan, the original author of containment, said that it was never designed for a military confrontation in Asia and opposed American entrance into the war: when the military effort did not go well, the anger over its many ill effects turned against the doctrine that had been drafted into service as the war's rationale and slogan. The task of the 1970s would therefore be to discover and defend a revised set of claims that could be sustained at home and abroad.

THE NIXON DOCTRINE AND THE
UNITED STATES' NATIONAL INTEREST

As the first administration to undertake this search, the Nixon administration arrived in Washington in early 1969 to find itself immediately confronted with the need to replace or alter the thinking that had led to a bad case of "pactitus" in general and the controversial intervention in Vietnam in particular. It set about the endeavor with less talk of the overall national interest than had accompanied the policy shifts of any of its postwar predecessors. Avowedly distrustful of "ideology" as a guide to foreign policy, Richard Nixon and his national security adviser, Henry Kissinger, may well have eschewed any defense of their actions couched in the rhetoric of the common good because they knew that such language would quickly lead to "ideological" debate on the character of the American regime as a necessary precondition of any agreement on the needs of the regime and therefore its requirements in the international realm.

Kissinger had long argued that a successful foreign policy could not be governed primarily by domestic considerations. It had been his contention that the greatest statesmen had been those who could transcend (without abandoning) the political traditions of their own society and relate them to the necessities of the international setting. The requirements of competition, indeed survival, in an anarchical world had to be taken into account by leaders of every state, whatever its domestic principles. To believe that one could guide one's actions solely by reference to the traditions and structure of one's own society would be, for a weak state, a prescription for irrelevance, isolation, or subjugation. For a major power, it could issue in an abdication of effective external influence, but it could also lead to a crusading or inflexible foreign policy that brought unnecessary conflict, even disaster, upon an international realm always tending in that direction in any case. It lent itself to moralizing on the unique virtues of one's political principles, but as Kissinger wrote of Czar Alexander, "The claim to moral superiority leads to an erosion of all moral restraint."[1] Likewise, the diplomatist who wished to solidify peace, order, and freedom in the international society of his day could not make policy dependent on the domestic practices of the states with which he had to work. Their views on liberty, equality, justice, the fundamental rights of the individual, and the legitimate claims of society—their philosophies of their public interest—were not the province of foreign statesmen; a workable arrangement among states guided by different ideas was. As his attitude toward the human-rights campaign would later demonstrate, Kissinger feared that constant public reference to one's own common good or public interest, or the attempt to define it for others, would result in self-righteousness or sterility.

All the same, Kissinger's writings before his assumption of office had dealt at length with one way in which domestic regimes unavoidably affected the character of great-power relations in succeeding eras. In his treat-

1. Henry A. Kissinger, *A World Restored: Metternich, Castlereagh and the Problems of Peace, 1812–1822* (Boston, 1973), 153.

ment of "revolutionary" leaders and "legitimate" international systems, he placed differing conceptions of justice and the public interest at the heart of the foreign policy a state could be expected to pursue. *A World Restored* began with a definition of the concepts that would serve as its framework. "'Legitimacy' as here used should not be confused with justice," Kissinger warned on his very first page. "It means no more than an international agreement about the nature of workable arrangements and about the permissible aims and methods of foreign policy. It implies the acceptance of the framework of the international order by all major powers, at least to the extent that no state is so dissatisfied that . . . it expresses its dissatisfaction in a revolutionary foreign policy. A legitimate order does not make conflicts impossible, but it limits their scope." What, then, was a revolutionary foreign policy?" According to Kissinger: "Whenever there exists a power which considers the international order or the manner of legitimizing it oppressive, relations between it and other powers will be revolutionary. In such cases, it is not the adjustment of differences within a given system which will be at issue, but the system itself. . . . [The] distinguishing feature of a revolutionary power is not that it feels threatened—such feeling is inherent in the nature of international relations based on sovereign states—*but that nothing can reassure it.*" In a revolutionary situation, diplomacy, understood as the art of restraining power in the search for a negotiated settlement, becomes impossible because of "the absence of an agreement on what constitutes a reasonable demand."[2]

Kissinger's hope was that a lessening of revolutionary ardor within the preeminent revolutionary power of his own day, the Soviet Union, combined with the skillful use of positive and negative inducements by the United States, would bring Moscow to believe that its interest would be best served by pursuing its goals and its continuing disputes with its superpower rival within the existing international order. Not convergence between Soviet and American ideologies, but a conviction by Moscow that its national interest would be advanced by relative international restraint: this was the goal to be achieved by demonstrating that the Soviet Union's national interest lay in developing its internal regime, rather than in exporting the tenets of its ideology. The general objective of bringing the Soviets to cease being a revolutionary power and to grant the existing society of states a measure of legiti-

2. *Ibid.*, 1–2.

macy would require changes in the Soviet regime that would cause it to accept that its national interest was not inevitably threatened by the continued existence of noncommunist states. Agreements on a number of specific issues on which the superpowers' specific interests clashed would also be necessary.

At the same time, Nixon and Kissinger had to respond to the possibility that the critics of containment as it had come to be practiced were correct—that the common good of the United States (its prosperity, its strength, and its continued ability to pursue its domestic search for justice) was being undermined by excessive involvement abroad. The comments and writings of both men before assuming office had contained implicit references to this theme. In an article published in *Foreign Affairs* in 1967, Nixon had described many Americans as "weary with war, disheartened with allies, disillusioned with aid, [and] dismayed at domestic crises," and predicted "a deep reluctance on the part of the United States to become involved once again in a similar intervention on a similar basis." "For the United States to go it alone in containing China would . . . place an unconscionable burden on our own country," he wrote. Rather, "the central pattern of the future in U.S.-Asian relations must be American support for Asian initiatives." Kissinger, too, in an essay written in 1968 before the election, noted, "Whatever the outcome of the war in Vietnam, it is clear that it has greatly diminished American willingness to become involved in this form of warfare elsewhere." Beyond Southeast Asia, the United States would be unwise to try to maintain its postwar burdens in a world now much more complex. "No nation can act wisely simultaneously in every part of the globe at every moment of time," he warned. "A more pluralistic world—especially in relationships with friends—is profoundly in our long-term interest."[3]

As suggested by the reference that both men made to American public opinion, a conviction that the United States should reduce its role abroad could spring not only from a cool, rational, and disinterested appraisal of the measures necessary to the common good of society, but also from calculations of electoral benefit. No more than the Marshall Plan or the Korean War could the Nixon Doctrine be separated from domestic politics. Surveys

3. Richard M. Nixon, "Asia After Vietnam," *Foreign Affairs*, XLVI (October, 1967), 111–25; Henry A. Kissinger, "Central Issues of American Foreign Policy," in *Agenda for the Nation*, ed. Kermit Gordon (Garden City, N.Y., 1968), 585–614.

for some time had shown public sentiment shifting against the continuation of the present policy in Vietnam. The president's political imperatives included the fact that his election victory had been narrow and that he took office as the first incoming chief executive in more than a century to face a Congress controlled in both houses by the opposition—a party that, relieved of the responsibility for the conduct of the war, was rapidly moving toward repudiating American participation in it. In such circumstances, it was useful that "domestically," as Kissinger said, the Nixon Doctrine "supplied a coherent answer to the charges of overextension; even those advocating a more far-reaching retrenchment had to take seriously the sweep and implications of Nixon's declaration." Through the contrast between its own statements and the more ambitious rhetoric of its predecessors, the administration could both preempt the position of those calling for even more drastic change—John Kenneth Galbraith, for example, admitted that the doctrine was "a recognition of the reality of the limits of American power"— and convince the voters that new policies, more cautious and prudent than the ones they replaced, were now at work.[4]

THE NIXON DOCTRINE AND NATIONAL CLAIMS ABROAD

It was in this atmosphere that the new president undertook a round-the-world trip in the summer of 1969, proceeding westward over the Pacific to greet the Apollo 11 astronauts on their return from their lunar mission, then going on to the Philippines, Indonesia, Thailand (where his stay was interrupted by a brief visit to South Vietnam), India, Pakistan, Romania, and the United Kingdom. Between the site of the splashdown and the first foreign stop at Manila lay the island of Guam, where the presidential party scheduled a one-night layover, which gained unexpected significance when Nixon chose it as the opportunity to reveal to the reporters accompanying him the results of the private policy reassessments in which his administration had been engaged.

The revelations came in a press conference at which the president spoke for attribution but not direct quotation, held at the Top O' The Mar Offi-

4. John Mueller, *War, Presidents and Public Opinion* (New York, 1973), 54–56; Henry A. Kissinger, *White House Years* (Boston, 1979), 225; New York *Times*, September 22, 1970, Sec. 1, p. 30.

cers' Club on the evening of July 25. He opened the session with a statement on the importance of Asia to the United States; he identified China, North Korea, and North Vietnam as the main threats to peace in the area and argued that "the way to avoid becoming involved in another war in Asia is for the United States to continue to play a significant role." Nevertheless, frustration in the United States over the war and increasing Asian nationalism made American involvement in Asian affairs much more difficult than before. How were these two apparently opposing requirements to be reconciled? In a series of answers to journalists' questions, widely scattered through the press conference, Nixon outlined a policy he felt would be able to tread the required fine line.[5]

The policy was based on advice the president recalled he had received in 1964 from President Ayub Khan of Pakistan: "The role of the United States in Vietnam or the Philippines or Thailand or any of these countries which have internal subversion is to help them fight the war but not fight the war for them." Nixon called Ayub's counsel "a good general principle" and said he hoped to ground all American policy on it. This did not mean that other countries should be left entirely to fend for themselves. The president promised that the United States would keep its treaty commitments, specifically mentioning SEATO; he noted that Washington would continue to bear a responsibility for deterrence if a friendly state was threatened by a major power possessing nuclear weapons; and he added that "where one of our friends in Asia asks for advice or assistance, under proper circumstances, we will provide it." Nevertheless, there were limits to American capabilities, which meant that there had to be limits to American commitments: "Where we must draw the line is in becoming involved heavily with our own personnel, doing the job for them, rather than helping them do the job for themselves. . . . [I]f the United States just continues down the road of responding to requests for assistance, of assuming the primary responsibility for defending these countries when they have internal problems or external problems, they are never going to take care of themselves."

All too often in prior years, Nixon said, Ayub's message of restraint had been ignored by American officials convinced that no one could perform a mission as well as Americans. That attitude the president proposed to

5. The transcript of the press conference was later released for publication. It appears in *Public Papers of the Presidents of the United States: Richard M. Nixon, 1969* (Washington, D.C., 1971), 544–46.

change. If the internal or external security of an Asian state was endangered, then, except in the case of a nuclear threat, "the United States is going to encourage and has a right to expect that this problem will be increasingly handled by, and the responsibility for it taken by, the Asian nations themselves." Thus, the hallmarks of the new policy would be cooperation with restraint: "I want to be sure that our policies in the future, all over the world, . . . reduce American involvement." Greatly heightened caution about involving American troops in conflict overseas, continued participation through military and economic assistance to friendly states, increased reliance on those states to preserve in their regions a distribution of power favorable to their own (and American) interests: these were the guides to policy by which the president proposed to navigate the treacherous shoals of the post-Vietnam era.

Were Nixon's remarks intended to reveal the product of his administration's policy reassessments, a new and more limited catalog of American national interests? Given the president's penchant for dramatic, surprise announcements, it is possible that this was a carefully prepared signal. But the setting seems an unlikely one for an enunciation of the administration's basic foreign-policy doctrine. "To this day," Kissinger has contended, "I do not think that Nixon intended a major policy pronouncement in Guam; his original purpose had been to make some news because of the empty period produced by the [presidential party's] crossing of the international dateline" earlier in the day. The national security adviser has acknowledged that the general ideas contained in the remarks at the press conference had been a topic of frequent discussion between the president and himself, and that their tenor was similar to that of his own background briefing for the press prior to the trip; but Kissinger has gone on to say that Nixon took up the theme "quite to my surprise" and has speculated that the president was "perhaps carried away by the occasion." Even at the time, press reports indicated some confusion over how seriously Nixon intended the remarks to be taken, given "the peculiar way" in which they were made. "From all that can be gathered," one press summary was to put it, "there was no elaborate staff work in advance, no carefully prepared position paper such as normally precedes a major policy pronouncement. Rather, the President announced the policy in a discursive news conference on an island in the Pacific and under the noncommittal terms that his statements could not be quoted directly." Henry Brandon, in describing the way Nixon "somewhat accidentally set the tone and stated the broad objectives of his stewardship of foreign policy," asserted that the State Department "had neither a hand in drafting the statement nor advance knowledge of the President's intention to deliver it to the world," and that several days elapsed before the State Department received a transcript.[6]

Despite what might be considered an unpropitious setting, the president's reflections aroused unexpectedly widespread interest. As Kissinger recalled, "Nixon made more news than he bargained for" with comments that "were a sensation, dominating his conversations everywhere he went in Asia" and that "surprised [the president] at first by their impact." In response to questions he received from his hosts at each stop and from the press, Nixon repeatedly alluded to the emerging American policy in his public statements. At his arrival in Manila on July 26 he warned, "The United States will play its part and provide its fair share. But peace in Asia cannot come from the United States. It must come from Asia." Upon his departure from the Philippines the following day, he spoke of "a new period" in which all the states of Asia had acquired "the independence that comes with economic strength, with political stability, and also with the means insofar as any threat internally that may occur in those countries—the ability to handle those internal problems without outside assistance, except that kind of assistance which is limited to material support and which, of course, would therefore exclude the kind of support which would involve a commitment of manpower." Some confusion arose when, in his remarks at a welcoming ceremony in Bangkok, the president seemed to contradict his assertion at

6. Kissinger, *White House Years*, 223–24; John W. Finney, "Nixon: What Does His 'Asian Doctrine' Mean?," New York *Times*, January 11, 1970, Sec. 5, p. 3; Henry Brandon, *The Retreat of American Power* (New York, 1973), 79; Roscoe Drummond, "Nixon's Big Foreign Policy Shift," *Christian Science Monitor*, August 12, 1969, p. 16; New York *Times*, January 18, 1971, Sec. 1, p. 1. That the press contingent traveling with the president, while aware of the ongoing White House review of policy, was unprepared for Nixon to unveil a new strategy may be seen from a typical dispatch filed from Guam the very day of the press conference: "No one expects startling announcements or policy departures during what will be essentially a goodwill and fact-finding trip. White House foreign-policy advisers, headed by Henry Kissinger, are making a broad study of American objectives overseas—with sweeping implications for future economic, military and political policies. But this study is still in the embryo stage, which means the present Nixon trip won't see any dramatic new ideas unveiled" ("Nixon's Journey: President Will Stress More Limited U.S. Role in Asia after Vietnam," *Wall Street Journal*, July 25, 1969, p. 1).

Guam that internal security would henceforth be treated as a local responsibility; he stated that as part of its SEATO obligations, the United States would "stand proudly with Thailand against those who might threaten it from abroad or from within." But a second statement issued later the same day by the presidential party reaffirmed the new policy: "Our determination to honor our commitments is fully consistent with our conviction that the nations of Asia can and must increasingly shoulder the responsibility for achieving peace and progress in the area. The challenge to our wisdom is to support the Asian countries' efforts to defend and develop themselves, without attempting to take from them the responsibilities which should be theirs. For if domination by the aggressor can destroy the freedom of a nation, too much dependence on a protector can eventually erode its dignity." Nixon reiterated in New Delhi that he and his administration "firmly believe that Asian problems must be resolved by the people of Asia [but that] we stand ready to help," and stated in Lahore that, because "Asian hands must shape the Asian future," foreign assistance had to "encourage self-reliance, not dependence."[7]

Meanwhile, press reports of the flurry overseas were arousing interest at home. Those reading newspaper accounts of the president's trip learned for the first time of a policy departure described as a "radical change," a "clear break with the past," a "new fully developed, clearcut policy which already is being put to the test," a "thoroughly new, firm, and comprehensive policy in hand," a "supple and adaptable program for applying basic concepts to events as they develop," a "historic assertion of political and civilian values over the great and often unchecked power that the American military establishment has accumulated since World War II," and "the articulation of a major shift in official American policy toward Asia." The White House press corps began a campaign—ultimately successful—to have the transcript of the Guam session released for direct quotation. Senator Mike Mansfield (Democrat, Montana), the majority leader, took the floor on July 28 to call his colleagues' attention to reports of the trip and to praise the president for "moving with caution and consideration but also with a sense of reality based on the changes which have occurred on the globe" toward "a sound long-range policy."[8]

7. See *Public Papers: Nixon, 1969*, 557–615 *passim*.
8. Saville R. Davis, "U.S. Asia Policy 'Supple, Adaptable,'" *Christian Science Monitor*,

In the face of this reception—generally favorable, but uncertain about where any new policy was meant to lead—the administration found it necessary, immediately upon the president's return on August 3, to give more substance to what was rapidly being transformed from a topic of private conversations with his national security adviser into the hallmark of American foreign policy, under the sobriquet "the Nixon Doctrine."[9] One of the first steps in this effort was a presidential meeting with a bipartisan group of congressional leaders on the morning of August 4; Senator Hugh Scott (Republican, Pennsylvania) summarized on the Senate floor the following day his understanding of the tenets of the doctrine as they then stood:

> The President has made clear that the new policy of the United States . . . is not to undertake intervention in the case of internal aggression or revolt within Asian countries. I think I should add that we understood the President to make the point quite clear that he was referring to intervention through U.S. military personnel.
>
> The President has made clear . . . that the United States intends to keep its commitments. But he has also made clear that the United States does not intend to expand those commitments to involve us in future confrontations with nonnuclear powers, such as that which occurred in Vietnam.

Much of this was, as Kissinger later admitted, already "the conventional wisdom." But the public announcement that Washington would no longer intervene in cases of internal subversion in Asia was new, and the briefing was apparently well received by the members of Congress who heard it, so that Senator Mansfield could "congratulate the President for this bold move,

---

July 29, 1969, p. 1; New York *Times*, July 28, 1969, Sec. 1, p. 10; *Congressional Record*, 91st Cong., 1st Sess., Vol. 115, p. 20958.

9. Perhaps not surprisingly, given their inception, the new foreign-policy principles enunciated on the president's tour entered the public domain under a variety of labels, including the "Guam Doctrine," the "Asian Doctrine," the "Pacific Doctrine," and the "Low-Profile Doctrine." Kissinger has recalled that "a considerable amount of [the president's] time was spent making sure that [these initial labels were] rapidly supplanted in the journalistic lexicon by a more impressive phrase commemorating the person rather than the place"—thus the "Nixon Doctrine" (*White House Years*, 224). See also *House Documents*, 91st Cong., 2nd Sess., No. 258, pp. 71–72.

this good move, this realistic move," and Senator George Aiken (Republican, Vermont) could commend the doctrine as "probably the most significant political development of this generation" and as something "which can be of inestimable value to the whole world in coming generations." [10]

The doctrine that drew these accolades remained imprecise, not least in the minds of Nixon, Kissinger, and the handful of senior aides on the NSC staff who were helping the president and the national security adviser formulate a set of principles that could keep up with the expectations that were being generated. A few things were clear: one was that the United States was pruning the list of countries where it might claim the right to introduce its ground forces to prevent developments it opposed. This could mean that Washington would henceforth regard fewer areas as "vital" interests, for the defense of which direct military action was warranted. Alternatively, it could mean that existing interests remained as important to American security, but that the United States would now employ different means for their protection as it turned over an increasing share of the responsibility for military action to the threatened country itself or to regional groupings of states. Yet again, the president's words could mean that while Washington would reduce its role in Asian security issues generally, it would vary its restraint according to the type of confrontation, maintaining its deterrent role unchanged in cases of overt threats by nuclear powers, restricting itself to support with naval and air forces in cases of conventional attack, and being willing to consider only material aid in cases of internal subversion or armed challenge from domestic opponents. This third interpretation would result in a lowered American profile in promising to respond to a narrower range of provocations, rather than in a shortened roster of locales. It seemed that the United States was trimming its list of asserted interests, but in what way was not yet known.

Two (or more) interpretations of the doctrine

Two further visitors to Asia in late 1969 undertook to clothe with specific applications the precepts announced thus far. Each clarified this narrowing

10. *Congressional Record*, 91st Cong., 1st Sess., No. 115, pp. 22271–72; Kissinger, *White House Years*, 225; New York *Times*, August 5, 1969, Sec. 1, p. 1.

of national interests, but in a fashion inconsistent with the other. The first was Senator Mansfield. Several months before, the president had asked the senator to undertake a journey to Cambodia in connection with the restoration of diplomatic relations with that country. On returning from his own trip, Nixon renewed the request and in addition asked Mansfield to visit other countries to gather reactions to the new doctrine. The senator agreed and left Washington on August 13 for a two-week tour of the Philippines, Indonesia, Burma, Cambodia, Laos, Okinawa, and Japan. Upon his return, he discussed his findings with the president at San Clemente and delivered to him a confidential report. Mansfield transmitted a second, public report to the Senate Foreign Relations Committee, of which he was a member, on September 13.

The Mansfield report, which was much the fullest definition of the new American role that had been made publicly available thus far, began with the latest in the shifting series of basic concepts of the Nixon Doctrine:

1. The United States will maintain its treaty commitments, but it is anticipated that Asian nations will be able to handle their own defense problems, perhaps with some outside material assistance but without outside manpower. Nuclear threats are another matter, and such threats will continue to be checked by counterpoised nuclear capacity.

2. As a Pacific power, the United States will not turn its back on nations of the Western Pacific and Asia; the countries of that region will not be denied a concerned and understanding ear in this Nation.

3. The United States will avoid the creation of situations in which there is such great dependence on us that, inevitably, we become enmeshed in what are essentially Asian problems and conflicts.

4. To the extent that material assistance may be forthcoming from the United States, more emphasis will be placed on economic help and less on military assistance.

5. The future role of the United States will continue to be significant in the affairs of Asia. It will be enacted, however, largely in the economic realm and on the basis of multilateral cooperation.

6. The United States will look with favor on multilateral

political, economic, and security arrangements among the Asian nations and, where appropriate, will assist in efforts which may be undertaken thereunder.

The report took up in turn each of the Asian countries on the senator's itinerary, giving an analysis of those aspects of its relations with Washington that seemed to come within the purview of the new policy. In general, it found a degree of "uncertainty as to what the new doctrine will mean in specific terms." The senator closed with three further recommendations for reducing uncertainty:

1. A contraction of bilateral U.S. aid efforts and a shift to expanding U.S. participation in multilateral efforts in the economic development of the region.
2. A rigid and immediate curb on military aid and no deepening of our direct military involvement with any Asian government, to be followed by a reexamination of longstanding treaty commitments and their organizational substructures, notably SEATO.
3. Official encouragement and support of commercial, cultural, technical, and all other forms of nonmilitary interchange on a mutual basis, scaled to the level of the capacity and the clearly expressed desires of the Asian nations.[11]

Despite the Mansfield report's bipartisan endorsement of the Nixon Doctrine, there is room for doubt that it was exactly what the administration would have wished. Policy differences between the president and the majority leader were too sharp to make it easy for any fair and unambiguous statement to represent the views of both. Nixon has said that at the leadership breakfast meeting on August 4, Mansfield "articulated [the] misunderstanding" that the doctrine signaled "a new policy that would lead to total American withdrawal from Asia and from other parts of the world as well;" the president "emphasized to him . . . that the Nixon Doctrine was not a formula for getting America *out* of Asia, but one that provided the only sound basis for America's staying *in* and continuing to play a respon-

11. Senate Committee on Foreign Relations, *Perspective on Asia: The New U.S. Doctrine and Southeast Asia* (1969) (hereinafter cited as Senate report, *Perspective on Asia*).

sible role in helping the non-communist nations and neutrals as well as our allies to defend their independence." [12] Nixon presumably retained this view when he and Mansfield met at the Western White House on August 27 before the release of the report, but points of divergence still appeared.

Thus it was that Vice-President Spiro Agnew was dispatched on behalf of the administration on December 26 for a three-week trip to Asian countries from the Philippines to Afghanistan, "prepared," in the president's words at a news briefing on the trip, "to talk to the leaders there with regard to the Nixon Doctrine." His mission appeared to be one of allaying fears, since at most stops he stressed continued American involvement—"the positive side" of administration policies—rather than limited American disengagement. In general, his message was that "the United States is not going to turn its back on Asia," and he talked of increased, not decreased, American aid to states in the region. He told Generalissimo Chiang Kai-Shek in Taipei that "we are pledged to stand firm to commitments to our allies." Speaking to reporters traveling with the vice-presidential party in Bangkok, he assessed his discussions with foreign leaders, saying, "They're frightened and they want reassurances that the American presence will continue," and adding that he had provided such assurances. (On the one occasion on which he stressed the "lowered profile" aspect of the doctrine—his stop in South Korea, where he told his hosts that the pulling out of twenty thousand American troops then under discussion between Seoul and Washington was only "the first step" toward withdrawal of all American ground forces there—his remarks were immediately disavowed by the White House.) Despite what some observers saw as contradictions between the vice-president's remarks at different stops and between Agnew's rhetoric and the administration's actions, he did seem to have achieved at least partial success in assuaging Asian apprehensions by convincing governments in the area that the United States would not embark on a precipitate withdrawal. [13]

Although Mansfield and Agnew were discussing the same "doctrine," they attached significantly different meanings to it and expected varying, not to say contradictory, policies to flow from it. Presumably, the president's

12. Richard M. Nixon, *RN: The Memoirs of Richard Nixon* (New York, 1978), 395.
13. *Public Papers: Nixon, 1969*, 1042; James M. Naughton, "Agnew: A Roving Envoy Comes on Strong," New York *Times*, January 11, 1970, Sec. 5, p. 3; Flora Lewis, "The Nixon Doctrine," *Atlantic*, CCXXVI (November, 1970), 6–16; Washington *Post*, January 3, 1970, p. 1, January 4, 1970, p. 19.

own interpretation would be authoritative, and Nixon devoted part of the autumn to filling in the outlines he had drawn in his remarks on Guam. He wished to establish an image of consistency, both between the new doctrine and the administration's domestic plans and between the doctrine's initial application to Asia and what the United States was trying to accomplish elsewhere around the world. As part of the first effort, Nixon began to draw parallels between the Nixon Doctrine and his "New Federalism," saying that both were intended to relieve the federal government of excessive commitments it had taken on in prior years, returning responsibilities to those best able to deal with problems locally, whether the states at home or allied countries abroad. In both cases Washington had preempted local initiative, created an expensive and burdensome bureaucracy, and ultimately failed to achieve its goals; in both cases, the proper corrective lay in a devolution of authority, coupled with continued aid from Washington (at least over a transitional period) to allow its newly reinvigorated recipients to take up the reins.[14]

The president also tried to achieve consistency by broadening the scope of the Nixon Doctrine beyond the region where it was announced. In his talks on August 8 with West German Chancellor Kurt Georg Kiesinger, Nixon indicated that his advocacy of greater self-reliance was meant for Europe as well as for Asia, though he would continue to oppose congressional moves to reduce the American troop presence in Europe unilaterally. His speech to the Inter American Press Association on October 31 dwelt on the same theme of transferring security responsibilities, this time to the countries of Latin America. Admitting that in the United States "we have sometimes imagined that we knew what was best for everyone else and that we could and should make it happen," Nixon called for "a more mature partnership" in which "the United States lectures less and listens more." Because "in each part of the world we can have lasting peace and progress only if the nations directly concerned take the lead themselves in achieving it," the most desirable pattern for future inter-American relations would be "U.S. support for Latin American initiatives." The expansion of the Nixon Doctrine's application reached its logical conclusion in November when, after a meeting with the president, Senator James B. Pearson (Republican, Kansas) announced that the doctrine was meant to extend to the world at

14. *Public Papers: Nixon, 1969,* 696–97, 700; James Reston, "Washington: The Turning of the Tide," New York *Times,* August 6, 1969, Sec. 1, p. 38; Max Frankel, "The Presidency: Nixon Tackles a Formidable Agenda," New York *Times,* August 10, 1969, Sec. 4, p. 1.

large. This interpretation was later supported by the vice-president, who remarked, as he left for his year-end tour of Asia, "I would think, as time goes on, the President would extend the doctrine to make it a worldwide posture."[15]

But when Nixon made the first comprehensive statement of his doctrine, it was in regard not to the world at large, but to the region of Asia, and within Asia to Vietnam. His reference to it came in the course of his November 3 "silent majority" address to the nation, in which he attempted to rally popular support for his policies in Southeast Asia. The scope of application thus came full circle, to the pressing problem of the war that had prompted the country's reexamination of its role in the beginning. By identifying the Nixon Doctrine with the progress of Vietnamization of the war, the president suggested that the new doctrine was simply an enlarged version of the American policy of turning the fighting of the war over to South Vietnamese troops financed and equipped by the United States. Or was the country's Vietnam policy only a specific application of the broader retrenchment promised in the doctrine? Nixon said that Vietnamization was "in line with a major shift in U.S. foreign policy" that he had announced on Guam, and he described the doctrine as "a policy which not only will help end the war in Vietnam, but which is an essential element of our program to prevent future Vietnams."

Calling Americans "a do-it-yourself" and "an impatient" people, the president said these traits had made Washington too willing to intervene itself instead of allowing problems to be handled by local governments, and cited the disproportionate American contribution to the wars in both Korea and Vietnam. A wiser course, he contended, would be the recognition that "the defense of freedom is everybody's business—not just America's business[—and is] particularly the responsibility of the people whose freedom is threatened." In accordance with this alternative, Nixon said that he had "laid down in Guam three principles as guidelines for future American policy toward Asia":

—First, the United States will keep all of its treaty commitments.
—Second, we shall provide a shield if a nuclear power threatens the

15. *Public Papers: Nixon, 1969*, 893–901; Richard Halloran, "Nixon Widens Aim on Self-Reliance," New York *Times*, August 9, 1969, Sec. 1, p. 5; New York *Times*, January 11, 1970, Sec. 5, p. 3, December 27, 1969, Sec. 1, p. 2.

freedom of a nation allied with us or of a nation whose survival we consider vital to our security.

—Third, in cases involving other types of aggression, we shall furnish military and economic assistance when requested in accordance with our treaty commitments. But we shall look to the nation directly threatened to assume the primary responsibility of providing the manpower for its defense.[16]

Interests as the connecting thread

Much of the debate going on in the fall of 1969 revolved around differences over the extent to which the United States ought to draw down its asserted interests, and the principles that described the proper stopping point. What claims did the country need to make on the states-system in the altered circumstances of the 1970s? National interests became a touchstone of administration diplomacy.

It made a difference whether the United States was to consider itself an "Asian power" (as the president often stated) or a "Pacific power" (as Mansfield preferred), because the former phrase implied more extended American claims to be taken into account on questions involving the Asian mainland. The senator, described by some as the coauthor of the doctrine, said that it called "for the sharp restriction of American military involvement in Asia . . . where our national interests are peripheral at most." This was the one idea of the most advantageous limit to American claims. Secretary of State William Rogers rejoined, "I don't think that we are overcommitted. . . . I think that our commitments are sound commitments [that] should be lived up to[, presumably by means including military involvement, and that] have contributed to the stability of the area." This was another. Nixon cited his policy of Vietnamization as an ongoing, successful application of the doctrine and decried immediate unilateral American withdrawal from the war as mistaken and wrong. Mansfield, asserting that he "agree[d] with [the president] 100 percent," argued that the "doctrine has not yet been applied anywhere on the [Asian] mainland" and that "the sooner it is applied by this Government in Vietnam [through publicly setting a date certain for the

16. *Public Papers: Nixon, 1969*, 901–909.

withdrawal of American forces] and throughout the Southeast Asia area, . . . the better it will be for this Nation and for all concerned." The senator insisted that the doctrine entailed reducing foreign assistance, and military assistance in particular, to countries where Washington was searching for a more modest role, and the president's initial comments on Guam seemed to bear him out. But Agnew implied that increased aid would be forthcoming, Nixon's later remarks took this side, and other observers believed that these states would not be able to step into the breach created by the recession of American power unless they were provided with more material and financial assistance. No one in the administration was saying, with Mansfield, that the doctrine meant that "the only way we would ever become involved again [in a land war in Asia] would be when our security was at stake and a nuclear showdown appeared to be in the offing. In other words, when there was no possible choice." [17] Until debates over these issues were resolved with public and private guidance from the White House, implementation of the doctrine would prove difficult. What interests should the United States claim? What were the legitimate interests of the other states involved?

That the debate over foreign policy should be couched so largely in terms of interests was itself an achievement for Nixon and Kissinger. National interests had long been a subject of Kissinger's academic work. [18] Dean Rusk, whose active public career had spanned the years of containment, had more than once been quoted as saying, "Other nations have interests, but the United States has responsibilities." In their 1970 foreign policy report, the president and his national security adviser turned this formulation on its head: "It is misleading . . . to pose the fundamental question so largely in terms of commitments. Our objective, in the first instance, is to support our *interests* over the long run with a sound foreign policy. The more that policy is based on a realistic assessment of ours and others' interests, the more

17. *Congressional Record*, 91st Cong., 1st Sess., No. 115, pp. 32782, 33043; U.S. Department of State, *Bulletin*, LXI (December 22, 1969), 580; Joint Economic Committee, *Economic Issues in Military Assistance* (1971) (hereinafter cited as Joint Economic Committee hearings, *Economic Issues*); "Building the Nixon Doctrine," *Christian Science Monitor*, September 16, 1970, p. 16; New York *Times*, January 5, 1970, p. 3; Senate report, *Perspective on Asia*, 4–5; Jerome K. Holloway, "East Asia and the Guam Doctrine," *Foreign Service Journal*, XLVII (November, 1970), 42; Wayne Wilcox, "Implications of a Foreign Policy of Restraint," *Foreign Service Journal*, XLVII (November, 1970), 37–38.

18. See, for example, Kissinger's article "The White Revolutionary: Reflections on Bismarck," *Daedalus*, XCVII (Summer, 1968), 888–924.

no
atmospherics ✓
or
personal relations

effective our role in the world can be." In their view, a diplomacy that kept interests uppermost would avoid the fascination with personal relations among leaders and "atmospherics" that Kissinger so much distrusted. It would also avoid the lack of differentiation that had made containment unworkably undiscriminating and trapped the country in the protracted struggle in Vietnam that Nixon wanted to escape. "Our objective was to purge our foreign policy of all sentimentality," the national security adviser stated afterwards. "Nixon and I wanted to found American foreign policy on a sober perception of permanent national interest, rather than on fluctuating emotions that in the past had led us to excesses of both intervention and abdication." An attitude toward the world based on interests would be cool, stable, and calculable; the statesmen that both men most admired had, they believed, made policy in this realistic fashion.[19]

Interests could now come to the forefront, first, because of the relative decline of American power. When the country had been at the height of its influence, in comparison to both allies and adversaries, it had had the luxury of asserting claims that sprang from principle (though critics said the proper term was *ideology*). Now that its margin of security was reduced, the United States had to calculate more carefully where its important material and strategic interests lay and define its commitments accordingly. Second, as the Soviet Union and China abandoned their stance of revolutionary powers, they would increasingly transact international business in the currency of interests, making, opposing, and allowing claims within the broad framework of a generally accepted system. The decline of tensions in this sort of interstate order would permit the United States to make the further reductions in its overseas obligations that the Nixon Doctrine foresaw.[20]

THE PRESIDENT'S FOREIGN POLICY REPORT

The start of 1970 gave the president three opportunities to address Congress, and through it the public, on the meaning and the benefits of his

19. Kissinger, "Central Issues of American Foreign Policy," in *Agenda for the Nation,* ed. Gordon, 610; Paul Seabury, "The Revolt Against Obligation," in *New Directions in U.S. Foreign Policy—A Symposium,* by Robert Strausz-Hupe *et al.,* Foreign Policy Association, no. 193 (February, 1969), 52–53; Kissinger, *White House Years,* 191, 914, 929; Richard M. Nixon, *Leaders* (New York, 1982).

20. *Cf.* Stephen D. Krasner, *Defending the National Interest: Raw Materials Investments and U.S. Foreign Policy* (Princeton, 1978), 329–47.

policy departure. The first two came in customary presidential messages to Congress—his State of the Union address and the message accompanying his proposed budget for the 1971 fiscal year. Neither discussed the Nixon Doctrine or indeed any aspect of foreign affairs at length, because an additional message dealing exclusively with international relations was to appear: the "First Annual Report to the Congress on United States Foreign Policy for the 1970's," or, as it and its three successors in 1971, 1972, and 1973 perhaps inevitably came to be called, the State of the World message. This separate presidential report reflected both Nixon's own interest in foreign affairs and Kissinger's bureaucratic skill in removing the message from the State Department—where the idea had been conceived and the initial work done—and making it a more purely presidential document. It also represented a chance to define with more rigor and emphasize with more force the place of the Nixon Doctrine in American foreign policy.

In the State of the Union message, delivered on January 22, Nixon promised that the administration would discuss in detail its foreign policy in a later report on that subject, saying at this time he would only "describe the directions" of American diplomacy. The president noted that he and his subordinates had "based our policies on an evaluation of the world as it is, not as it was 25 years ago at the conclusion of World War II," and called the contrast between 1945, when the United States needed to assume most of the burden for defense and development in an otherwise ruined world, and 1970, when the United States needed to share that burden with its rejuvenated allies and the newly confident younger nations of the less developed world, "the basis of the doctrine I announced at Guam." He then briefly sketched the conclusions for American foreign policy to be drawn from these changed conditions:

> Neither the defense nor the development of other nations can be exclusively or primarily an American undertaking.
> The nations of each part of the world should assume the primary responsibility for their own well-being; and they themselves should determine the terms of that well-being.
> We shall be faithful to our treaty commitments, but we shall reduce our involvement and our presence in other nations' affairs.

The president also took up the challenge of his critics, saying, "To insist that other nations play a role is not a retreat from responsibility; it is a sharing of responsibility. The result of this new policy has been not to weaken our alliances, but to give them new life, new strength, a new sense of common purpose." He illustrated his case with assertions about specific regions, noting that American relations with Western Europe were "strong and healthy," that Americans were now acting in Latin America "as partners rather than patrons," and that "the new partnership concept has been welcomed in Asia."[21]

What this sharing of responsibility meant to the United States' own expenditures could be seen in a February 2 budget message proposing to spend $6.3 billion less on defense in 1971 than had been estimated by the Johnson administration. An even more abbreviated mention of foreign policy than had been contained in the State of the Union message credited the Nixon Doctrine with the savings: "The strategy of this Administration, as I stated at Guam, is based on the expectation that our allies will shoulder substantial responsibility for their own defense. With this posture, we can safely meet our defense requirements with fewer resources."[22]

The minimal treatment given the doctrine in the two earlier messages left the field open for its fullest explication in the foreign policy message, which was transmitted to Congress and released to the public on February 18. A bulky document—it was issued by the White House as a 160-page booklet—it reflected, as the president stated in a news briefing on February 16, "my best view at this time of where we are and where we ought to go." It contended that the surest road to lasting peace lay through American policies based on three basic principles: partnership, strength, and a willingness to negotiate. The Nixon Doctrine was the administration's means of approaching the first of these principles; with it, the president hoped to remold the nation's partnership with its allies in ways that would receive lasting domestic support.

Such a redefinition, in the administration's eyes, required a shifting of burdens to others now capable of bearing them, and this theme of a new and more equitable division of labor ran through most of the report's six sections, each of which discussed a different region of the world. With regard to Western Europe, Nixon called for "a more balanced association and a more genuine partnership" in which "the balance of burdens and respon-

21. *Public Papers: Nixon, 1970*, 8–16.
22. *Ibid.*, 60.

sibilities [was to be] gradually . . . adjusted, to reflect the economic and political realities of European progress." In Latin America, he saw the need for the United States to exhibit a less "directive and tutorial style." While offering to aid African countries threatened by outside forces—though only after "consulting our own interests"—the report called attention to the "lesson of the 1960's . . . that African defense against subversion, like African development, must be borne most directly by Africans rather than by outsiders."[23]

The doctrine received its fullest treatment in the section dealing with the region where it had first been announced—Asia. Nixon repeated the doctrine's three key elements as he had outlined them in his speech of November 3—maintenance of all treaty commitments, a shield offered to countries threatened by a nuclear power, and the offer of military and economic assistance but no American troops to states facing other types of aggression. He pointed to the political progress and economic development that allowed Washington to reduce its presence in the area, and said that "the fostering of self-reliance is the new purpose and direction of American involvement in Asia." But he also spoke of his determination that the United States "remain involved in Asia. . . . We have learned that peace for us is much less likely if there is no peace in Asia." The proper American response, therefore, was not simple withdrawal, but a different kind of involvement, one that required local governments to assume more of the costs of their own defense and development and encouraged them to make more use of their own creativity and resourcefulness: "While we will maintain our interests in Asia and the commitments that flow from them, the changes taking place in that region enable us to change the character of our involvement. The responsibilities once borne by the United States at such great cost can now be shared. America *can* be effective in helping the peoples of Asia harness the forces of change to peaceful progress, and in supporting them as they defend themselves from those who would subvert this process and fling Asia again into conflict."

Such help and support was "not only a more effective use of common resources, but also an American policy which can best be sustained over the long run." But the general guideline the doctrine provided did not—could

23. *Ibid.*, 116–90. Subsequent quotations from Nixon's 1970 foreign policy message also *ibid.*

not—supply detailed responses to specific events; its effectiveness was hostage to the wisdom of any succeeding administration that chose to apply it. Moreover, it posed again what had been the dilemma all along—the level of American activity, in this region and others. If, as the administration and its critics agreed, the United States had been doing too much, then how much was enough? The report could say only that the answer lay in "a careful balance" or "a basic and delicate choice." If Washington continued on the course of active, intimate involvement, "we promote dependence rather than independence" and "risk stifling the local contribution which is the key to our long-run commitment to Asia." If, on the other hand, the United States' profile was so low that allied and friendly nations could neither obtain the assistance they needed to protect themselves nor rely on American pledges, "they may lose the necessary will to conduct their own self-defense or become disheartened about prospects of development," and should the threat turn out "to have been more serious that we had judged, we will only have created still more dangerous choices."

Questions on these issues were to dog the Nixon Doctrine all its days. Because the first foreign policy report laid out for Americans and for other countries all the major arguments for the claims that the administration thought the United States should make in the society of states, however, it can be taken as the case for the interests asserted under the doctrine. In the eyes of a number of opponents, it was a case undermined by the doctrine's lack of clarity. Some charged that it was nothing more than a "pastiche" or a bit of "muddy rhetoric." One was prompted to adopt a musical metaphor: "The Doctrine is little more than a political accordian [*sic*]; the administration's traveling minstrels, playing by ear, stretch it out or squeeze it tight depending on their particular audience. Invasion of Cambodia? *Rapprochement* with China? The Nixon Doctrine in action." The vice-president himself noted on his Asian trip, "I don't know how specific any doctrine can be," and there were indications in the press that the lack of clarity was a deliberate tactic to "keep options open."[24]

24. John Dower, "Asia and the Nixon Doctrine: The New Face of Empire," in *Open Secret: The Kissinger-Nixon Doctrine in Asia (Why We Are Never Leaving)*, ed. Virginia Brodine and Mark Selden (New York, 1972), 129, 135; George W. Ball, *Diplomacy for a Crowded World: An American Foreign Policy* (Boston, 1976), 9; New York *Times*, January 11, 1970, Sec. 5, p. 3, January 14, 1970, Sec. 1, p. 8. For a more sympathetic appraisal of the doctrine's lack of clarity, see Thomas P. Thornton, "The Nixon Doctrine and Beyond," *Foreign Service*

A desire for national freedom of action may well have been the driving force behind the Nixon Doctrine, for what seemed most necessary to Nixon and Kissinger was a reduction not in interests but in commitments. As we have seen, they sharply distinguished between the two. Dean Acheson, speaking in the midst of the Korean War, had argued that the one followed from the other in logic, as it ought to do in policy: "What we must do is to be conscious of our national interests. A commitment is a national vital interest of which we have become conscious and for which we have made provision, but we may have national interests, which are just as valid, of which we have not become conscious and for which we have not made provision—about which we should immediately become conscious and about which we should immediately make provision." Acheson granted, "I have no doubt there is a point beyond which the United States cannot go [in turning interests into commitments through the pledge of American power], but I am equally sure that we are not anywhere near that point." By contrast, Nixon and Kissinger suspected the country had passed that point. "We will view new commitments in the light of a careful assessment of our own national interests and those of other countries, of the specific threats to those interests, and of our capacity to counter those threats at an acceptable risk and cost," Nixon warned in his foreign policy report, with the clear implication that this threefold test would be highly difficult to meet. In the more straitened circumstances of the 1970s, he and his aide saw a sharper dividing line between prudent interests and expansive commitments. "We are not involved in the world because we have commitments; we have commitments because we are involved," they insisted in the foreign policy report. "Our interests must shape our commitments, rather than the other way around."[25] The burden from which the United States needed relief was to be found not so much in its claims on the society of states as in its promises to other members of that society.

The president and the national security adviser recognized that as it drew down its forces abroad, Washington would have to accommodate it-

---

Journal, XLVII (November, 1970), 19–21; for a balanced and comprehensive survey and critique of the Nixon Doctrine, see Cecil V. Crabb, Jr., *The Doctrines of American Foreign Policy: Their Meaning, Role, and Future* (Baton Rouge, 1982), 278–324.

25. U.S. Department of State, *Bulletin*, XXV (July 23, 1951), 126; *Public Papers: Nixon, 1970*, 119.

self to exercising less influence over the policies of other states and the outcomes of international disputes: in that sense, they were willing to accept a contraction of American interests. While their retreat would be less rapid and less complete than the withdrawal urged by Mansfield, they were reconciled to a world in which the United States would have to concentrate its energies in a smaller compass than had been the case for a generation.

But there were bounds to this process of self-limitation. The list of interests important to the United States was dictated in part by the thinking of the country and its leaders, but also by the exigencies of the international environment, and in particular by the competition for power with the Soviets. As Nixon would later put it, "Under the Nixon Doctrine we should certainly do as much for those who are fighting to defend their independence as the Soviet Union does for those who are attempting to destroy it." The relationship between Washington and Moscow remained an adversarial one, and in some regions, such as the Middle East, the increasing reach of Soviet military power was a more serious threat to American interests than it had been in the 1950s and 1960s.[26]

The most important change under the doctrine, therefore, was not in the number of interests to be asserted but in the manner in which they would be protected. Considerably reduced capabilities and readiness to employ them; modestly pruned objectives: this was the combination that led some to charge that the administration was recklessly unbalancing means and ends. Nixon and Kissinger proposed to square the circle by shifting much of the burden to others: "The United States will participate in the defense and development of allies and friends, but . . . America cannot—and will not—conceive *all* the plans, design *all* the programs, execute *all* the decisions and undertake *all* the defense of the free nations of the world. We will help where it makes a real difference and is considered in our interest." Countries in areas Washington considered to be of interest would be expected to defend themselves, led by regional alliances and relatively strong American surrogate states, supplied materially by the United States but strengthened psychologically by their own sense of nationalism, which would be bolstered by a less obtrusive role for their great-power patron. These steps were all sanctioned by the doctrine; together, they amounted to what the secretary of defense, Melvin Laird, called "a process of shifting

26. Richard M. Nixon, *The Real War* (New York, 1980), 123.

from direct to indirect means for defending American and allied interests (quite a different process, incidentally, from complete withdrawal)." For those skeptical that small states could fill the gap left by the end of direct American involvement, Nixon and Kissinger pointed to detente, which was closely linked to the doctrine. Bringing the great Communist powers to believe that they had more to gain from pursuing interests within the present international order than from seeking to overturn the system out of ideological compulsion, the United States could hope that the challenge posed by their attempts to expand their influence would be reduced enough not to be beyond the capacity of their intended targets to meet.[27]

A policy that depended so heavily on other states either to contain a common adversary or to contain themselves had to recognize that they would press their own interests, to which the United States would have to accommodate itself, at least to some extent. In the case of friendly states being asked to assume more of the burden of defense, the counterclaims were likely to be for a measured pace of American withdrawal to give them time to adjust, for a residual American presence, and for increased American material and financial assistance. Yasuhiro Nakasone, the director general of the Japanese Defense Agency, said in Washington that he hoped for "a form of soft landing" for the countries of Asia, and the application of the doctrine in other regions provoked similar reactions. As for rivals and foes, Washington would be willing to bargain over their interests and to pay less attention to the ideological formulas their leaders espoused: "It will be the policy of the United States . . . not to employ negotiations as a forum for cold-war invective, or ideological debate. We will regard our Communist adversaries first and foremost as nations pursuing their own interests as *they* perceive these interests, just as we follow our own interests as we see them. We will judge them by their actions as we expect to be judged by our own.

27. Earl C. Ravenal, "The Nixon Doctrine and Our Asian Commitments," *Foreign Affairs*, XLIX (July, 1971), 201–217; Ravenal, *Large-Scale Foreign Policy Change: The Nixon Doctrine as History and Portent* (Berkeley, 1989), No. 35 of Institute of International Studies, *Policy Papers in International Affairs*, Joint Economic Committee hearings, *Economic Issues; Public Papers: Nixon, 1970*, 141; Melvin R. Laird, "The Nixon Doctrine: From Potential Despair to New Opportunities," in Laird *et al., The Nixon Doctrine* (Washington, D.C., 1972), 12; Robert S. Litwak, *Detente and the Nixon Doctrine: American Foreign Policy and the Pursuit of Stability, 1969–1976* (Cambridge, Mass., 1984); Robert W. Tucker, "The American Outlook: Change and Continuity," in *Retreat from Empire? The First Nixon Administration*, ed. Robert E. Osgood (Baltimore, 1973), 43–44.

Specific agreements, and the structure of peace they help build, will come from a realistic accommodation of conflicting interests." [28]

State interests provided a rough sort of equality in Washington's relations with all countries. With the Soviet Union, the United States would work toward an accommodation of interests, but it would remain unimpressed by any transitory warming of the climate produced by the "Spirit of" whatever location was chosen as the site of a summit. It would allow the Western allies to be the best judges of their own interests and would refrain from the faintly self-righteous pronouncements that had so grated on them in the past, but it would no longer place alliance interests above American national interests. In both instances, relations would be correct but cool, constrained neither by the rivalry of old ideological enmities nor by the sentiments of old partnerships. In his doctrine, Nixon sought to set the United States entirely at liberty to act as it saw fit, unencumbered by the diplomatic alignments of the past, guided only by its interests as it saw them. [29]

In addition to the question of *how* American interests were to be protected, the doctrine spoke to the issue of *where* interests would be fought for, even by United States troops. For all the assertions that combatting internal subversion would henceforth be a local responsibility, a close examination of the administration's foreign-policy pronouncements suggested that the introduction of American ground forces would not depend on the type of triggering action by an opponent. Although the term *aggression* was often used, it did not seem to be a juridically defined concept whose occurrence would guarantee American involvement and whose absence would forestall such involvement. Likewise, the dividing line was not between places where treaty commitments applied and places where they did not. Some controversy had arisen over the second of the administration's frequently cited three principles explaining the doctrine, concerning just this

28. "Nixon Doctrine: Questions About U.S. Policy for Asia," *Congressional Quarterly Weekly Report*, XXIX (February 12, 1971), 383–86; *Public Papers: Nixon, 1970*, 179.

29. Anthony Hartley, *American Foreign Policy in the Nixon Era*, Adelphi Paper no. 110 (London, 1975); Werner Kaltefleiter, "Europe and the Nixon Doctrine: A German Point of View," *Orbis*, XVII (Spring, 1973), 75–94; Walter F. Hahn, "The Nixon Doctrine: Design and Dilemmas," *Orbis*, XVI (Summer, 1972), 361–76; "Mr. Nixon's Philosophy of Foreign Policy," *Round Table*, CCXLVIII (October, 1972), 403–10; *European Security and the Nixon Doctrine*, International Security Series, I (Medford, Mass., 1972); Franz Schurmann, *The Foreign Politics of Richard Nixon: The Grand Design* (Berkeley, 1987).

point. The pledge that "we shall provide a shield if a nuclear power threatens the freedom of a nation allied with us or of a nation whose survival we consider vital to our security" raised the fear among some that the doctrine "widened . . . the declared obligations of American policy" by promising aid to countries not formally allied with Washington. In reality, it was an effort to downplay obligations and substitute for the test of treaty commitments the test of national interests. Kissinger had castigated "the argument that we do not oppose the fact of particular changes but the method by which they are brought about." This thinking had led to a dangerously abstract attitude toward power: "We find it hard to articulate a truly vital interest which we would defend however 'legal' the challenge." Geopolitically defined interests, not overfastidiousness about methods or the perusal of treaty wording, ought to determine the (henceforth rarer) occasions of American military intervention.[30]

It was on this point that the Nixon Doctrine staked its new claim on the states-system: for national freedom of action. Despite its frequent pledges of fidelity to existing American commitments, the administration wished to regain flexibility for the United States to maneuver in a world in which it could no longer rely on predominance. Freed from an obligation to intervene found in legal documents or ideological fears, the United States could pick and choose the occasions of its action to make it effective. "By . . . scaling down the nation's ambitions to match its capacities, the President intends *not* to promote a new isolationism, but to prevent it," wrote one commentator. "By promising cold calculation of American interests abroad, he intends not a random disengagement but a more credible involvement where it counts." Skeptics like George Ball viewed this effort at increased freedom of action as a misguided attempt "to avoid the partnership implications of an alliance policy, and to maintain supremacy by setting one nation off against another"—in short, "to convert the Delian League into the Athenian Empire." Kissinger, on the other hand, saw it as a return to normal foreign policy after the special necessities of the deepest Cold War.[31]

30. David Landau, *Kissinger: The Uses of Power* (Boston, 1972), 111–14; House Committee on Foreign Affairs, *Hearings before the Committee on Foreign Affairs on H.R. 19845* (1970) (hereinafter cited as House hearings, *H.R. 19845*), 220; Kissinger, "Central Issues of American Foreign Policy," in *Agenda for the Nation*, ed. Gordon, 611.

31. Ball, *Diplomacy for a Crowded World*, 3–17; Henry A. Kissinger, "The Moral

Like any interest, this claim of increased flexibility would have to be justified to other members of the international society, since it would impose costs on them. The most obvious price would lie in replacing the material efforts Washington was no longer willing to make. So often was the theme sounded that the Nixon Doctrine would save the United States Treasury money that one observer called it "a policy . . . designed principally to reduce the cost of conflict for America." (A less sympathetic writer insisted that Kissinger had given a blunter definition during a private White House discussion of Indochina: "The Nixon Doctrine means that Asian boys will fight Asian boys.") Beyond calls on their men, money, and materiel, states that had been American partners feared the effects of an unpredictable United States playing a lone hand with little regard for the needs of others.[32]

To these concerns, the administration tried to give reassuring responses. While holding out to the domestic audience hopes for an eventual reduction in foreign assistance, it requested an increase in these funds in its 1971 budget, directly attributing to the doctrine the rises in expenditures that it sought. To assuage fears of abandonment, time and again Nixon stressed, "This doctrine is designed for the specific purpose of maintaining a U.S. policy role in the world rather than a withdrawal from the world and international responsibilities." And he and his national security adviser strongly denied that a state that governed its actions by its own interests was an undependable ally. Just the opposite was true, they contended: "A concept of our fundamental national interests would provide a ballast of restraint and an assurance of continuity." (Kissinger later asserted that because the doctrine contained "clear-cut criteria for friend and foe[,] . . . nations in Asia dreading American withdrawal found in the Guam pronouncements considerable reassurance once they had understood them.") Nixon and Kis-

Foundations of Foreign Policy," U.S. Department of State, *Bulletin,* LXXIII (August 4, 1975), 163–64.

32. Lewis, "The Nixon Doctrine," 16; Tad Szulc, *The Illusion of Peace: Foreign Policy in the Nixon Years* (New York, 1978), 298; "Asian Reaction to Prodding?," *Christian Science Monitor,* July 28, 1969, p. 1; Maximo Soliven, "Reactions to Nixon Trip Mixed," *Christian Science Monitor,* July 29, 1969, p. 4; Sung Wen-ming, "Nixon Doctrine in America's Asian Policy," *Asian Outlook,* V (May, 1970), 15–17; Joo-Hong Nam, *America's Commitment to South Korea: The First Decade of the Nixon Doctrine* (Cambridge, Mass., 1986); Kissinger, *White House Years,* 460. Cf. David P. Calleo, *The Imperious Economy* (Cambridge, Mass., 1982).

singer thus reiterated the argument Kissinger had made in 1968: "We have a tendency to offer our altruism as a guarantee of our reliability. . . . Such an attitude makes it difficult to develop a conception of our role in the world. It inhibits other nations from gearing their policy to ours in a confident way—a 'disinterested' policy is likely to be considered 'unreliable.' . . . The abstract concept of aggression causes us to multiply our commitments. But the denial that our interests are involved diminishes our staying power when we try to carry out those commitments." If the administration could persuade the American people to think about foreign policy in terms of interests, and convince them that a specific objective was, not a high-minded assignment, but a vital necessity, they would support the sacrifices necessary to attain the objective. If Nixon and Kissinger could demonstrate to American allies that a policy grounded in interests was a dependable policy, those countries could gain the confidence necessary to provide for their own security. If the United States could convince its adversaries that it would be resolute in sustaining its interests, they would give up any effort to outlast it and agree to a settlement of armed conflicts (thereby lowering the costs borne by the American public). And if Washington and other capitals could meet "the greatest need of the contemporary international system[,] . . . an agreed concept of order," clashes of interests might be commonly resolved without clashes of arms. In the language of the 1970 foreign policy report, "We must recognize national interests may indeed diverge from ours rather than merge. Our joint task is to construct a community of institutions and interests broad and resilient enough to accommodate our national divergencies."[33]

Thus, for all its emphasis on interests, the Nixon Doctrine could not—and did not try to—do away with the role of ideas. In its proclaimed prudence, its concern for costs, and its concentration on the relations among the great powers, the doctrine was not startlingly new; in its determination to devolve responsibilities onto the partners of the United States, its heightened desire for American freedom of action, and its reliance on the vocabulary of traditional European statecraft, it was a marked departure. By put-

33. House hearings, *H.R. 19845*, 6–7, 57, 109, 151; Lewis Sorley, *Arms Transfers Under Nixon: A Policy Analysis* (Lexington, Ky., 1983); "Building the Nixon Doctrine," *Christian Science Monitor*, September 16, 1970, p. 16; New York *Times*, March 10, 1971, Sec. 1, p. 14; Kissinger, "Central Issues of American Foreign Policy," 610–11; *Public Papers: Nixon, 1970*, 139; Kissinger, *White House Years*, 65, 225.

ting up a conceptual barrier between interests and commitments—saying implicitly and sometimes explicitly that the country might have interests where it had no commitments, and, in a more novel twist, commitments where it had no interests—Nixon and Kissinger endeavored to respond to changed international and domestic circumstances by advocating a revised list of American national interests, one that was shortened somewhat from its predecessors and, more importantly, drawn up according to different announced principles. A response to a crisis every bit as much as the decisions to offer the Marshall Plan or to enter the war in Korea had been, the Nixon Doctrine was both an acknowledgment that the postwar world was ending and a set of suggestions for the type of policy that would be suited to the period ahead. Its authors granted from the beginning that its ideas ran counter to much of the American tradition in foreign policy. Within half a dozen years, the country would swing back toward that tradition, and toward a different cluster of ideas governing its national interests.

IX The Carter Human-Rights Policy

Wɪᴛʜ ᴛʜᴇ ᴀʀʀɪᴠᴀʟ of the Carter administration in Washington, the presidential search for an enduring roster of national interests took a new tack and acquired new assumptions that were seen—and were meant to be seen—as quite unlike those of the Republican era from 1969 to 1977. In no case was the break sharper than the new administration's emphasis on human rights. Where the Nixon Doctrine had presupposed a world in which states would continue to be the primary actors and diplomacy was the instrument for carrying on their relations, "human rights" as a policy would embrace a challenge to the traditional world of states; the idea that a government had a legitimate concern with the treatment of noncitizens living outside its territory, simply because of their status as human beings. Where the Nixon Doctrine had proudly claimed the sophistication to deal only in interests, the new concern for human rights adopted the fervor of an attachment to the values of freedom. The one had been attracted (some said mesmerized) by the "European" qualities of caution, balance, and skepticism; the other would demand a return to the more traditionally "American" traits of confidence, boldness, and faith. The earlier policy had been a justification for the retrenchment of American power; the later one would support the expansion of American values.

HUMAN RIGHTS AND THE COMMON GOOD

Among the four departures in policy discussed here, the Carter administration's effort to promote respect for human rights abroad stands out as the case in which officials made the most insistent argument that their policy was not simply compatible with the common good of American society but almost equivalent to it. Repeatedly, Jimmy Carter and his lieutenants contended that in seeking to advance the human rights of others, the United States was only being true to itself, for a respect for individual liberty and an opposition to arbitrary government were what defined the domestic society that American foreign policy was obligated to protect. In his inaugural address, Carter proclaimed that "to be true to ourselves, we must be true to others." "Ours was the first society openly to define itself in terms of both spirituality and human liberty," the new president declared. "It is that unique self definition which has given us an exceptional appeal, but it also imposes on us a special obligation" to uphold the universality of the principle that all men were indeed endowed with certain inalienable rights. Likewise, Carter said in his second State of the Union address, in January, 1978, "The very heart of our identity as a nation is our firm commitment to human rights." Declarations like these came also from other figures in the administration, such as Undersecretary of State Warren Christopher, who would be closely involved in the daily operation of the new human-rights policy.[1]

Even allowing for some degree of bicentennial-era oratory, these statements indicated a conviction that ultimately the public interest of the United States lay in respect for a body of ideas that underlay the political regime. This was the common good of Americans, and the accumulation of wealth and the cultivation of power were means to the safeguarding of that end. In the external realm, "respect for" the rights of individuals meant the "promotion of" them among governments that often fell far short of observing such rights. Whatever the difficulties, however, to follow Kissinger's advice and behave as other great powers behaved would, in the professed view of the Carter administration, be a betrayal of the only real common good Americans shared among themselves.

Nevertheless, the debate over human rights in American foreign policy also witnessed a determined effort to prove that the vigorous advocacy of human rights would advance the national interest defined in terms of power—the power of the United States to influence others and to avoid being threatened by others. It was a line of reasoning that was to be repeated often as advocates of an outspoken human-rights policy tried to demonstrate that it

1. *Public Papers of the Presidents of the United States: Jimmy Carter, 1977* (Washington, D.C., 1977), I, 1–4, 954–62; *Public Papers: Carter, 1978*, I, 95; U.S. Department of State, *Bulletin*, LXXVII (August 29, 1977), 269–73, LXXVIII (March, 1978), 30–33. See also Jimmy Carter, *A Government as Good as Its People* (New York, 1977), 166–71.

would be neither an irrelevance, nor a distraction, nor a danger to American security and prosperity.[2]

A human-rights policy, it was argued, would be not only right but useful in a number of ways. One was that, by appealing to long-standing American political traditions, the policy would strengthen domestic support for government actions abroad. The president told his listeners in a 1977 speech he delivered at Notre Dame that it was "a policy that I hope will make you proud to be Americans." Its confidence restored by the reestablishment of a close communion between officialdom and the populace, the United States could act abroad with all the strength that came from domestic unity.[3]

Second, advocacy of human rights would also appeal to popular opinion abroad and improve Washington's international image. "Without a human rights commitment," the International League for Human Rights said in a statement in the spring of 1977, "the United States presents to the world a posture of power and self-interested entrepreneurism hardly likely to keep friends or win converts. By contrast, the vision of maintaining human rights and enlarging individual welfare and freedom remains a potent means to generate popular support abroad among masses of people—a support critical to any position of world leadership." Of course, this optimism assumed that third-world governments would themselves be interested in pursuing human rights as Washington understood them, an assertion that critics questioned. The president, however, was publicly confident that this was true, telling the UN General Assembly in March of 1977, "I see a hopeful world, a world dominated by increasing demands for basic freedoms, for fundamental rights, for higher standards of human existence. . . . The basic thrust of human affairs points toward a more universal demand for fundamental human rights." Christopher reported the following February, "Surveys conducted abroad have shown time and time again that the renewed interest in human values expressed by the President and implemented by our diplomatic efforts has had an enormously positive impact on the view people in foreign countries hold of America and our role in the world."[4]

2. Tom Farer, "United States Foreign Policy and the Protection of Human Rights: Observations and Proposals," *Virginia Journal of International Law*, XIV (Summer, 1974), 625. See also Richard B. Lillich, "Human Rights, the National Interest, and U.S. Foreign Policy: Some Preliminary Observations," *ibid.*, 591–96.

3. *Public Papers: Carter, 1977*, I, 954–62.

4. International League for Human Rights, "Report of the Conference on Implementing

Finally, the human-rights policy was said to serve the national interest by making for a more peaceable world. As the International League for Human Rights saw it, violations of human rights often provoked internal revolts, which could spill across state boundaries; countries that observed their citizens' rights did not spread such contagion. If states lived up to the various international agreements on human rights, they set a precedent that might be followed in other areas of international life; countries that observed "restraints on arbitrary and irresponsible government action" domestically were likely to be law-abiding international citizens as well. The United States was a satisfied power; its prosperity, if nothing else, would be harmed by the disruption of the international economy. Its interest would be served by the stability of a world made up of human-rights-friendly states.[5]

All of the attempts to connect human rights to the national interest did not mean that the administration was unaware of, or unconcerned with, the domestic political benefits that championing human rights might bring. "I think it's good politics," Carter's chief political confidant, Hamilton Jordan, told an interviewer in the early weeks of the administration. "The people who are upset are people who would prefer international relations conducted in a traditional way. This is a break with tradition. His international style of doing business is as different as his domestic style."[6]

a Human Rights Commitment in United States Foreign Policy," March 4, 1977, pp. 10–11; James Petras, "President Carter and the 'New Morality,'" *Monthly Review*, XXIX (June, 1977), 42–50; Ernst B. Haas, "Human Rights: To Act or Not to Act?," in *Eagle Entangled*, ed. Kenneth Oye *et al.* (New York, 1979), 167–96; *Public Papers: Carter, 1977*, I, 444–51.

5. International League for Human Rights, "Implementing a Human Rights Commitment," 9–10; Sandra Vogelgesang, *American Dream, Global Nightmare* (New York, 1980), 80–88.

6. Robert Shogan, *Promises to Keep: Carter's First Hundred Days* (New York, 1977), 219–20, 224; Memorandum, Jordan to Carter, March 12, 1977, "Human Rights Policy, 1977," in Box 34, Jimmy Carter Library, Atlanta, Ga. (hereinafter cited as JCL); Carter, *A Government as Good as Its People*, 71–72, 115–22, 166–71, 214; Jimmy Carter, *Why Not the Best? Why One Man Is Optimistic About America's Future* (Nashville, 1975), 123; Elizabeth Drew, "A Reporter at Large: Human Rights," *New Yorker*, July 18, 1977, pp. 36–38; Mark L. Schneider, "A New Administration's New Policy: The Rise to Power of Human Rights," in *Human Rights and U.S. Foreign Policy: Principles and Applications*, ed. Peter G. Brown and Douglas Maclean (Lexington, Mass., 1979), 3–13; David Weissbrodt, "Human Rights Legislation and U.S. Foreign Policy," *Georgia Journal of International and Comparative*

HUMAN RIGHTS AND THE UNITED STATES' CLAIMS ABROAD

"In human rights we have the problem of everybody having a vague nice feeling about it," said Patricia Derian, the new coordinator of the State Department's Office of Human Rights and Humanitarian Affairs, in the spring of 1977. Making a general claim of concern about respect for human rights abroad entailed making a whole series of specific claims to do things involved in implementing such a national commitment. What the justifiable limits of these subsidiary claims might be was a matter of some considerable dispute, not least because they were of a new type.[7] The administration asserted four interests in its policy: the claim to define a standard of human rights to which all states could be held; the claim to pass judgment publicly on other states' human-rights performance; the claim to make foreign assistance contingent on that performance (though not to make human rights the sole consideration in allocating aid or in assessing requests for aid from international financial institutions); and the claim to carry on the campaign for human rights without having it linked to other issues that Washington wished to keep separate.

Defining human rights

A basic difficulty was the absence of any universally agreed-on definition of human rights. Yet this was the claim the administration had to make before it could assert any others: that it could define the rights its policy would endeavor to protect. The international agreements to which Carter often referred—the UN Charter, the UN's Universal Declaration of Human Rights, and the Helsinki Accords, among others—contained great numbers of supposed rights. Would the United States act on behalf of all of them? The definitional question occupied much of the new administration's first months in office, beginning at least with the State Department transition

---

Law, VII (Summer, 1977), 231–32; International League for Human Rights, "Implementing a Human Rights Commitment," 41.

7. House Committee on Banking, Finance, and Urban Affairs, *International Development Institutions Authorizations—1977* (hereinafter cited as House hearings, *International Development Institutions*) III, 66.

briefing paper for the incoming team that "stressed a need for greater definition of human rights objectives." In response, soon after assuming office,
Secretary of State Cyrus Vance instructed Christopher to establish the Human Rights Coordinating Group and directed the Policy Planning Staff "to
formulate a broad human rights policy for my review."[8] The most basic
issue to be settled was whether the American government would confine its
use of the term *human rights* (and thereby its efforts to promote their respect) to the "rights of the person"—at bottom, the right to be free of the
threat of torture or arbitrary detention or execution—or would expand its
operative definition to include civil and political rights—the right to due
process of law, the right to vote, freedom of the press, of speech, of assembly—or would adopt a still-more inclusive definition of human rights encompassing the so-called economic and social rights—the right to a minimum standard of food, clothing, and shelter, and to various other measures
of social security obligating the state to provide to those unable to provide
for themselves certain benefits assuring their physical and economic well-
being. Debate on the issue of definition had been going on for years among
those concerned to analyze and to promote human rights and had come to
center around two predominant views: one that followed the classical liberal tradition in saying that civil and political rights constituted the outer-
most boundaries to which true, basic human rights could be considered to
extend, and the other that accepted newer egalitarian currents of thought
and argued that provision of the physical sustenance of life constituted a
human right (or a series of human rights) as well.[9]

Vance tried his hand at resolving the issue in an address at the University of Georgia Law School on April 30, Law Day. His speech included all
three of the major categories of rights, listing the integrity of the person first,
social and economic rights second, and civil and political rights third. Far
from emphasizing one category of rights over another, the secretary said,
"our policy is to promote all the rights. . . . There may be disagreement on

8. Schneider, "A New Administration's New Policy," in *Human Rights and U.S. Foreign
Policy,* ed. Brown and Maclean, 9; Memorandum from Vance for all assistant secretaries,
February 11, 1977, reprinted in *Checklist of Human Rights Documents,* I (December, 1976),
Appendix D, 18.
9. See Maurice Cranston, *What Are Human Rights?* (London, 1973); Brown and
Maclean, eds., *Human Rights and U.S. Foreign Policy.*

the priorities these rights deserve. But I believe that, with work, all of these rights can become complementary and mutually reinforcing."[10]

It is unclear how carefully thought-out the inclusion of economic and social rights was. Elizabeth Drew reports that the decision to proceed with a broadly inclusive definition of human rights was the product of "much deliberation and struggle," while Sandra Vogelgesang, at that time a special assistant for policy planning in the Office of the Assistant Secretary of State for European Affairs, later recalled that the section on economic and social rights "was a belated addition to the draft text" that "may have emerged more by accident than design." Some in the administration, like Hendrik Hertzberg, took the view that the inclusion of social and economic rights was little more than a sop to those who did not believe in civil and political rights: "I think the main motivation behind it was a desire to get the Third World to buy a package, [as if] this was the toy inside the Cracker Jack box. [It] was supposed to pull them into the idea of human rights . . . and then they would find that there was this package that involved freedom of speech and stuff like that." Others, including Derian and UN Ambassador Andrew Young, were more persuaded by the view that a minimum of economic and social well-being was indeed a human right. The Vance speech may have been broadly phrased so as to satisfy the widest range of views. Nor is it certain that the order in which the three categories were listed was intended to indicate their priority, though this order became virtually formulaic in public statements by members of the administration. (Some thought was given to including on the list the right to live in peace, which would make it easier to continue to deal with countries such as South Korea that pleaded threats to their security as excusing their violation of other rights. In the end it was decided to include as a standard for any action the question, "Have we been sensitive to genuine security interests, realizing that outbreak of armed conflict or terrorism could in itself pose a serious threat to human rights?")[11]

In an effort to give more specific meaning and more powerful bureaucratic impetus to Vance's guidelines, the White House put out a Policy Re-

10. U.S. Department of State, *Bulletin*, LXXVI (May 23, 1977), 505–508.

11. Drew, "Human Rights," 42–43; Vogelgesang, *American Dream, Global Nightmare*, 184; Joshua Muravchik, *The Uncertain Crusade: Jimmy Carter and the Dilemmas of Human Rights Policy* (Lanham, Md., 1986), 75–111.

view Memorandum (PRM-28) on May 20.[12] Addressed to all agencies significantly concerned with human rights, it called for responses to several questions, including the meaning of the test of "consistent pattern of gross violations of internationally recognized human rights." Congress also directed, with the acquiescence of the administration, that the secretaries of state and treasury open consultations with other countries, beginning with the industrialized democracies, to arrive at an international standard for human rights.

Presidential Directive/NSC-30 (PD-30) was issued over Carter's signature on February 17, 1978. It retained the threefold classification of human rights the United States was to promote. Two reasons suggest themselves, one domestic, one foreign. Domestically, the administration may have wished to retain the notion of economic rights as a rationale for continuing to provide aid to governments that violated civil and political rights—aid that otherwise would have been cut off under congressional mandates that many in the executive found increasingly irksome. The hope may also have been present that if the administration included in its definition of human rights an element comparatively palatable to third-world countries, those countries would be more likely to accept the validity of the United States' claim to the authority to employ a human-rights test in its relations with them.[13]

12. PRM 28 was partially declassified and released April 6, 1983, at the request of this author, under the Freedom of Information Act. It is on file at the NSC Library. It is also described in Lincoln Bloomfield, "The Carter Human Rights Policy: A Provisional Appraisal" (March, 1981), 9–10, in Center for International Studies, Massachusetts Institute of Technology. Bloomfield served in 1979–80 as a senior NSC staff member in charge of global issues, including human rights. He followed Jessica Tuchman in that post and was succeeded by Roger Molander. The resulting presidential directive, PD-30, was declassified January 8, 1981, and is on file at the Military Archives Division, Modern Military Headquarters Branch, National Archives, Washington, D.C.

13. U.S. Department of State, *Bulletin*, LXXVII (August 29, 1977), 269–73, (October 24, 1977), 556–61, LXXVIII (March, 1978), 30–33; Jimmy Carter, *Keeping Faith: Memoirs of a President* (New York, 1982), 144; Zbigniew Brzezinski, *Power and Principle: Memoirs of the National Security Adviser, 1977–1981* (New York, 1983), 558; Senate Committee on Foreign Relations, *Human Rights and U.S. Foreign Assistance: Experiences and Issues in Policy Implementation (1977–1978)* (1979) (hereinafter cited as Senate report, *Human Rights and Foreign Assistance*), 49–51; *Public Papers: Carter, 1977*, I, 4–5. But see also J. L. S. Girling, "Carter's Foreign Policy: Realism or Ideology?," *The World Today*, XXXIII (November, 1977), 421.

Public statements

A second claim asserted by the administration was the authority to comment publicly on the human-rights records of other states. While some dismissed this change from Kissinger's quiet diplomacy as "merely" verbal, Carter insisted, particularly in the early months of his presidency, that criticism and exhortation were meaningful and legitimate interests that the United States could press on other members of the states-system. As he said in his 1977 speech at Notre Dame, "In the life of the human spirit, words *are* action, much more so than many of us realize who live in countries where freedom of expression is taken for granted. The leaders of totalitarian nations understand this very well. The proof is that words are precisely the action for which dissidents in those countries are being persecuted."

The occasions on which the president and others could act through words ranged from passing references in answers to questions from reporters or in speeches, through written communications and statements in international gatherings, to carefully prepared evaluations issued with official imprimatur. The administration tried all of these, though with more vigor and more frequency in its initial period in office. Within its first week, the State Department issued a statement condemning the harassment and detention by the Czech government of the signers of Chapter 77, a petition calling for the respect of human rights in Czechoslovakia. A day later, the department followed this unprecedented statement—the first occasion on which it had ever publicly charged a signatory of the Helsinki Accords with their violation—with an equally stern warning to the Soviet government against trying to silence Andrei Sakharov; and it made headlines for the third successive day by releasing upon its receipt a letter to Carter from Sakharov requesting the president's help in protecting Sakharov's and others' human rights in the Soviet Union. All this brought agitated protests from the Soviet ambassador, Anatoly Dobrynin. Yet, sharp as it was, the furor created by Sakharov's letter to Carter was mild compared with that touched off on February 17, when, in Moscow, Sakharov received and released to the press the president's reply indicating his sympathy with Sakharov's plight and his determination to press for human rights.[14]

14. Drew, "Human Rights," 38–41; U.S. Department of State, *Bulletin*, LXXVI (February 21, 1977), 137–46, 154; New York *Times*, January 27, 1977, Sec. 1, p. 1, January 28,

Criticism from the Kremlin and further visits from Dobrynin followed, but Carter stood on American rights under the Helsinki agreement. At a news conference on February 8, the president asserted that "I have made clear," both in communications with Soviet General Secretary Leonid Brezhnev and in the meeting with Dobrynin, "that I was reserving the right to speak out strongly and forcefully whenever human rights are threatened—not every instance, but when I think it is advisable." He added, "This is not intended as a public relations attack on the Soviet Union," and the statement that the administration did not wish to "single out" Moscow was a regular feature of presidential news conferences for months, even as dramatic messages like the letter to Sakharov or off-the-cuff remarks on human rights became less frequent.[15]

Sometimes such interventions led to embarrassment because the United States seemed to back down after initially taking a strong stance. Sometimes they backfired because the publicity revealed divisions within the administration. Yet through it all the president maintained his claim to comment on the state of human rights in other countries—"the arousing of public condemnation around the world for the violation of these principles of human freedom is a legitimate role for me as a leader and for the people of our country. . . . [O]ur voice will not be stilled"—even though he would exercise that claim less often.[16]

More formal and far more comprehensive than these occasional remarks were the annual country reports on human rights. These had originated in legislation in 1975 and 1976 requiring that the secretary of state submit to Congress an evaluation of the state of human rights in each country receiving economic and military assistance. The Ford administration had

1977, Sec. 1, p. 1, January 29, 1977, Sec. 1, pp. 1, 2, January 31, 1977, Sec. 1, p. 1; *Economist,* February 5, 1977, p. 49.

15. *Public Papers: Carter, 1977,* I, 100, 220, 341.

16. *Ibid.,* 1109, 220; *Public Papers: Carter, 1978,* II, 1281, 1282–83, 1323, 1325; Commission on Security and Cooperation in Europe, *Basket Three: Implementation of the Helsinki Accords* (1977) (hereinafter cited as CSCE hearings, *Basket Three*), Pt. 4, pp. 94–100; Carter, *Keeping Faith,* 220; New York *Times,* February 28, 1977, Sec. 1, pp. 1, 6, February 27, 1977, Sec. 1, p. 1, February 28, 1977, Sec. 1, p. 4, March 1, 1977, Sec. 1, p. 1, June 2, 1977, Sec. 1, p. 14, July 13, 1978, Sec. 1, pp. 1, 3, 45, July 14, 1978, Sec. 1, pp. 1, 7, 8, 9, 26, July 15, 1978, Sec. 1, p. 1, 3; U.S. Department of State, *Bulletin,* LXXVI (March 21, 1977), 245–46, 250, 252, (April 4, 1977), 314.

opposed the mandate, fearing that by bathing the issue in worldwide publicity, the reports might well provoke to resistance the targets of American disapproval, worsening the chances for improvement in their attitude toward human rights. At the direction of the State Department, all American diplomatic missions had over the course of 1975 submitted classified analyses of human-rights conditions in their host countries, and an overall report compiling these assessments had apparently been drafted in Washington. But it had been killed by Kissinger, who had substituted a more general document that contained specific references to neither countries nor rights violations and called for a continuation of "quiet but forceful diplomacy." Such discretion had not been appreciated on Capitol Hill; speaking of the report, Senator Hubert Humphrey (Democrat, Minnesota) had cracked, "It was about as bland . . . as swallowing a bucket of sawdust."[17]

Carter was expected to be much more sympathetic to the use of publicity in the second set of reports, which the State Department sent to Congress in early March of 1977. The reports had in fact been prepared by December, 1976, in the closing months of the Ford presidency, and the new administration had had only a few weeks in late January and February to conduct a hurried review and introduce small changes in the format and text. Nevertheless, because they were made available in the midst of its many other human-rights initiatives, they were received at home and abroad as part of its campaign and taken as representative of its thinking. James Wilson, director of the office of humanitarian affairs under Ford, who had overseen most of the preparation of the reports before Carter's inauguration, described them as "tactfully drafted." Some human-rights activists angrily agreed, castigating the reports as "vague," "extremely general," and "a scandal—inaccurate, tendentious, evasive and shoddily researched." The states whose human-rights practices were being described, on the other hand, were furious, not just that, in their opinion, the wording was inflammatory and the conclusions overdrawn, but that the issuance of the reports itself had challenged their domestic sovereignty.[18]

17. Senate report, *Human Rights and Foreign Assistance*, 17–18; Weissbrodt, "Human Rights Legislation," 244–45; Thomas A. Balmer, "The Use of Conditions in Foreign Relations Legislation," *Denver Journal of International Law and Policy*, VII (Spring, 1978), 227–28; New York *Times*, November 19, 1975, Sec. 1, p. 14.

18. Senate Committee on Foreign Relations, *Human Rights Reports prepared by the Department of State in accordance with Section 502(B) of the Foreign Assistance Act, as*

Release of the following year's country reports on January 31, 1978, made for interesting comparisons. Although these were the first evaluations drafted entirely under the Carter administration, they did not differ greatly from their 1977 predecessors, other than being more complete and more practiced as a result of their authors' having gone through the exercise before. Perhaps officials were less fervent in 1978 than in 1977; the complaints from nongovernmental groups that the documents were too diplomatic were just as loud. Yet the protests of the countries that were the subjects of the reports were more muted. Joshua Muravchik has speculated that "the rest of the world has gotten used to them, or has realized that this is something the United States is determined to continue doing, so there is no point in protesting"—in other words, that the society of states largely acceded to the American claim to speak out in this regularized way.[19]

A final venue in which the United States claimed the competence to assess publicly the human-rights records of other states was the continuing follow-up process to the Helsinki Accords. Like the issuance of the country reports, the evaluation of the operation of the agreements reached at Helsinki was a task left to the members of the new administration by their predecessors. The accords themselves had been agreed to by the United States, Canada, and the European states, East and West, in 1975. Congress, in 1976, concerned that the Ford administration might lack vigilance in monitoring the observance of the accords' provisions, particularly those regarding human rights, established an independent advisory agency to do so. The Commission on Security and Cooperation in Europe (CSCE) was to be composed of six members of the Senate, six members of the House, and one member each from the Departments of State, Defense, and Commerce, and was to receive reports twice a year from the president (compiled by the State Department) on compliance by the signatory states.[20]

amended (1977); Drew, "Human Rights," 42; Weissbrodt, "Human Rights Legislation," 260, 263–64; Balmer, "The Use of Conditions," 230–31; Washington Post, February 27, 1977, Sec. C, pp. 1, 4.

19. House Committee on International Relations and Senate Committee on Foreign Relations, Country Reports on Human Rights Practices (1978); House Committee on International Relations, Foreign Assistance Legislation for Fiscal Year 1979 (1978) (hereinafter cited as House hearings, 1979 Foreign Assistance), Pt. 2, p. 140, Pt. 4, pp. 4–6, 27, 142, Pt. 5, pp. 573, 590; New York Times, February 10, 1978, Sec. 1, p. 14; Muravchik, Uncertain Crusade, 230–32.

20. The congressionally mandated advisory panel, the Commission on Security and Co-

By the time Vance presented the president's report on implementation of the accords to the commission on June 3, 1977, and testified on it three days later, the administration's early ardor for public discussion of the Soviet Union's human-rights failings in this forum had begun to cool. Some within the executive had not wished to issue the report at all, but the legislation gave them no alternative.[21] Moreover, stung by charges that their early statements had been directed solely against Moscow, Carter and his appointees had been making certain to include criticisms of other states, including American allies, in their statements. But the primary purpose of CSCE was precisely to make public comments and to bring the light of public attention to bear on human-rights abuses still practiced by states that had pledged at Helsinki to abjure them. And because the Helsinki Accords had been confined to European states, Moscow and its East European allies—as the countries where most violations of human rights occurred—were inevitably the target of most of the indictments in the reports of the commission.[22]

As a result, the administration soon found itself under attack in Congress for lacking vigor in pressing the claim to speak out in the venue that Helsinki provided. When he appeared before the Senate Foreign Relations Committee on June 6, Vance outlined an approach that employed the unobtrusive and emollient methods of the diplomatist, pledging to "avoid grandiose new proposals that have little chance of being acceptable," "propaganda ploys," and "debating points." By contrast, Senator Clifford Case (Republican, New Jersey) came down strongly on the side of public advocacy and debate: "There is only one thing, Mr. Secretary, that really concerns us related to our discussions with the executive branch at this

---

operation in Europe, should not be confused with the group of thirty-five states that approved the agreement in Helsinki in 1975 and would meet later in Belgrade, the *Conference* on Security and Cooperation in Europe. Unless otherwise indicated, whenever the initials CSCE are used here, they will refer to the commission. See CSCE hearings, *Basket Three;* Commission on Security and Cooperation in Europe, *Basket II—Helsinki Final Act: East-West Cooperation* (1977); House Committee on International Relations, *Report of the Study Mission to Europe to the Commission on Security and Cooperation in Europe* (1977).

21. House Committee on International Relations, *Second Semiannual Report by the President to the Commission on Security and Cooperation in Europe* (1977) (hereinafter cited as House report, *Second Seminannual Report*); CSCE hearings, *Basket Three*, IV, 85–104; Brzezinski, *Power and Principle*, 126, 150.

22. *Public Papers: Carter, 1977*, I, 782, 1107; *Washington Post*, June 3, 1977, Sec. A, p. 4; A. Glenn Mower, Jr., *The United States, the United Nations, and Human Rights: The Eleanor Roosevelt and Jimmy Carter Eras* (Westport, Conn., 1979), 141.

time. . . . That is whether this is going to be an exercise in who can be the nicest to the other side and how we can show that all the world is one—or will it be a real airing of the situation, particularly in respect to [the human rights in] Basket Three?"[23]

Despite its heightened reservations about public criticism of the human-rights record of the Soviet Union and its East European allies, the administration frankly concluded in its report to CSCE, "The overall basket three implementation by the Warsaw Pact countries, though varying among individual states, remained well below the objectives of the final act." Still, the report pointed to what areas of progress it could, such as an increase in cultural and educational exchanges, and Vance generally counseled patience: "One cannot judge the ultimate effect of our statements with respect to human rights and the actions which we take with respect to human rights, including quiet diplomacy, in the short run. . . . One has to judge this over a period of time."[24]

While the president was defending himself against charges made in Congress that statements such as this showed that his administration had abandoned human rights, he was being attacked in Moscow for being strident in his public comments on the subject. On June 19, *Pravda* described the human-rights campaign as a pretext for an American arms buildup. (Carter's immediate response did not go beyond saying, "Our commitment to human rights is independent of other motives and will not be changed.") In August the CSCE's own report on the Eastern countries' lack of compliance with the accords in the two years since their signing—a toughly worded document, to be sure, that portrayed a dismal record in damning terms—was greeted by *Tass* as "a collection of lies and slander."[25]

The president summed up his own attitude in a news conference in War-

23. CSCE hearings, *Basket Three,* IV, 86–88, 95–96, 102–104; *Public Papers: Carter, 1977,* I, 1085; CSCE hearings, *Basket Three,* V–VII.

24. House report, *Second Semiannual Report,* 23, 24–32 *passim;* CSCE hearings, *Basket Three,* IV, 90, 93–94.

25. House Committee on International Relations, *Implementation of the Final Act of the Conference on Security and Cooperation in Europe: Findings and Recommendations Two Years after Helsinki* (1977); U.S. Department of State, *Third Semiannual Report to the Commission on Security and Cooperation in Europe,* Special Report No. 39, December, 1977; Brzezinski, *Power and Principle,* 559; New York *Times,* June 20, 1977, Sec. 1, p. 10, June 26, 1977, Sec. 1, p. 1, August 7, 1977, Sec. 1, p. 7, October 11, 1977, Sec. 1, p. 14, October 14, 1977, Sec. 1, p. 3, November 12, 1977, Sec. 1, p. 9, December 6, 1977, Sec. 1, p. 3.

saw on December 30, when he described the Belgrade conference, called to assess performance of the obligations undertaken at Helsinki, "productive" and asserted that spirited debate was an intrinsic part of the accords: "The treaty terms provide for open and frank criticism of other signatories when [human-rights] standards are not met." The public discussion of abuses was valuable as "a constant reminder . . . of the importance of . . . the preservation of basic human rights" and would ensure "that this issue of human rights will never be forgotten."[26]

Carter also mentioned at the news conference his hope that the Belgrade sessions would "come to a rapid and successful conclusion." How this was to be done was a matter that increasingly preoccupied the delegates as the early months of 1978 passed and the conference remained deadlocked on the contents of the session's final document. As had been the case from the start, the basic line of division ran between East and West: the United States and the other NATO countries wished the final document to reflect all subjects, including human rights, that had been reviewed at the conference. The Soviet Union and its allies, still smarting over the attention given in the sessions to their human-rights violations, were adamant in their refusal to allow that subject into the concluding statement. The impasse persisted through January and February, until the West at length conceded the issue and agreed to a closing statement on March 2 that made no mention of human rights. Clearly stung by its defeat, the White House issued a sharp statement of its own the following day in which it expressed regret that the Soviet Union "was not prepared to engage in a serious discussion of new proposals" to further the goals expressed at Helsinki, and that it "failed to permit the conference to proceed to its proper conclusion [by agreeing] to a final document that would take note of the full review of implementation—including human rights—that was the centerpiece of the conference." The statement claimed success in that a "full and frank review" of all aspects of the accords, "including specific country-performance and individual cases" of human rights, meant that "human rights has now been firmly inscribed as a legitimate and proper concern on the agenda of international discussion." The White House asserted, "What has been done cannot be ignored, whether or not the Soviet Union is prepared to see it recog-

26. *Public Papers: Carter, 1977*, II, 2206–209; New York *Times*, December 31, 1977, Sec. 1, p. 2.

nized in a formal document," and warned, "We intend to press the Soviet Union to fulfill its commitment to respect human rights."[27] Whether or not this language had been toughened to fend off criticism that the president was letting Moscow off the hook (as was alleged at the time), it certainly reflected the administration's frustration, in Brzezinski's words, at "the problem inherent in fitting human-rights criteria into the framework of American interests."[28]

During this period of 1977 and 1978, then, important states did not acquiesce in the United States' asserted interest in publicizing human-rights records in fora such as Belgrade. Perhaps they found the examination more intrusive in a multilateral setting than in the country reports issued by the State Department, which could be more easily dismissed as an idiosyncrasy of the United States and were, after all, written documents without the immediacy and force of a spoken presentation at an international gathering before the world's television cameras. Despite the doubts by figures within the American government itself about the usefulness of the documents, however, the president and the human rights bureau maintained their claim to this form of public examination.

Foreign assistance

In addition to propounding a definition of human rights and calling others to account for failing to live up to the standard that definition suggested, many wished the United States to assert that it had an interest in distributing its foreign assistance with the human-rights record of potential recipients in mind. This might have been thought a minimal claim to make, since every sovereign state could allocate its aid resources (or allocate none at all) as it chose. Such a theoretical freedom does not prevent every aid donor from

27. *Public Papers: Carter, 1978*, I, 453–55; House Committee on International Relations, *The Belgrade Followup Meeting to the Conference on Security and Cooperation in Europe: A Report and Appraisal, by the Commission on Security and Cooperation in Europe* (1978); U.S. Department of State, *The Belgrade Followup Meeting to the Conference on Security and Cooperation in Europe, October 4, 1977—March 9, 1978*, Special Report No. 43, June, 1978; New York *Times*, March 3, 1978, Sec. 1, p. 3, March 4, 1978, Sec. 1, p. 1, March 9, 1978, Sec. 1, p. 7.

28. Brzezinski, *Power and Principle*, 144.

finding it politic to announce some rationale for its distribution of assistance, both to secure political support at home for aid funding and to set finite resources against infinite demands and deny the unsuccessful requests with some measure of grace. Moreover, "foreign aid" does not start each year with a clean slate: political expectations have been formed around an existing allocation, and political coalitions have been mustered behind it. A serious change in the pattern will require a serious justification if it is not to appear wholly arbitrary and incur political costs. Human-rights advocates believed they had the necessary justification.

As in the case of the country reports, the Carter administration found a fairly substantial body of law on foreign assistance and human rights already in place when it took office. A renewed interest in human rights had gripped Congress for some four years, and throughout the early and mid-1970s it had enacted into law an increasing number of restrictions on aid of various kinds to countries with demonstrably poor human-rights records.[29] Beyond these limits, Congress also wrote into law a series of tight constraints on executive decisions in allocating foreign assistance generally.

How often would the incoming administration find it in the national interest to provide aid to countries with less than perfect records on human rights? How would it decide? Answers to these questions were necessary to put the general directives of Congress into practice. Vance had advised Carter on foreign issues during the campaign and on October 24, 1976, at Carter's request, had sent the candidate a memorandum suggesting goals for a possible Carter administration. The document argued that human rights should be one of the "primary elements" of Carter's diplomacy, but opposed further tightening of the human-rights requirements in foreign-assistance legislation. Establishing a human-rights hurdle without exceptions, it contended, would appear to be an "intrusion" into the domestic affairs of other countries and would harm the well-being of the poor. In a

29. House Committee on Foreign Affairs, *International Protection of Human Rights: The Work of International Organizations and the Role of U.S. Foreign Policy* (1973); House Committee on Foreign Affairs, Subcommittee on International Organizations and Movements, *Human Rights in the World Community: A Call for U.S. Leadership* (1974) (hereinafter cited as House, *Human Rights in the World Community*); John Salzberg and Donald D. Young, "The Parliamentary Role in Implementing International Human Rights: A U.S. Example," *Texas International Law Journal*, XII (Spring–Summer, 1977), 251–78; Weissbrodt, "Human Rights Legislation," 231–87; Balmer, "The Use of Conditions," 197–238.

post-election press conference on November 16, Carter declared, somewhat ambiguously, "I think the allocation of foreign aid and the normal friendship of our country would be determined or affected certainly by the attitude of those countries toward human rights."[30]

Vance announced the administration's first application of the new standard after just over a month in office, on February 24, telling a Senate hearing that military assistance to Ethiopia and Uruguay was being eliminated and arms sales credits to Argentina were being reduced to $15 million—one-third the level proposed the previous year by Ford. Aid to other countries that had been considered for cuts—Zaire, South Korea, the Philippines, Brazil, and others—would be spared because of overriding political or security concerns. A series of human-rights activists appearing before a Senate subcommittee praised some aspects of the administration's outspoken public stand as "impressive" and "forthright," but called the cuts in military assistance "not very significant," termed Vance's refusal to recommend cuts in aid to other countries "disturbing," warned that unless the administration asked for further reductions, "questions will arise about the depth of its commitment to human rights," and demanded an announced overall strategy, saying, "Ad hoc action is not policy." On the other hand, the targets of the cuts felt that the administration had already gone much too far. Stung by the cutoff or reduction of aid requests and by the publication of the human-rights country reports, El Salvador, Guatemala, Argentina, Uruguay, and Brazil angrily rejected all American military assistance (though in several of these cases both sides later quietly agreed to restart the flow of aid), and Brazil renounced its mutual defense pact with the United States.[31]

If they were to go beyond ad-hoc actions, the State Department's coordinator on human rights, the former civil-rights activist Patricia Derian, and the interagency groups established to review economic and military assistance requests needed standards for deciding when to invoke the claim that foreign assistance could be reduced or denied on human-rights grounds.[32]

30. Cyrus Vance, *Hard Choices: Critical Years in America's Foreign Policy* (New York, 1983), 441–62; House hearings, *International Development Institutions,* 86.

31. Drew, "Human Rights," 41–42; Patrick Breslin, "Human Rights: Rhetoric or Action?," Washington *Post,* February 27, 1977, Sec. A, pp. 1, 3; Senate Committee on Foreign Relations, Subcommittee on Foreign Assistance, *Human Rights* (1977) (hereinafter cited as Senate hearings, *Human rights and foreign assistance*), 3–41 *passim.*

32. Donald P. Kommers and Gilbert D. Loescher, eds., *Human Rights and American*

Outside the administration, there were calls for making human rights the controlling issue.[33] Clearly, these views went beyond what Vance and others were prepared to accept, but the administration needed an alternative. As a step toward creating a standard, PRM-28 in May of 1977 asked its respondents to evaluate "changes in levels of security and economic assistance and food aid—as both sanctions and incentives." In the end, it proved impossible to obtain agreement on anything more specific than the mandate in Presidential Directive/NSC-30 the following February that "countries with a poor or deteriorating record will receive less favorable consideration" in the allocation of foreign assistance. This general direction was consistent with Vance's admonition in his Law Day speech that "no mechanistic formula produces an automatic answer." Yet a case-by-case approach could also be a formula for delay, as the P.L. 480, or "Food for Peace," program demonstrated.

By late September, 1977, the committee of representatives of the state, commerce, and agriculture departments that nominated P.L. 480 recipient countries was ready to begin signing contracts as usual; but because this was the first year that the new human-rights tests applied (under the International Development and Food Assistance Act of 1977), all potential buyers had first to pass before the Christopher Group (the new Interagency Group on Human Rights and Foreign Assistance, under Christopher's chairmanship) for inspection and approval of their human-rights records. The applications quickly bogged down in what seemed to the waiting recipients and to many of the participants an almost interminable series of delays. In general, officials in the regional bureaus favored the continuation of food aid to countries with which they were concerned, even when the governments involved were violating some human rights (and they became quite skilled at finding "needy-people" justifications for almost any sales), while

---

Foreign Policy (Notre Dame, 1979), 226; Senate hearings, *Human rights and foreign assistance*, 72–73; Brzezinski, *Power and Principle*, 125; Senate report, *Human Rights and Foreign Assistance*, 36–42; Memorandum from Vance, reprinted in *Checklist of Human Rights Documents*, Appendix D, 18; Bloomfield, "The Carter Human Rights Policy," 15–18; Cedric W. Tarr, Jr., "Human Rights and Arms Transfer Policy," *Denver Journal of International Law and Policy*, VIII (1979), 573–90.

33. *Renewed Concern for Democracy and Human Rights*, Report of the 10th meeting of Members of Congress and of the European Parliament (September, 1976), 53, cited in Mower, *The United States, the United Nations and Human Rights*, 119; Statement of Bruce Cameron, Senate hearings, *Human rights and foreign assistance*, 18–33.

the human rights bureau believed in strict enforcement of the human-rights standard across the board. All these disputes were thrown into the Christopher Group, which struggled to decide each sale "on its own merits." Since there was no body of precedent to guide these labors, their results tended not only to appear arbitrary but also to be repeatedly postponed.[34]

A number of members of Congress, including Humphrey and Representatives Clement Zablocki (Democrat, Wisconsin, and chairman of the Committee on International Relations) and Thomas Foley (Democrat, Washington, and chairman of the Agriculture Committee) wrote Vance to ask about the delay, and Humphrey later called on the executive branch to "implement these [human-rights] laws in such a way that the poor people of a country are not punished because of the repressive action's [sic] of their leaders." The requests of more than twenty countries were delayed while their human-rights records were examined, and Guinea, Indonesia, Bangladesh, South Korea, and Zaire were placed in the Christopher Group's troublesome category. It was not until December 17, nearly three months after the group had begun its work, that two of the dubious cases, concerning Indonesia and Guinea, were resolved, and other cases were still pending the following February. A proposed increase in food assistance to what was described simply as "a West African country" was rejected; on the other hand, the improvement in Peru's record was rewarded by a rise in its allotment. Administration witnesses before Congress denied "that anybody was disadvantaged by the delay," but the episode continued to trouble those who feared that the human-rights policy was too loosely defined.[35]

As a practical matter, the United States could not bind itself in all cases either to make the human-rights criterion controlling on aid decisions or to set it aside whenever any other considerations were present. Vance was entirely correct that the decision had to be a matter of informed judgment. But "informed and concerned discretion for policy-makers" as a rule for making decisions on aid was unpopular with Congress, difficult to justify to other countries, and often time-consuming for the officials involved. American decision-makers themselves were not satisfied with the way that this claim was enforced primarily through punishments. They would have preferred, in the language of PD-30, that "great reliance . . . be placed on positive in-

34. House hearings, 1979 Foreign Assistance, Pt. 1, p. 167; Drew, "Human Rights," 44.
35. House hearings, 1979 Foreign Assistance, Pt. 1, p. 166–67; Congressional Record, 95th Cong., 2nd Sess., 38671, 38673; New York Times, December 18, 1977, Sec. 1, p. 3.

ducements and incentives acknowledging improvements in human rights . . . through preferential treatment in political relations and economic benefits" to "countries with a good or substantially improving record." As long as resources for such a program of rewards were lacking, however, those in the executive branch were prepared to defend the general claim that the American government could justifiably reduce or eliminate foreign assistance with human rights in mind, though they regularly disagreed on specific instances in which the claim might be applied.

International financial institutions

By contrast, the case of the international financial institutions (IFIs) was one in which most executive officials did not favor making a claim that the United States could and should employ a human-rights standard equivalent to that governing bilateral aid. Members of Congress were much more likely to favor such a claim, and the differences led to struggles in 1977.

Congress had always been somewhat suspicious of the multilateral lending agencies because of their power to disburse American contributions free from congressional control once the lump-sum contributions had been made, and this long-standing worry had been exacerbated in the mid-1970s by what many members of Congress saw as indifference on the part of these agencies toward the human-rights practices in countries that received loans. "Especially troublesome," in the words of Representative Donald Fraser (Democrat, Minnesota), were cases such as the International Monetary Fund (IMF) loans to the Pinochet government in Chile after Congress had cut off American aid to that regime. This seemed to signal an executive willingness to vitiate congressionally mandated human-rights sanctions by making up any lost funds for other sources. In 1976, Congress had required the American representatives to two of these multinational institutions—the Inter-American Development Bank (IADB) and the African Development Fund (ADF)—to vote against any loan or extension of financial or technical assistance to any country that engaged (in the standard phrasing) "in a consistent pattern of gross violations of internationally recognized human rights," unless such assistance would directly benefit the needy people in that country. In its February/March, 1977, report, the International League for Human Rights had recommended that this mandate be extended to the

World Bank. It should not have been surprising, then, that when the bill to replenish and increase the American contribution to these agencies—the IADB, the ADF, the World Bank, the Asian Development Bank, and the International Finance Corporation—came before the Congress in the early spring of 1977, it would become the subject of an intense battle over human rights.[36]

HR 5262 provided $5.2 billion over three years for these five institutions, but the sums involved provoked little controversy compared with the bill's new section, Title V, on human rights. The wording of Title V was the product of long negotiations between the administration (which had at first stiffly opposed any mention of human rights) and Representative Henry S. Reuss (Democrat, Wisconsin). Reuss had met with Carter on this subject just prior to Inauguration Day, and broader meetings involving a number of congressional leaders and representatives of the White House, the State Department, and the Treasury had followed. Their labors—described by one State Department official as "rather tense"—had resulted in language that pledged the American government to use "its voice and vote" in these five institutions to "advance the cause of human rights," and allowed, but did not require, American representatives to the five agencies to follow this mandate "by seeking to channel assistance toward countries other than" human-rights violators. This was the form in which the bill emerged from hearings and markup before the Subcommittee on International Development Institutions and Finance and Reuss' full Committee on Banking, Finance, and Urban Affairs.[37]

The administration suffered a sharp setback when the bill was brought to the House floor on April 6, however. The language to which it had agreed with Reuss was assailed as too weak by Congressman Herman Badillo (Democrat, New York), who offered an amendment that would reinstate the tougher language of the previous year mandating that the United States vote against assistance to human-rights violators in the IADB and the ADF and

---

36. Donald Fraser, "Freedom and Foreign Policy," *Foreign Policy*, XXVI (Spring, 1977), 153; Inter-American Bank and African Development Fund, Title I, secs. 101, 103, 104, 90 Stat. 591–593 (1976); International League for Human Rights, "Implementing a Human Rights Commitment," 73.

37. House hearings, *International Development Institutions*, 2, 65–67; Drew, "Human Rights," 44, 46; Reuss to Brzezinski, February 15, 1977, and accompanying draft bill by Reuss, and Brzezinski to Reuss, February 28, 1977, in White House Central File, Box FO-33, Folder FO 4-2 1/20/77–12/31/77, JCL.

extending it to the other institutions. Despite the circulation of an April 2 letter from Carter to Reuss opposing such a provision as "an overly rigid approach which would subvert the integrity and effectiveness of the institutions," the Badillo language was adopted. The entire bill then passed, 194–156.[38]

The floor debate on the Badillo amendments drew the lines of battle clearly. Both sides in a sense saw themselves as defenders of institutional integrity. On one side were those who portrayed the issue as the preservation of the nonpolitical character of the IFIs. They pointed to Article 4, Section 10, of the Articles of Agreement of the World Bank, promising that the bank would not interfere in the internal affairs of any member and that only "economic considerations" and not "the political character" of the states concerned would weigh in its decisions. If this provision, and its nearly identical counterparts in the charters of the other international agencies, were disregarded by the United States in its promotion of human rights, other states would feel free to lodge similar claims, making their votes on assistance contingent on the recipient country's adoption of their preferred position on political questions of interest to them. The IFIs would become entirely politicized, and questions of economic need and the effectiveness of the proposed assistance would become secondary. This was not the place for Washington to stake a claim on the states-system, even for a subject as important as human rights.

Proponents of the more stringent Badillo language, on the other hand, also believed themselves to be protecting institutional prerogatives—those of Congress. Having painfully wrested power from the presidency in the mid-1970s, they had no intention of letting it slip from them now. They were therefore extremely reluctant to allow the president—any president— the discretion that the Reuss language provided. (Ironically, this suspicion was strongest among members of Carter's own party.) If Congress did not insist that the United States assert an interest in determining its votes in the IFIs on human-rights grounds, the executive branch would acquiesce as multilateral agencies made up for cuts in bilateral American aid imposed on human-rights violators. All the other claims asserted in the area of human rights would be vitiated.

Meanwhile, the administration was going through a similar internal de-

38. *Congressional Record,* 95th Cong., 1st Sess., 10761–94; Drew, "Human Rights," 46, 51–52.

bate. On one hand were Brzezinski, Vance and much of the State Department, and Secretary of the Treasury Michael Blumenthal and his department, who favored executive discretion. They argued that the "wooden" Badillo language would undermine efforts to promote human-rights objectives in the IFIs. If it were known that the United States would automatically vote "no" on any loan, "neither donor nor recipient countries [would] have any incentive to work with us on improving the human rights situation." Alone, Washington did not have the votes to block loans, so that "virtually all loans would go ahead over our objections." There were cases in which the United States should vote for loans to countries that abused human rights: "For example, we could 'ransom' some prisoners or reduce other offensive practices by calibrating our positions on particular loans—even if the offending country maintained some offensive practices." The United States could most easily work quietly with other donor states to have loans denied, or withdrawn before even coming to a vote, if it did not take a position "offensive to the integrity of the institutions" by enacting a "unilateral amendment of the . . . charters" of the IFIs.[39]

On the other hand was Robert Lipshutz, the White House counsel, acting as the advocate for the human rights bureau, who favored mandatory opposition to all loans to states that fell within the human-rights standard, except loans that advanced basic human needs. He argued that a fight against the Badillo language "well might undermine much of our credibility in our espousal of Human Rights as a fundamental cornerstone of our foreign policy." The United States had "only a few means of implementing this policy," and it should not throw away the leverage that the IFIs represented. Approval of the Badillo language would still leave the "needy peoples" exception for the president to use at his discretion, along with bilateral assistance and the option of going to Congress on truly "urgent" matters. If taking human-rights violations into account was inconsistent with the IFI charters, "then presumably [Washington] could *never* consider Human Rights violations relative to a loan application—whether our vote was mandatory or discretionary under our law." The conjectures that the United

39. Memorandum from the Treasury, April 14, 1977, Memorandum from Vance to the president and accompanying draft letter from the president to Humphrey, Badillo and Humphrey amendments to HR 5262, April 15, 1977, Memorandum from Brzezinski and Frank Moore to the president, April 16, 1977, Memorandum from Rick Hutcheson to Frank Moore, April 18, 1977, all in White House Central File, Box HU-1, Folder HU 4-1-77–4-30-77, JCL.

States would lose its ability to bargain or would be isolated were "no more than arguable opinions."[40]

Vance and Brezezinski carried the day, however, and the administration redoubled its efforts as the debate moved to the Senate. At an April 15 press conference the president called the Badillo amendment "a mistake" and argued that a mandated negative vote on loans deprived potential recipients of any incentive to negotiate improvements in human-rights practices in return for assistance. He followed that with a memorandum to Senator Humphrey during the markup session of the Senate Foreign Relations Committee, in which he said that the bill was passed by the House was "weak and ineffective" and "would handicap our efforts to encourage human rights improvements in other countries." Lobbying by Carter and his subordinates was rewarded by the vote of the committee on April 19 not only to reject the House provisions and return to the language agreed on by Reuss and the administration but also to retain the "needy people" provision. Even so, the president admitted that he was having "a very hard time" in the fight.[41]

HR 5262 came to the Senate floor June 14. Senator James Abourezk (Democrat, South Dakota) offered an amendment restoring the requirements approved by the House; anything less exacting, he said, would be undermined by "certain people" in the administration who did not wish to support the president's words with actions. Unlike the House, the Senate was apparently convinced by the administration and its supporters, and the Abourezk amendment was defeated, 43–50—a margin closer than those supporting the president had expected, but still enough to carry the day. The Senate then approved the entire bill, 59–30. Three days later, the president scored another victory when, in the House, a motion by Representative Joun Rousselot (Republican, California), instructing the House members of the Senate-House conference committee on HR 5262 to stand by the Badillo language, failed, 161–200.[42]

Having won in the Senate and apparently having persuaded the House to reverse itself, the administration could look forward to a report from the

40. Memorandum from Lipshutz to the president, April 17, 1977, in Staff Offices—Counsel—Lipshutz series, Box 19, "Human Rights (Re International Financial Institutions Legislation), 4/8/77 (Cf, O/A, 120)" folder, JCL.

41. *Public Papers: Carter,* 1977, I, 636, 766; *Congressional Record,* 95th Cong., 1st Sess., 18924–19007; New York *Times,* April 20, 1977, Sec. 1, p. 5.

42. New York *Times,* June 15, 1977, Sec. 4, p. 5, June 19, 1977, Sec. 3, p. 5.

conference committee that gave it the latitude to promote human rights as it saw fit. The negotiations over a compromise were arduous—an exasperated Carter on July 16 called his own stance on human rights "fairly moderate" compared with that of some members of Congress—but in the end the president's hopes were not disappointed. The conference report made gestures to both bodies, but it clearly leaned in the direction of the Senate. It provided (1) that American representatives on the financial institutions were to use their voice and vote to channel funds away from consistent human-rights violators (the Senate's language), and (2) that they were to oppose loans to violators unless the assistance served basic human needs (the language of the House), but only (3) "where other means have proved ineffective," and not if (4) "the President verifies that the cause of international human rights would be more effectively served by actions other than voting against such assistance" (both new compromise provisions that had been passed by neither house but were in the spirit of the Senate's tolerance for executive discretion). Recognizing in the conference report its own handiwork, the Senate approved it by voice vote on July 27.

What followed confirmed the administration's worst fears about the extent to which the human-rights campaign, including its own pronouncements, had aroused the House. That body, following the summer recess, took up the bill on September 16 and, in a serious setback for the president, voted 153–230 against the conference report. Representative Tom Harkin (Democrat, Iowa) immediately moved to substitute for the defeated bill one that removed the two new provisions drafted by the conference committee. Shorn of these two loopholes, the bill had now returned to what was basically the original Badillo language. Nevertheless, the president's supporters, in no mood to continue the fight for executive discretion any longer, were prepared to accept it. Reuss acceded to the Harkin language, and the House passed the bill by voice vote. On September 21, after Foreign Relations Committee chairman John Sparkman (Democrat, Alabama) had also reversed himself and urged acceptance of the House version, the Senate followed suit. (Sparkman and others who argued against tying the president's hands too closely took what comfort they could from the broad interpretation they said would be given to the requirement that American representatives "oppose" loans to human-rights violators. Straining the limits of the dictionary, they insisted that while to "oppose" could mean to vote no, it could also mean to vote "present," to abstain, or to do anything else but vote yes.)

Carter signed HR 5262 into law on October 3 with no public statement. It could not have been a triumphant occasion for him. Far from leading the human-rights charge, he was now in danger of being trampled by it. Instead of persuading Congress to trust him with the leeway to promote human rights as he thought best, his rhetoric had helped to spur it into writing new restrictions on presidential power. He would now have to administer a human-rights policy in the international lending agencies that he himself had called "weak" and "ineffective," while fending off new challenges from a Congress whose appetite for intervention seemed to grow by what it fed on. He was in the odd situation of making a claim on other states that he considered excessive and likely to be rejected.[43]

De-linking human rights

Carter's predicament might have seemed even more troubling to him if he were not putting forth one final claim: that human rights could be separated from other issues. Those advocating that this interest be asserted believed that even though the United States linked its stance on human rights with its aid policies or its positions in the international financial institutions, other states would not tie human rights to matters of interest to them. It was perhaps the most difficult claim for the administration to make.

One issue from which Carter tried to isolate human-rights concerns was arms control. The Soviet Union was one of the world's more serious violators of human rights. It was also the United States' necessary partner in the control of strategic arms. Could pressure on the one issue coexist with collaboration on the other? In Vance's first press conference, on January 31, 1977, three days after Dobrynin's telephone call to him to protest the State Department's warning on Sakharov, the secretary told his questioners, "I do not believe that it will have a negative impact [on arms control]. . . . I am sure that our discussions with the Soviet Union on a whole range of matters will not be adversely affected by what we have said."[44] When Vance arrived in Moscow for his negotiations on SALT two months later, however, this confidence came into question; on the second day of the talks, March 30,

43. G. D. Loescher, "U.S. Human Rights Policy and International Financial Institutions," *The World Today*, XXXIII (December, 1977), 453–63.

44. U.S. Department of State, *Bulletin*, LXXVI (February 21, 1977), 148; New York *Times*, February 5, 1977, Sec. I, p. I.

the Russians showed where they stood by curtly—and publicly—rejecting the new proposals Vance had brought and breaking off the discussions. A serious setback for arms control and a deep personal disappointment to the president, the episode forced a reexamination of policy.

There were indeed other explanations for the Kremlin's sharp rejection. The new proposals Vance brought to Moscow were a bold step that represented a considerable departure from the tentative agreement reached at Vladivostock in the Ford years. When the rejection came, then, administration officials consistently denied that any connection had existed between American pressures on human rights and Soviet suspicions on arms control. At his news conference in Moscow immediately after the Soviets' dismissal of the American plan, Vance maintained that there had been no link: "Human rights did not come up after the first day. We never discussed it again. . . . I don't believe that it did [affect the Soviets' thinking on the American proposals]. . . . I think it stood on its own feet." Carter spoke with reporters in Washington the same day; while he admitted that he could not "certify" that the breakoff of the talks was not due to his human-rights stand, he insisted, "I will not modify my human rights statements. My human rights statements are compatible with the consciousness of this country. . . . I don't think that it's accurate to link the human rights concept with the SALT negotiations. . . . I'm not discouraged at all."[45]

By the following month, the president, in a slight shift, was saying, not that it was untrue that the Soviets were linking the two issues, but that it would be a mistake for the Americans to do so. In an NBC interview on April 14, he noted that it would be a "step backward" to abandon human rights in order to improve the chances for arms control. On June 11, he returned to the issue, telling the Magazine Publishers Association that the United States should "aggressively challenge" the Soviet Union for influence by proclaiming its beliefs on human rights. While granting that some targets of his human-rights criticisms had been annoyed, he insisted, "We ought not to be timid about putting our best foot forward. . . . I think that if we stand for something we ought to be forceful about it. We might win some and lose

45. New York *Times*, March 31, 1977, Sec. 1, pp. 1, 10, 11, 12, April 15, 1977, Sec. 1, p. 11; *Public Papers: Carter, 1977*, I, 541, 560; Senate report, *Human Rights and Foreign Assistance*, 69; Carter, *Keeping Faith*, 149; Vance, *Hard Choices*, 54; Brzezinski, *Power and Principle*, 557; Malcolm Toon, "In Defense of the Foreign Service," *New York Times Magazine*, December 12, 1982, p. 96.

some in relationships with other countries. But in general, though, I have been pleased." Two weeks later, he was reported to have told Vance, Brzezinski, and Mondale that he doubted that Soviet-American relations would improve in the next few months, until the leaders in the Kremlin accustomed themselves to his human-rights and other initiatives. Along with other disputes, the issue of human rights had "provided a greater obstacle to other friendly pursuits" than he had expected, he told a gathering of news editors.[46]

A year afterward, the controversy within the administration was over charges that the State Department was undermining the campaign for human rights, precisely in order to improve Soviet-American ties. Following the end of the Belgrade meeting, a memorandum of June 19, 1978, from Joyce Starr, an associate director of the White House Office of Public Liaison with primary responsibility for contacts with Soviet Jewry, to Lipshutz and Stuart Eizenstat, the president's chief domestic adviser, called the Helsinki process "a failure of U.S. diplomacy." She charged American embassy officials in most of Eastern Europe and the Soviet Union with side-stepping human-rights concerns: "While the Secretary of State and the President were both confirming publicly and privately our general commitment to human rights and the Helsinki Agreement, our diplomats were not providing official explanations (demarches) of precise expectations." American representatives were able to slough off their responsibilities, she said, because Marshall Shulman, the chairman of the Inter-Agency Task Force on Soviet Affairs, and George Vest, the assistant secretary for European affairs, "consistently overruled" Derian and provided "no follow-through" for the president's concerns, in the interest of conciliating Moscow.[47]

The administration had begun by staking a claim to isolate human rights from other issues of interest to the United States, especially arms control. It had then denied that setbacks in arms-control talks were caused by its human-rights stance. Later, while admitting that Moscow might be delaying progress on SALT in retaliation for human-rights criticisms, it had suggested that this was a price worth paying for human rights, and that

46. *Public Papers: Carter,* 1977, I, 1088–89, 1166–67, 1210; New York *Times,* April 15, 1977, Sec. 1, p. 11, June 12, 1977, Sec. 1, p. 15, June 20, 1977, Sec. 1, p. 10, June 26, 1977, Sec. 1, p. 1.

47. Starr to Lipshutz and Eizenstat, June 18, 1978, Starr and Cliff Brody to Lipshutz, Eizenstat, and Joe Aragon, June 19, 1978, both in Staff Offices—Counsel—Lipshutz series, Box 46, "Soviet Jewry, 4/78–4/79" folder, JCL.

eventually the Soviets would accommodate themselves to the two-track American approach. Eighteen months into the president's term, senior officials were softening their stance on human rights so as to encourage movement on arms control. This was the story of a claim being abandoned.

A SUMMING-UP FROM THE WHITE HOUSE

The disappearance of the subsidiary claim that foreign states should not hold other matters hostage to American human-rights concerns made it all the more important to stand by the basic claim that the United States would expect the countries with which it did business to respect human rights. On October 27, 1978, Brzezinski told Carter that the election of Pope John Paul II could "be viewed as part of a new era of human rights" and that "the worldwide demand for human rights is a growing political force." The national security adviser counseled, "You should reaffirm the U.S. commitment." An opportunity presented itself on December 6, the thirtieth anniversary of the signing of the Universal Declaration of Human Rights. A White House ceremony would be a fitting way to commemorate this milestone. It would provide a convenient occasion to lobby members of Congress on the human-rights covenants submitted by the president to the Senate for ratification. It would remind both domestic and foreign audiences of the importance the administration attached to human rights and counteract the impression that it had lost its enthusiasm for their promotion.[48]

Anne Wexler, assistant to the president, arranged a briefing in the East Room for members of Congress, private citizens, and officials in organizations interested in the human-rights cause. Lasting about an hour and a half, the midday meeting began with short statements by Vance and Wexler, continued with longer remarks by Brzezinski and Derian and a question-and-answer period conducted by Derian, and concluded with an appearance by the president, who gave his own brief address.[49] In the ceremony, the five

48. Brzezinski, *Power and Principle*, 127, 563; Washington *Post*, December 7, 1978, Sec. A, p. 2; Memorandum, Brzezinski and Gerald Rafshoon to Carter, December 4, 1978, in Rafshoon Files, Box 14, "Human Rights Speech, 12/6/78" folder, JCL.

49. Carter's remarks may be found in Carter *Public Papers*, 1978, pp. 2161–65. The transcript of the remainder of the program was issued by the office of the White House press secretary as Press Release No. 2723. The speeches given on the occasion were compiled in a

speakers attempted to convince their listeners, and their wider audience, that human-rights issues had won for themselves a place in the administration's conception of the national interest and in the country's foreign policy. Now at the midpoint of the president's term, they spoke less of bold new approaches and more of a settled policy arrived at over the preceding two years. At the same time, they repeated their long-range goals and argued for continued efforts by pointing to the results that had already been achieved.

These statements were a distillation of the arguments that members of the administration had been making to justify their new set of claims on the states-system, as well as the accommodations that two years of contact with the pressures of the system had forced them to make. There was a good deal of emphasis, as there had always been, on the close connection between human rights in foreign policy and the general national common good. The president employed this argument: "Human rights is the soul of our foreign policy. And I say this with assurance, because human rights is the soul of our sense of nationhood. . . . What unites us—what makes us Americans— is a common belief in peace, in a free society, and a common devotion to the liberties enshrined in our Constitution." Brzezinski also spoke of the nation's having "consciously . . . shape[d] itself around a central philosophical idea, namely, the idea of the independence and freedom of man."

Given this heavy reliance by the American national community on a shared adherence to inalienable rights, the failure to promote those rights abroad had endangered the American community at home. The American regime could not survive schizophrenia, Derian argued: it could not follow one set of standards in domestic affairs and another in foreign affairs. Therefore, the administration's human-rights policy was "important to the health and integrity of this society within the United States. Support for or indifference to oppression in other countries weakens the foundation of our democracy at home." Opposition to human-rights violations provided a way for the country to redeem its heritage by rising above traditional power politics to display altruism. "I'm very proud that our Nation stands for more than military might or political might. It stands for ideals," said Carter.

---

booklet, *The White House Commemoration of the 30th Anniversary of the Universal Declaration of Human Rights* (Washington, D.C., 1978). See also *Checklist of Human Rights Documents*, IV (March, 1979), 13.

The argument that pressing for respect for human rights served particular American interests by increasing American power also reappeared. Derian contended, "Human rights is an area where our ideals and our self-interest strongly coincide," because an effective human-rights policy "strengthens our position and influence in the world." It was, in Brzezinski's words, "politically useful—and I am not hesitant in saying that—for the United States to carry high the standard of human rights, for we are then in the forefront of a powerful movement which indeed has worldwide appeal. And we gain from it."

Several of the speakers pressed the point that the definition of the human rights they hoped to protect was justifiable to the other members of the states-system—that is, that it was not a purely idiosyncratic American invention. "When I say 'human rights,'" Brzezinski granted, "I recognize the fact that in a globally diverse world, there will be different emphases, and what we stress may be defined and stressed differently in different parts of the world." At bottom, however, all states had the same obligations toward their citizens. Vance grounded these obligations in international law. "Although the policy reflects basic American ideals, it is not an attempt to impose uniquely American values," he insisted, noting that the very occasion for the White House session was an international statement that had been approved by almost every UN member state. "The rights about which we are concerned, the right to be free from torture, to be free from arbitrary arrest, rights of political expression, the rights to basic economic needs, are recognized in the U.N. Carter and in other international agreements as being universal in their application throughout the world," the secretary argued.

Carter also spoke of governments' legal responsibilities as well as their ethical duties. He appealed to the Universal Declaration's withdrawal of every state's "cloak of sovereignty" and to its requirement that "our Nation fulfill . . . its own international obligations" by furthering human rights elsewhere. In the only explicit effort on this occasion at ranking the three categories of rights, he put the "rights of the person" first, while social and economic rights seemed to eclipse civil and political rights, which might help to make human rights more attractive to illiberal regimes.

If the United States had a right, a responsibility, and an interest in promoting a human-rights standard that it claimed was internationally sanctioned, it also had an interest in speaking out on violations and remonstrating with violators. Derian claimed that discussions of human rights had been accepted as a legitimate part of diplomatic negotiations, both by American representatives and by other countries, though she added that everyone remained "a little bit uneasy and nervous about it." Quiet diplomacy was supplemented by "symbolic [public] affirmations of our concern": "The president says something, the Secretary says something, it is in a speech, it is in a press conference, it is in a press release, it is in a casual comment, it is in a letter, it is whatever way you can find at some point when it seems like the right instrument to have a strong public gesture." While neither Vance nor Brzezinski endorsed public appraisals and condemnations, the president pledged to "speak out when individual rights are violated in other lands."

Carter and Derian were also the most explicit in laying claim to the position that Washington could unapologetically take human rights into account when allocating foreign aid. The assistant secretary made reductions in aid seem a last resort: "When there is no response to quiet expressions of human rights concerns, there is no response to a symbolic speaking out, our law and our policy demand that we examine . . . our Assistants' [sic] relationship, economic and military." The president accentuated the positive rewards that could come to countries with superior or improving records on human rights: "In distributing the scarce resources of our foreign assistance programs, we will demonstrate that our deepest affinities are with nations that commit themselves to a democratic path to development." Neither chose to emphasize reductions in assistance as a way of punishing states that failed to respect human rights, and no one at the briefing spoke in favor of using the IFIs as an instrument of human-rights policy.

All of these steps had become possible, not only because of the heritage of American political thought, and not only because of the evolving demands by citizens on governments in other states, but also because of the changing terms of discourse among states. Domestic awareness of and adherence to notions of human rights had spilled over into international diplomacy; most of the speakers did not even feel it was necessary to demonstrate this was the case, so clear did the penetration of human-rights concerns into the dialogue of governments seem to them. Human rights—"the genuine . . . historical inevitability of our time," according to Brzezinski—had established itself as a claim that one state could make on another. Like any other interest, such a specific claim might or might not be considered justifiable by the state against which it was directed, and that state might or might not accept it, but it was no longer considered at the outset a violation of the unwritten norms of the society of states to raise the issue.

Yet while "human rights now sits at the table," in Derian's words, its place was not wholly secure. The assistant secretary feared its abandonment if outside activists did not continue to apply pressures on governments; in this sense, even unrealistic demands would be useful as a spur. "If that doesn't continue, then 15 or 20 years down the pike this will just be something else that happened or still has a little office percolating somewhere," she warned. "There is no question that we have got it and that we intend to hang onto it. Just make sure that everybody else who comes wants to hang onto it or is caused to." If an American administration less friendly to human rights came to power, claims regarding the issue could still slip out of the vocabulary of state interests once more.

Even if human-rights practices remained an accepted subject for claims among states, policy makers could still decline to press these interests because they believed other interests to be more important. The president referred to the inevitability of such choices in an oblique way: "We do live in a difficult and complicated world, a world in which peace is literally a matter of survival. . . . Often, a choice that moves us toward one goal tends to move us further away from another goal. Seldom do circumstances permit me or you to take actions that are wholly satisfactory to everyone."

Brzezinski made a more pointed parenthetical reminder when he said that every government was aware that its human-rights record would "affect its relationship with us," adding, "I use my words advisedly—will affect, not determine in its entirety, because we have to be cognizant of the fact that there are other considerations also involved in dealing with other governments, regional interests, specific bilateral interests, security concerns which may dictate different arrangements, even if these governments in some cases are unresponsive." Derian herself, who had reportedly clashed with Vance over allowing security interests ever to override human-rights issues, and who opposed Shulman's application of "quiet diplomacy" to the Soviet Union, granted that it was "incredibly complex to balance all of the things that are of great concern to the United States with all the other things." In these cautionary statements, the officials were injecting what had often been missing from the exuberant pronouncements of the administration's early days: a sense of the limitations on what the United States could do for human rights, because it had other, sometimes conflicting, interests.

Recognition of the risks that might arise in the pursuit of human rights, and of the legitimacy of claims that might run athwart a human-rights campaign, tempered the administration's policy. It also demonstrated the difficulties that could accompany the transmutation of human rights into state interests. As they were frequently defined, the "human rights" of individuals belonged to them through no one's gift and could be denied them only for the gravest of causes; in most cases, when human rights came into conflict with other rights, privileges, or conveniences, these other considerations had to give way and the privileged status of human rights had to be upheld. But the promotion of human rights, understood as a state's interest, did not automatically trump other interests, even in an administration as consciously protective of human rights as Carter's. Although its refusal to decide every case of competing interests in favor of human rights led to the appearance (and the reality) of inconsistency, the administration assumed that other needs and dangers in the international environment often had to take precedence; while human rights, in the president's phrase, could be the "soul," it could not safely and wisely be made the whole, of American foreign policy.[50]

Indeed, to a greater extent than any of the other policy departures examined here, the Carter human-rights initiative demonstrates the possibilities and limits of placing new types of claims on the international agenda as interests. The president and his subordinates could encourage already-existing domestic and foreign trends of opinion that legitimized the kinds of arguments that supported demands for other governments to change the way they treated their own citizens. They could sometimes make those claims stick, particularly against countries that were neither strong enough nor vital enough to other American interests to have countervailing leverage. What they could not do was to ignore the requirements of surviving, prospering, and countering threats to those other interests; they could not make human-rights policy coterminous with the whole of American foreign policy. They felt they could not make all the human-rights claims they might have made (as in the case of the IFIs), and they were unable to prevail on all the human-rights claims they did make (as in the case of the Helsinki review

---

50. Muravchik, *Uncertain Crusade*, 113–60; Susan L. Shirk, "Human Rights: What About China?," *Foreign Policy*, XXIX (Winter, 1977–78), 109–27.

conference), because other interests, more traditionally defined, circumscribed Washington's perceived freedom of action. Even in the midst of a concerted effort to introduce a new interest in the society of states, the administration had to recognize the legitimacy of a host of older understandings that defined the limits of a supportable claim on the system.

CONCLUSION: A Sense of Limits

THE NATIONAL INTEREST has received a prolonged working-over in these pages. It has been criticized, defined, defended, argued over, and dissected; it has served as the backdrop for the retelling of four familiar stories from American foreign policy. Without recapitulating what is already a bulky book, one ought not leave the reader without a summing-up.

Is the national interest ambiguous? The three presidents and their top subordinates who have appeared in these examples certainly used the words *national interest* frequently. Does this imply anything more than their skill at mouthing the term? Truman, Nixon, and Carter all said that the policy departures they were proposing would serve the national interest. Despite their invocation of the national interest, however, neither they nor their subordinates explicitly defined it, and they sometimes employed it in contradictory ways. Presumably, all knew that reliance on a popular term would ease their job of cajoling the political system into following their lead. Perhaps they could more readily milk the term of the favorable reactions it inspired if it remained vague enough to allow different publics to define it in their preferred ways.

Still, such political considerations do not mean that these officials lacked an appreciation for the national autonomy that would allow Americans to reason over and argue about their shared well-being.[1] C. B. Marshall has recalled that in a public career spanning most of the events described in this book, "I know of no case . . . in which the settlement of an issue of our national policy . . . would have been facilitated by injecting the question: Shall we or shall we not try to serve the national interest?"[2] Yet Marshall

---

1. See Henry Fairlie, "Does It Matter Whether America Matters?," *New Republic*, September 22, 1979, pp. 16–18.

2. C. B. Marshall, "National Interest and National Responsibility," *Annals of the American Academy of Political and Social Science*, CCLXXXII (July, 1952), 85.

clearly did not mean that decision makers decided to ignore the common good of the United States; just the opposite: the obligation to consider the national interest—to strive to elucidate it—was regarded as so obvious that it did not have to be discussed. This was true of even the most practical and politically astute policy-makers.

In questioning the adequacy of personal or intragovernmental interests, demands by extragovernmental interest groups, or ideological preconceptions as full explanations for why policy makers acted as they did, one need not conclude that officials always sought the national interest or were uniformly successful in discovering it. Indeed, it is the assertion that the national interest is whatever those in positions of power say it is—simultaneously relieving political figures of any risk of error and draining the concept of all substantive content—that deprives it of any usefulness. If, by contrast, the national interest is not determined by contemporary political actors, but only sought and (perhaps) discovered by them, then it can serve as a standard by which to assess particular policies. The national interest is defined by prudence and good judgment, not by official authority or by any particular political process; it allows the observer to place specific actions in a broader context and to judge them by a consistent measure.

The four cases described here illustrate the value of Kennan's understanding of the national interest—the continued ability of Americans (or any people) to carry on their domestic search for their common good without undue hindrance or danger from outside. Here is another sense in which Marshall's observation is correct. In their everyday discussions of specific policies, decision makers are not usually dealing with the national interest, because no serious prospect of foreign interference is present. Not all the specific national interests that leaders may assert stem from the overall national interest: in the words of Kenneth Waltz, "If the preservation of the state is not in question, national goals easily fluctuate between the grandiose and the frivolous."[3] If these asserted goals or interests are to be defended, it must be on grounds other than the securing from foreign interference of the society's never-completed quest for the common weal. Likewise, as long as the domestic community is not directly or indirectly interfered with, no one policy within that range or margin of safety can be said to be recommended

3. Kenneth N. Waltz, *Foreign Policy and Democratic Politics: The American and British Experience* (Boston, 1967), 15–16. See also Barry Buzan, *People, States and Fear: An Agenda for International Security Studies in the Post–Cold War Era* (2nd ed.; Boulder, 1991), 57–111.

over another by considerations of the national interest. When policy options are debated, the choice must be made for other reasons. What that choice should be in any specific instance, of course, would vary with the circumstances. Reliance on the national interest should not predispose the observer to believe that any policy-maker or institution always has the clearest insight into the policies dictated by the national interest. That is a matter for informed debate. What the adherent of analysis based on the national interest must insist on is that the participants in the policy process be clear on what they are debating—when they are discussing the national interest and when, the security of the country from outside threats being assured, they are deciding policy on other terms. Many times—perhaps most of the time in a country with the United States' margin of security—they are deciding on grounds other than the national interest.

An adherence to Kennan's conception of the national interest need not lead others to follow Kennan into the posture of a self-described isolationist, however. The domestic requirements of the regime found in its fundamental principles may impel it to act in certain ways in its foreign policy, taking on further tasks after the minimal requirements of the national interest have been met. While the Carter administration embraced the clearest example of this phenomenon, the Marshall Plan can also be seen as a broad-gauged initiative that went beyond the basic duty of self-preservation, both because its framers could see that in the long run European economic collapse could bring great dangers to America's safety from outside interference, and because the American conscience responded to the "humanitarian interest," as the report of the Harriman Committee put it, in a way demanded by the ethical maxims that Americans said they lived by.

I would argue that in none of these four instances did policy makers stray so far outside the range described by the United States' requirements for security that they could be said to be acting against the national interest. In three of the four, they advanced the national interest in Kennan's narrow understanding of it, though the administration's case for intervention in Korea went well beyond language based on the nation's duty to itself and would ultimately provoke the corrective sought through the Nixon Doctrine. The Carter campaign for human rights exceeded this limited definition of national interest in substance as well as rhetoric, but competing interests ensured that the policy was not carried so far as to undermine the country's power. Administration figures were reduced to taking limited, ameliorative steps, though the logic of the human-rights movement, and in some cases their own prior history, had suggested much bolder measures. (And delays over reconciling these positions help to explain why a settled policy on human rights did not emerge until almost two years into the president's term.)

Similarly, when one asks whether the national interest is dangerous, and especially whether it is amorally exclusivist, the least one can say after reviewing these four cases is that interest-based thinking is not incompatible with the application of ethical principles. The need to bring other countries along in support of the claims that the United States was making in each instance, and the character of the American polity itself, meant that the conception of the common good and the specific interests being asserted had to be associated with broader goals than simple unshared gain. Gain was certainly aimed at, but the principles that also influenced policy made these episodes efforts at what Michael Donelan has called "interest considered right."[4] As Tocqueville and Madison argued, self-interest is concerned with wealth and power, but also with the uses to which wealth and power may be put: with the preservation of the system or society within which the mundane scrabbling for again goes on, or with the achievement of lasting renown for achieving great (and at least somewhat unselfish) deeds. Farsightedness can make both a concern for the institutional health of the system and a desire for fame elements in one's calculus of self-interest, because, as Walter Lippmann recognized, "There is no one self always at work. . . . And so while it is so true as to be mere tautology that 'self-interest' determines opinion, the statement is not illuminating, until we know which self out of many selects and directs the interest so conceived."[5]

In each of these four instances, policy makers tried to mold their asserted claims around a central virtue as well as power and plenty—to appeal to self-interest broadly understood. In the case of the Marshall Plan, one sees the national interest clothed in generosity. Here were peoples in serious need. Here, too, were circumstances that come but rarely; one can detect the sense by those involved that the history of the United States was at a turning point, that what they did would be remembered for a very long time, and that for the sake of their appearance to posterity if nothing else, they should pursue the self-interest of the United States in a large-minded and

4. Michael Donelan, "A Community of Mankind," in *The Community of States: A Study in International Political Theory,* ed. James Mayall (London, 1982), 140–57.

5. Walter Lippmann, *Public Opinion* (1922; rpr. New York, 1946), 173.

generous way. That the United States did benefit, and hugely, from the economic recovery of and its political alliance with Western Europe is not to be denied. That Washington, in concert with the Europeans, found ways of broadening its national interest to include generosity to its future partners was no less helpful to Western Europe because American policy-makers did *generosity* not forget their own national interest. That the Marshall Plan is still remembered as a great act of statesmanship shows that its framers were not mistaken in thinking they were serving the country's longer-term interest in its ✓ reputation.

Truman's decision to intervene in the Korean War demonstrates the na- *national* tional interest understood as national honor. The United States had seen *honor* nothing intrinsically valuable in the Korean Peninsula, and it had been making that estimation clear through its actions for more than two years by the summer of 1950. Brought by the invasion to change its calculation and to accept that the proximity of Japan, and the need to deter whatever danger existed of other military contests supported by the Soviet Union, made the defense of South Korea a claim that Washington could reasonably make on the states-system, the Americans surely had their own security in mind as they came to their decisions. "To back away from this challenge, in view of our capacity for meeting it, would be highly destructive of the power and prestige of the United States," Acheson recalled thinking at the time. "By prestige I mean the shadow cast by power, which is of great deterrent importance."[6] As the secretary's remarks imply, decision makers were thinking of the American reputation as well. Through its defeat of Japan, Washington had helped to create a vacuum of power in the area of the Japanese home islands. In Kennan's words, it had thereby taken on a responsibility for the security of the region, until Japan could recover. While this was not a responsibility or duty the United States owed to anyone in a legal sense—and it does not seem to have been a moral obligation owed to the United Nations, given the assiduousness with which Americans had been trying to shift responsibility for Korean affairs to the international body since 1947—it was an obligation Kennan believed Americans owed to themselves, if they were to continue to call themselves an honorable (a "responsible") people. Immediate interests of the United States were at risk in the summer of 1950; so was the country's honor. Honor was a long-term inter-

6. Dean Acheson, *The Korean War* (New York, 1971), 20.

est that went beyond the autonomy demanded by the overall national interest; it was a particular interest that could not be understood without a grasp of the kind of people Truman and his associates thought Americans to be. Honorable action in this sense coincided with action intended to keep up the country's side in its power competition with Moscow, and with action to vindicate the universal principles of peace, collective security, and opposition to aggression wherever it might occur.

Attachment to these general values can become addictive, of course. The Nixon administration took office with the belief that during the nearly twenty years since the outbreak of war in Korea, American policy-makers had become so accustomed to justifying their actions under beneficent principles of universal scope that they had ceased to consider the possibility that abstract moral maxims might run counter to important national interests. Nixon and Kissinger proposed to wean American foreign policy away from intoxicating grand moralistic gestures and replace them with a diet of material interests mixed with the homelier virtue of prudence. They were convinced that the rhetoric and the actions demanded by the direct application to foreign policy of ethical rules of universal import had led Washington to intervene or pledge to intervene in too many areas for its resources to support and had deprived it of the flexibility necessary to any successful diplomacy. Too many obligations to others, entered into under the aegis of broad statements of principle, had blinded the United States to the duties it owed itself. The resources demanded by these obligations threatened the country's ability to pursue its domestic goals unhindered by outside forces—that is, its national interest. Nixon and Kissinger—nationalists before they were ideologues—attempted to bring American power and commitments back into balance by shifting responsibilities to others and regaining freedom of action for the United States. Their aim went beyond the husbanding of American assets, however. "In the absence of agreement as to what constitutes a 'just' or 'reasonable' claim," Kissinger had contended only the year before taking office, "no basis for negotiation exists."[7] By placing renewed public emphasis on the role of interests, or specific, justifiable claims, as the medium of exchange in international politics, they tried to solidify an understanding with their major adversaries that would make challenges and collisions less frequent and less serious. It was in this effort to "manage"

7. Henry A. Kissinger, "The White Revolutionary: Reflections on Bismarck," *Daedalus,* XCVII (Summer, 1968), 900.

American resources with more care that their endeavor to associate national interest with prudence lay.

Perhaps Nixon, Kissinger, and Ford were too prudential. In any event, the Carter administration chose to go in another direction, aiming at combining self-interest and justice. It argued that it could hardly do otherwise and remain consistent with the United States' domestic search for its common good as embodied in its fundamental belief in inalienable human rights. Because the human-rights campaign, of all the policy departures examined here, seemed closest to pure disinterestedness, the administration made special efforts to demonstrate that the specific claims upon other states and upon the states-system that a concern for human rights entailed would serve other more material interests of the United States, especially if these national interests included a concern for reputation. If the American government did what it could to see that justice was done by other states to their nationals, at least in the comparatively narrow and irreducible category of rights known as "human" rights, it would be rewarded with goodwill from peoples around the world and lasting fame as the country that opened a new range of international cooperation in advancing the well-being of individuals everywhere. Under the circumstances, Carter contended, the United States would forfeit its self-respect—it would run the risk of losing its own "soul"—if it declined to promote respect for the rights of others outside its borders. In that sense, the human-rights campaign was a test of the country's fidelity to its own constantly reiterated domestic standards, rather than an exercise in compassion for strangers.

Yet if the Nixon Doctrine ran the risk of infusing self-interest with too little high-mindedness, the Carter campaign for human rights, at least in its early days, courted the opposite danger. The *via media* that both may have missed is to be found in magnanimity, the sort of high-mindedness that is engendered by self-respect. Again, the generosity, honor, prudence, and justice for which American decision-makers strove in these cases were first and foremost duties they owed to the American people, or to the kind of people they believed Americans were. These qualities are the product of universal moral laws filtered through the circumstances of time and place characteristic of a particular national community to give them specific content, reflected in the claimed national interests of that state.[8]

8. See Joseph Cropsey, "The Moral Basis of International Action," in *America Armed: Essays on United States Military Policy,* ed. Robert A. Goldwin (Chicago, 1969), 71–91; Marshall, "National Interest and National Responsibility," 84–90.

Thinking of ethical obligations in this way reinforces the picture of interest-based politics as a complex compromise, more subtle than either unvarnished self-assertion and cupidity or pure altruism resting directly on abstract moral principles. This compound character makes the politics of interest suited to an international setting that is a mixture of anarchy and society. Looking at a state's moral opportunity in this way also helps to guard against the sense of self-righteousness that tempts officials who conceive they are acting on principle pure and simple. It is too neat to say, as Lyndon Johnson did, quoting Jefferson, that "America's only interests in the world today are those that we regard as inseparable from our moral duty to mankind."[9] By recalling that they are working under a duty to the national interest, "qualified," as Madison cautioned, "with every necessary moral ingredient," and granting the same privilege to other leaders striving on behalf of other societies, statesmen may save themselves from the temptation to believe they have a special commission for the reform or punishment of a recalcitrant world, while at the same time they pursue large-minded goals out of a noble sense of self-respect.

A magnanimous devotion to right conduct—conduct that will bring luster to the state—is not the only restraint in place in international politics, however. Nor is the framework that is supplied by a political and cultural heritage. There are also other national or state interests, the specific claims made upon the state's environment in furtherance of policy. Each of these interests runs a gauntlet of other states as they judge it on its necessity to the claimant and the effect on the safety of others if the claim is allowed. It is striking how many of these asserted claims were rejected, even when they were put forth by the most powerful state in the system, which conceived itself to be acting for the benefit or protection of others. The many suggestions that the United States be repaid for Marshall Plan aid through preferential access to raw materials almost all came to naught, and Washington proved unable to use its assistance to maneuver Western Europe under some sort of supranational institution. The United States did not succeed in delivering South Korea into the custody of the UN and washing its hands of the peninsula before war broke out, and afterward Truman was persuaded not even to ask for as many troops from other countries as he might have. Washington did not withdraw from its position on the Asian mainland as rapidly

9. U.S. Department of State, *Bulletin*, LXIV (June 28, 1965), 1026.

as Mansfield would have done under his interpretation of the Nixon Doctrine, and it found its commitments more difficult to relinquish than even Nixon and Kissinger wished. Carter discovered that other countries refused to accept an American claim to separate the United States' stance on human rights from other aspects of any bilateral relationship, and the administration feared that a purely American definition of a human-rights standard would not be granted legitimacy by the states that would be expected to abide by it.

In all these instances one sees national interests at work as restraints. Thinking in the terms of national interests—of balancing power and commitments—forced policy makers to be calculators rather than crusaders. It limited their aims by inducing them to compare ends and means. Policy discussions within the administration or between the executive and legislative branches often brought these considerations to light. Because they knew that Congress would be resistant to an aid program bearing excessive costs, Lovett and others could be persuasive in bringing the Europeans to lower their request, which the administration itself considered inflated. Speaking in the terms of national interests—making claims on the international setting that would be convincing to others—forced policy makers to think of others' reactions as well as the United States' requirements and to mold and describe those requirements in ways that would not pinch the interests of other states too sharply. When policy soared too far above the identifiable needs of the countries that Washington had to bring along with it if it was to achieve its aims, as happened in the initial expectations on human rights, the recalcitrance of outside forces made the Americans reconsider. "I think," one member of the Carter administration said when the human-rights policy had been under way for some six months, "that the mulish world has noticed the two-by-four."[10] True, change had occurred, due in large part to the determination with which the American advocates for human rights had pressed their case. But this period and the months that followed also saw a reduction in the demands made on others as the continuing mulishness of the world encouraged Washington to whittle down its claims. The intractability of the issues and the recalcitrance of other states meant that as the Americans turned the principles of human rights into

10. Elizabeth Drew, "A Reporter at Large: Human Rights," *New Yorker*, July 18, 1977, p. 62.

concrete policies they had to review their asserted interests, make them more modest, and think hard about the case for them that the United States needed to make before the society of states. Why did Washington need to advocate this change? What interests of other states would be helped or harmed if they acceded to American pressure on the issue? If fellow members of the states-system were uncertain of the answers to these questions, as they were at least initially in the case of the Nixon Doctrine, they could decline to take the actions necessary to its success; thus, the Nixon administration found it had to pull back the American military presence more slowly, and supply American security partners more assistance, than it had originally hoped.

The role here of debate, of making a case, with supporting justification, before skeptical audiences, is crucial. Decision makers could assume they were part of a national community, in which they would be expected to argue for their position, not simply declaim it, and in which they could in turn expect that their arguments would be understood, even if they were not always accepted, because they drew on a shared body of knowledge and conventions (including ethical expectations). Each of the four departures in policy treated here—even the Nixon policy of retrenchment—required resources and thereby competed with American domestic needs and desires, whether public or private. Each of the three presidents who oversaw these departures could anticipate that he and his subordinates would be required to show how his policy was preferable to the alternatives. Parochial and shortsighted as they may sometimes appear, subnational interests carry on a continuous contest that forces leaders to sharpen their thinking and their arguments.

Somewhat more surprisingly, these American administrations found themselves engaged in an international debate as well. Carter was correct when he said in his speech at Notre Dame in 1978 that it was "a mistake to undervalue the power of words and of the ideas that words embody." In the society of states, the degree of understanding fostered by a sense of a shared history and destiny was less than in domestic public discourse, and the role of unvarnished power was greater; but Washington did not feel itself free to do whatever it pleased, without justifying its actions to others. The influence of international society was enough to create an expectation here too that the Americans would act in reference to interests and not to simple self-gratification. When Truman made his televised address on Korea, when

Nixon sent Congress his State of the World message, when Vance gave his Law Day speech, they were speaking not only to a domestic audience but also to the other members of the states-system.

It might be wondered how an overall national interest conceived as a duty to oneself can be reconciled with a clutch of asserted particular interests justified by making a convincing case to others. Why should foreign states accede to American wishes so that the United States can satisfy its own sense of honor? While the deliberation over the common interest of a national society and the bargaining among the participants in international society do proceed on different planes, the two conversations intermingle. As noted in Chapter III, political actors in one state are not unaware of the definition of the national interest that obtains in another. A member of international society that espouses an ideology that leads it to be hostile, aggressive, or insensitive to the interests of others is likely to find that they will combine to resist its claim of specific interests. In their tripartite meeting in Paris in June of 1947, Bevin and Bidault knew that one of the most damaging charges Molotov could make against the tentative American offer of aid was that the nature of capitalism in the United States required Washington to present a package of assistance that was in fact a Trojan Horse—an immediate infusion of resources concealing requirements that would ensnare the recipients in the service of the American economy. Similarly, those who were skeptical of the Carter policy on human rights argued that it was, or could be made to appear, a manifestation of "cultural imperialism," which √ would provoke foreign hostility toward other American interests.

Aware of these risks, policy makers in Washington could try to assuage concerns in other capitals by revising their list of American claims. As noted in Chapter IV, they could broaden their asserted interests by including points of shared benefit that others would also find in their interest, or they could narrow their range so as to avoid unnecessary conflicts with others. Truman wished to preserve the fiction that MacArthur would act at the orders of the UN rather than those of the White House, precisely to sidestep the self-damaging broad claim that military action in Korea was an American show run solely by the United States. Nixon asserted that reducing Washington's commitments would make it easier to come to an accommodation with Moscow. Efforts at broadening included the economic argument that Marshall Plan aid would make everyone, on both sides of the Atlantic, better off, and the political argument that foreign regimes would make themselves more stable if they responded to the rising universal demand for the respect of human rights.

All these considerations reinforce the picture of national interest as less than a right but more than a whim. Interests cannot claim the same moral warrant as rights; they are not so ethically exalted as actions taken in conformity with moral laws unmediated by the worldly influences of history, power, and the limitations on human reason and virtue. At the same time, true interests are real needs, sustainable by reasoned discourse, which requires taking the needs of others into account. Interest is in fact inextricably bound up with societies, both domestic and international, whose common understandings can sustain discourse, and with the interplay between them.

Interests are therefore difficult to generalize about, because they are tied to the nature of particular societies. This study has concentrated primarily on the formulation of claims by the United States. Equally important would be detailed examinations of the responses to those asserted interests by the other governments involved in these cases, and analyses of the forces that have led different states, with different regimes, to make the claims they have in different circumstances. The interaction between domestic and international society would vary with each situation.

In the late 1970s, when a representative of Amnesty International interviewed a group of Iranian dissidents about to go on trial and asked them about the circumstances under which their confessions had been obtained, they were prevented from answering by an official of the Shah's government, who told the interviewer that his question was "not in the national interest." On November 30, 1950, speaking to the House of Commons on the Korean War, Winston Churchill offered interest as a useful if imperfect guide to understanding:

> It is impossible to prophesy what [the Soviets] will do, or when, or how they will do it. One can only judge these matters by estimating what is in their interest. The great Duke of Marlborough quoted a saying in his day: "Interest never lies": and there is no doubt that trying to put oneself in the position of the other party to see how things look to him is one way, and perhaps the best way, of being able to feel and peer dimly into the unknowable future. It is, at any rate, the only guide—and it does not include accident, passion, folly

or madness, madness which may arise from some error, some blunder, or from the results of some internal convulsion.[11]

These two quotations illustrate what we should fairly expect from the concept of national interest. It is a way of making the international political world more intelligible—but it gives no guarantee that leaders will always see their states' interests clearly or act rationally. It prods the statesman to consider the claims and views of others—but there is no assurance that it will not be misused for low ends. As a standard of judgment and a tool of observation, it necessarily partakes of the ambiguities of the real phenomena it describes and the uniqueness of each case. In the difficult meeting of national societies with the society of states, these are no great faults; indeed, they are no mean virtues.

While this conclusion was being composed, the United States became involved in a new contest. Its relations much improved with the Soviet Union, its antagonist through all of the episodes in this book, it now confronted a regional power. Iraq staked a claim—to the territory of Kuwait, to the emirate's oil production, and to increased influence within OPEC and in the gulf. It adduced reasons legal (its previously announced claims to Kuwait), moral (its desire to redistribute wealth within the Arab world), and political (its hope to reunite the Arab nation against outside threats). Washington and most of the other members of the states-system remained unconvinced by these arguments and were not disposed to accede to Baghdad's definition of its legitimate interests. While assembling and then employing a large military force, the United States stated its own demands, including Iraq's withdrawal from Kuwait, and added several subsidiary interests, such as compensation for American war expenses from the oil-producing countries of the gulf and from its allies elsewhere. With no generally acceptable compromise in sight, the extent to which conflicting claims were honored was settled, not only by argument, but by force. Yet even as they employed the military "argument," these states showed themselves concerned to win the verbal and written argument as well, testifying to the hold that common understandings of legitimate interests have on international and domestic

11. House Committee on International Relations, *Foreign Assistance Legislation, Fiscal Year 1979* (1978), Pt. 4, pp. 216–17; *Parliamentary Debates* (Commons), 5th ser., 481 (1950), 1333.

societies. The interplay of interests goes on—though not without collisions and conflicts, not always skillfully managed—in a rough-and-ready accommodation characteristic of the setting within which it takes place. It may proceed the more smoothly if the nature of national interests is more clearly understood.

SELECTED BIBLIOGRAPHY
ON NATIONAL INTEREST

BOOKS

Arkes, Hadley. *Bureaucracy, the Marshall Plan, and the National Interest*. Princeton, 1972.

Beard, Charles A. *The Idea of National Interest: An Analytical Study in American Foreign Policy*. New York, 1934.

———. *The Open Door at Home: A Trial Philosophy of National Interest*. New York, 1934.

Beitz, Charles R. *Political Theory and International Relations*. Princeton, 1979.

Bentley, Arthur. *The Process of Government*. Edited by Peter Odegard. 1908; rpr. Cambridge, Mass., 1967.

Bloomfield, Lincoln P. *Vital Interests and Objectives of the United States*. Washington, D.C., 1963.

Brower, Michael J. *The U.S. National Interest—Assertions and Definitions*. Cambridge, Mass., 1959.

Carr, E. H. *The Twenty Years' Crisis, 1919–1939*. 1939; rpr. New York, 1964.

Cook, Thomas, and Malcolm Moos. *Power Through Purpose: The Realism of Idealism as a Basis for Foreign Policy*. Baltimore, 1954.

Crick, Bernard. *In Defence of Politics*. 2nd ed. Chicago, 1972.

Flathman, Richard E. *The Public Interest: An Essay Concerning the Normative Discourse of Politics*. New York, 1966.

Frankel, Joseph. *National Interest*. New York, 1970.

Friedrich, Carl J., ed. *The Public Interest*. New York, 1962.

Gaddis, John L. *Strategies of Containment: A Critical Appraisal of Postwar American National Security Policy*. New York, 1982.

Grossack, Irvin Millman. *The International Economy and the National Interest*. Bloomington, 1979.

Gulick, Edward V. *Europe's Classical Balance of Power: A Case History of the Theory and Practice of One of the Great Concepts of European Statecraft*. New York, 1967.

Hatch, Richard W. *Notes on Congress and the National Interest, 1945–1951.* Cambridge, Mass., 1957.

Held, Virginia. *The Public Interest and Individual Interests.* New York, 1970.

Herz, John H. *The Nation-State and the Crisis of World Politics: Essays on International Politics in the Twentieth Century.* New York, 1976.

Hirschmann, Albert O. *The Passions and the Interests: Political Arguments for Capitalism Before Its Triumph.* Princeton, 1977.

Johansen, Robert C. *The National Interest and the Human Interest: An Analysis of U.S. Foreign Policy.* Princeton, 1980.

Kennan, George F. *American Diplomacy, 1900–1950.* New York, 1951.

Kissinger, Henry A. *A World Restored: Metternich, Castlereagh and the Problems of Peace, 1812–1822.* Boston, 1973.

Krasner, Stephen D. *Defending the National Interest: Raw Materials Investments and U.S. Foreign Policy.* Princeton, 1978.

Kratochwil, Friedrich V. *International Order and Foreign Policy: A Theoretical Sketch of Post-War International Politics.* Boulder, 1978.

Leys, Wayne A. R., and Charner Perry. *Philosophy and the Public Interest.* Chicago, 1959.

Lippmann, Walter. *Essays in the Public Philosophy.* New York, 1955.

———. *Public Opinion.* New York, 1922.

Lowi, Theodore J. *The End of Liberalism: The Second Republic of the United States.* 2nd ed. New York, 1979.

Meinecke, Friedrich. *Machiavellism: The Doctrine of Raison d'Etat and Its Place in Modern History.* Translated by Douglas Scott. London, 1957.

Morgenthau, Hans J. *In Defense of the National Interest: A Critical Examination of American Foreign Policy.* New York, 1951.

———. *Politics Among Nations: The Struggle for Power and Peace.* 5th ed. New York, 1978.

Nuechterlein, Donald E. *America Overcommitted: United States National Interests in the 1980s.* Lexington, Ky., 1985.

———. *National Interests and Presidential Leadership: The Setting of Priorities.* Boulder, 1978.

———. *United States National Interests in a Changing World.* Lexington, Ky., 1973.

Osgood, Robert E. *Ideals and Self-Interest in America's Foreign Relations: The Great Transformation of the Twentieth Century.* Chicago, 1953.

Public Agenda Foundation/Carnegie Endowment for International Peace. *U.S. Foreign Policy: Principles for Defining the National Interest.* New York, 1976.

Reitzel, William, *et al. United States Foreign Policy, 1945–1955.* Washington, D.C., 1956.

Rohan, Henri, duc de. *A Treatise of the Interest of the Princes and States of Christendome.* London, 1643.

Schubert, Glendon. *The Public Interest: A Critique of the Theory of a Political Concept.* Glencoe, Ill., 1960.

Schultze, Charles L. *The Public Use of Private Interest.* Washington, D.C., 1977.

Truman, David B. *The Governmental Process: Political Interests and Public Opinion.* New York, 1951.

Van Dyke, Vernon, ed. *Some Approaches and Concepts Used in the Teaching of International Politics: Outlines Stemming from a Seminar on the Teaching of International Politics.* Iowa City, Iowa, 1957.

von Vorys, Karl. *American National Interest: Virtue and Power in Foreign Policy.* New York, 1990.

Waltz, Kenneth N. *Theory of International Politics.* Reading, Mass., 1979.

Wolfers, Arnold, and Laurence W. Martin, eds. *The Anglo-American Tradition in Foreign Affairs: Readings from Thomas More to Woodrow Wilson.* New Haven, 1956.

ARTICLES

Adler, Mortimer. "Parties and the Common Good." *Review of Politics,* I (January, 1939), 51–83.

Barnes, Harry Elmer. "National Interest and World War III." *American Perspective,* IV (Fall, 1950), 383–90.

Barnet, Richard J. "The National Security Managers and the National Interest." *Politics and Society,* I (February, 1971), 257–68.

Barry, Brian. "The Public Interest." In *The Bias of Pluralism,* edited by William E. Connolly. New York, 1969.

Bartlett, Ruhl J. "The Principles of National Interest." *American Perspective,* IV (Fall, 1950), 373–82.

Benn, S. I. "'Interests' in Politics." In *Proceedings of the Aristotelian Society.* London, 1960. N.s., LX, 123–40.

Bulbus, Isaac D. "The Concept of Interest in Pluralist and Marxian Analysis." *Politics and Society,* I (February, 1971), 151–77.

Carleton, William. "National Interest and the Balance of Power." *American Perspective,* IV (Fall, 1950), 346–58.

Cassinelli, C. W. "Some Reflections on the Concept of the Public Interest." *Ethics,* XXXXIX (October, 1958), 48–61.

Chase, John L. "Defining the National Interest of the United States." *Journal of Politics,* XVIII (November, 1956), 720–24.

Cochran, Clarke E. "Political Science and 'the Public Interest.'" *Journal of Politics,* XXXVI (May, 1974), 327–55.

———. "The Politics of Interest: Philosophy and the Limitations of the Science of Politics." *American Journal of Political Science,* XVII (November, 1973), 745–66.

———. "Yves R. Simon and 'the Common Good': A Note on the Concept." *Ethics,* LXXXVIII (April, 1978), 229–39.

Cole, Allan B. "National Interest in the Far East." *American Perspective,* IV (Fall, 1950), 391–401.

Colm, Gerhard. "In Defense of the Public Interest." *Social Research,* XXVII (Autumn, 1960), 295–307.

Connolly, William E. "On 'Interests' in Politics." *Politics and Society,* II (Summer, 1972), 459–77.

Cook, Thomas, and Malcolm Moos. "The American Idea of International Interest." *American Political Science Review,* XLVII (March, 1953), 28–44.

———. "Foreign Policy: The Realism of Idealism." *American Political Science Review,* XLVI (June, 1952), 343–56.

———. "Hindrances to Foreign Policy: Individualism and Legalism." *Journal of Politics,* XV (February, 1953), 114–39.

Corbett, P. E. "National Interest, International Organization, and American Foreign Policy." *World Politics,* V (October, 1952), 46–65.

Diggs, B. J. "The Common Good as Reason for Political Action." *Ethics,* LXXXIII (July, 1973), 283–93.

Donelan, Michael. "A Community of Mankind." In *The Community of States: A Study in International Political Theory,* edited by James Mayall. London, 1982.

Downs, Anthony. "The Public Interest: Its Meaning in a Democracy." *Social Research,* XXIX (Spring, 1962), 1–36.

Fox, William T. R. "The Reconciliation of the Desirable and the Possible." *American Scholar,* XVIII (Spring, 1949), 212–16.

Frankel, Joseph. "National Interest: A Vindication." *International Journal,* XXIV (Autumn, 1969), 717–25.

Garson, G. David. "On the Origins of Interest-Group Theory: A Critique of a Process." *American Political Science Review,* LXVIII (December, 1974), 1505–19.

George, Alexander L., and Robert O. Keohane. "The Concept of National Interest: Uses and Limitations." In *Presidential Decisionmaking in Foreign Policy: The Effective Use of Information and Advice,* edited by Alexander L. George. Boulder, 1980.

Good, Robert C. "The National Interest and Political Realism: Niebuhr's 'Debate' with Morgenthau and Kennan." *Journal of Politics,* XXII (November, 1960), 597–619.

Gunn, J. A. W. "'Interest Will Not Lie': A Seventeenth-Century Political Maxim."

Journal of the History of Ideas, XXIX (October–December, 1968), 551–64.

———. "Jeremy Bentham and the Public Interest." *Canadian Journal of Political Science*, I (December, 1968), 398–413.

Harmon, Michael Mont. "Administrative Policy Formation and the Public Interest." *Public Administration Review*, XXIX (September–October, 1969), 483–91.

Harrington, Fred Harvey. "Beard's Idea of National Interest and New Interpretations." *American Perspective*, IV (Fall, 1950), 335–45.

Hehir, J. Bryan. "Human Rights and the National Interest." *Worldview*, XXV (May, 1982), 18–21.

Kautsky, John H. "The National Interest: The Entomologist and the Beetle." *Midwest Journal of Political Science*, X (May, 1966), 222–31.

Kennan, George F. "Lectures on Foreign Policy." *Illinois Law Review*, XLV (January–February, 1951), 718–42.

Kirk, Grayson L. "In Search of the National Interest." *World Politics*, V (October, 1952), 110–15.

Knudsen, Olav. "National Interests and Foreign Policy: On the National Pursuit of Material Interests." *Conflict and Cooperation*, XIV (1979), 11–19.

Kratochwil, Friedrich. "On the Notion of 'Interest' in International Relations." *International Organization*, XXXVI (Winter, 1982), 1–30.

Krislov, Samuel. "What Is an Interest? The Rival Answers of Bentley, Pound, and MacIver." *Western Political Quarterly*, XVI (December, 1963), 830–43.

Latham, Earl. "The Group Basis of Politics: Notes for a Theory." *American Political Science Review*, XLVI (June, 1952), 376–97.

Licklider, Roy E., and Ploughman, Piers. "Soviet Control of Eastern Europe: Morality versus American National Interest—Advancing American Interests Through Soviet Control: A Modest Proposal—Rejoinder to Piers." *Political Science Quarterly*, XCI (Winter, 1976–77), 619–29.

Lilla, Mark. "What Is the Civic Interest?" *Public Interest*, no. 81 (Fall, 1985), 64–81.

Liska, Jiri. "The Multiple Equilibrium and the American National Interest in International Organization." *Harvard Studies in International Affairs*, IV (February, 1954), 35–50.

Lowi, Theodore. "The Public Philosophy: Interest-Group Liberalism." *American Political Science Review*, LX (March, 1967), 5–24.

Lundberg, George A. "Conflicting Concepts of National Interest." *American Perspective*, IV (Fall, 1950), 359–72.

Marchant, P. D. "Realism and Foreign Policy." *International Relations*, I (April, 1959), 557–76.

Morgenthau, Hans J. "Another 'Great Debate': The National Interest of the United States." *American Political Science Review*, XLVI (December, 1952), 961–88.

————. "The Mainsprings of American Foreign Policy: The National Interest vs. Moral Abstractions." *American Political Science Review*, XLIV (December, 1950), 833–45.

————. "Old Superstitions, New Realities: Defining the National Interest—Again." *New Republic*, January 22, 1977, pp. 50–55.

————. "The Primacy of the National Interest." *American Scholar*, XVIII (Spring, 1949), 207–12.

————. "The Reality of the National Interest." *Partisan Review*, XLVII (1980), 578–80.

————. "The Yardstick of National Interest." *Annals of the American Academy of Political and Social Science*, CCXCVI (November, 1954), 77–84.

Morgenthau, Hans J., and Noam Chomsky. "The National Interest and the Pentagon Papers." *Partisan Review*, XXXIX (1972), 336–75.

"National Interests." In *International Encyclopedia of the Social Sciences*. Vol. XI, pp. 35–39.

"The National Interest—Alone or with Others?" *Annals of the American Academy of Political and Social Science*, CCLXXXIII (July, 1952).

Neuchterlein, Donald E. "The Concept of 'National Interest': A Time for New Approaches." *Orbis*, XXIII (Spring, 1979), 73–92.

————. "National Interests and Foreign Policy: A Conceptual Framework for Analysis and Decision-Making." *British Journal of International Studies*, II (October, 1976), 246–66.

Orwin, Clifford. "The Just and the Advantageous in Thucydides: The Case of the Mytilenaian Debate." *American Political Science Review*, LXXVIII (June, 1984), 485–94.

Packenham, Robert A. "Foreign Aid and the National Interest." *Midwest Journal of Political Science*, X (May, 1966), 214–21.

Puchala, Donald J. "American Interests and the United Nations." *Political Science Quarterly*, XCVII (Winter, 1982–83), 571–88.

Relyea, Harold C. "National Security and Information." *Government Information Quarterly*, IV (1987), 11–28.

Riley, Patrick. "A Possible Explanation of Rousseau's General Will." *American Political Science Review*, LXIV (March, 1970), 86–97.

Rochester, J. Martin. "The 'National Interest' and Contemporary World Politics." *Review of Politics*, XL (January, 1978), 77–96.

————. "The Paradigm Debate in International Relations and Its Implications for Foreign Policy Making: Toward a Redefinition of the 'National Interest.'" *Western Political Quarterly*, XXXI (March, 1978), 48–58.

Ruggie, John Gerard. "Collective Goods and Future International Collaboration." *American Political Science Review*, LXVI (September, 1972), 874–93.

Schilling, Warner R. "The Clarification of Ends: Or, Which Interest Is the National?" *World Politics*, VII (July, 1956), 566–78.

Schubert, Glendon A. "'The Public Interest' in Administrative Decision-Making: Theorem, Theosophy, or Theory?" *American Political Science Review*, LI (June, 1957), 346–68.

Sears, Richard D. "The Classical Understanding of International Politics." In *Power, Principles & Interests: A Reader in World Politics*, edited by Jeffrey Salmon *et al.* Lexington, Mass., 1985.

Sestanovich, Stephen. "Inventing the Soviet National Interest." *National Interest*, XX (Summer, 1990), 3–16.

Skidelsky, Robert. "Politics Is Not Enough: On the 'Dying Metaphor' of National Interest." *Encounter*, XXXII (January, 1969), 25–35.

Smith, Michael Joseph. "Hans Morgenthau and the American National Interest in the Early Cold War." *Social Research*, XLVIII (Winter, 1981), 766–85.

Sondermann, Fred A. "The Concept of the National Interest." *Orbis*, XXI (Spring, 1977), 121–38.

Sorauf, Frank J. "The Public Interest Reconsidered." *Journal of Politics*, XIX (November, 1957), 616–39.

Storing, Herbert. "The Crucial Link: Public Administration, Responsibility, and the Public Interest." *Public Administration Review*, XXIV (March, 1964), 39–46.

Thompson, Kenneth W. "Beyond National Interest: A Critical Evaluation of Reinhold Niebuhr's Theory of International Politics." *Review of Politics*, XVII (April, 1955), 167–88.

———. "The Limits of Principle in International Politics: Necessity and the New Balance of Power." *Journal of Politics*, XX (August, 1958), 437–67.

Tonelson, Alan. "The Real National Interest." *Foreign Policy*, LXI (Winter, 1985–86), 49–72.

Tucker, Robert W. "Faith, Reason, and Power Politics." *World Politics*, V (April, 1953), 392–413.

———. "Professor Morgenthau's Theory of Political 'Realism.'" *American Political Science Review*, XLVI (March, 1952), 214–24.

Twitchett, Kenneth J. "The American National Interest and the Anti-Colonial Crusade." *International Relations*, III (October, 1967), 273–94.

Van Dyke, Vernon. "Values and Interests." *American Political Science Review*, LVI (September, 1962), 567–76.

Wall, Grenville. "The Concept of Interest in Politics." *Politics and Society*, V (1975), 487–510.

Wolfers, Arnold. "Disarmament, Peacekeeping, and the National Interest." In *The United States in a Disarmed World: A Study of the U.S. Outline for General and Complete Disarmament,* edited by Arnold Wolfers and Robert E. Osgood. Baltimore, 1966.

————. "National Security as an Ambiguous Symbol." *Political Science Quarterly,* LXVII (December, 1952), 481–502.

DISSERTATIONS

Holly, David C. "The National Interest as Perceived by United States Policy-Makers." Ph.D. dissertation, The American University, 1964.

Jung, Yong Suk. "The Rise of American National Interest in Korea: 1845–1950." Ph.D. dissertation, Claremont Graduate School and University, 1970.

Kwak, Tae-Hwan. "United States-Korean Relations: A Core Interest Analysis Prior to U.S. Intervention in the Korean War." Ph.D. dissertation, Claremont Graduate School and University, 1969.

Weinstein, Eugene David. "The Ignoble Lie—National Interest Ideology in American Civilization." Ph.D. dissertation, University of Minnesota, 1967.

INDEX